VIDEO IN HIGHER EDUCATION

Acknowledgements

I wish to thank Reg Hardwick, Director of the Audio-Visual Services at the University of Queensland, for his expert advice on video matters related to this book and Kim McAllister for typing the manuscript.

Ortrun Zuber-Skerritt

VIDEO IN HIGHER EDUCATION

Edited by Ortrun Zuber-Skerritt

NP

Kogan Page, London
Nichols Publishing Company, New York

First published in Great Britain 1984
by Kogan Page Limited
120 Pentonville Road, London N1 9JN
and by Nichols Publishing Company
PO Box 96, New York, NY 10024

British Library Cataloguing in Publication Data

Zuber-Skerritt, Ortrun
   Video in higher education.
   1. Video tapes in education
   I. Title
   371.33'5   LB1044.75

   ISBN 0-85038-749-3

American Library of Congress Cataloging in Publication Data

Video in higher education.

   1. Video tapes in education. 2. Education, Higher—
   Audio-visual aids. I. Zuber-Skerritt, Ortrun.
   LB1044.75.V5 1983   378'.1735   83-6301

   ISBN 0-89397-165-0

Printed in Great Britain by Billing & Sons Limited, Worcester.

Contents

Introduction

Ortrun Zuber-Skerritt

The aims of this book are:

1. To make a contribution to the understanding of video, a medium which has frequently been misused, or ignored altogether, but which has great potential for influencing the learning process;
2. To show that the various uses of videotape which are discussed are appropriate and potentially effective in educational practice only if acted upon and viewed from a theoretical framework;
3. To stimulate readers to make more and better use of video technology for their own educational purposes.

This book examines the use of video in higher education to improve learning, teaching, interaction, personal behaviour and communication. It contains contributions from researchers, teachers, educational technologists, staff developers, consultants, student counsellors and psychologists from many parts of the world (Australia, Canada, England, Germany, Israel, New Zealand, Scotland, USA). Some contributors are theorists while others are practitioners; all are concerned with exploring the potential of video technology.

The term 'video technology' is used in this book not in the limited sense of 'hardware and software' but as a part of 'educational technology' in the wider sense.

Earlier books on video technology have mainly been concerned with the relative attributes of software, equipment and professional production techniques. The application of video production and recording in terms of educational theory has been neglected, particularly in tertiary education. The contributions contained in this book are, in essence, theoretical statements deduced from experiments or case studies, or they present applications of theories to educational practice. Their focus is on the use of videotape, videocassette and videodisc — not of celluloid film or broadcast television — in higher education.

A definition of terms, for the purpose of this publication, might be appropriate. Television is considered to be the reception of information transmitted either through cable or by electro-magnetic waves. Video is taken to mean material stored on tape or disc as magnetic or optical impressions. Some universities have broadcast television facilities, some have their own closed-circuit television (CCTV) or cable television which can simultaneously be video recorded. But most institutions use video recording and playback equipment only.

The advantage of video over television is that it is not transitory; it can be stopped and wound forward or backward, and thus it can be used more effectively by the individual learner at his/her own pace and by groups of students for in-depth discussion and analysis. It is accepted that motion picture film has similar attributes, but videotape has several advantages over film: firstly, videotape is much cheaper; secondly, videotape can be viewed while the recording is in progress as well as immediately after it has been completed, which gives it an immediacy lacking in film. Videotape is, up to a certain point, of reasonable quality. The main disadvantage of videotape is its low resolution factor. However, in most educational situations, this is outweighed by the advantages. It is true that most educational (or instructional) TV programs are pre-recorded video productions, and that we can record TV programs off-air onto videotape, but the purpose of this book is to focus on the medium of video as such, and to present a comprehensive discussion of its uses and applications in higher education.

Video is not considered in a vacuum, detached from the learning task and the learner. It is seen as a medium by which specific educational objectives can be achieved under certain appropriate conditions. It is not assumed, for example, that video — even if appropriately used — guarantees a positive learning outcome. The other important variables in any instructional design system, besides its medium, are always taken into account. The three components to be considered by the instructional designer are the content, the cognitive organization of the individual learner, and the medium. Statements about the use of video in higher education are therefore most meaningful when they specify the learning task or the specific learning situation.

A student's task is not only to acquire factual information, but to learn to apply knowledge and learning strategies to other contexts. The instructional medium can influence the learner's internal information processing. It should not, therefore, be regarded as a neutral vehicle of information. In education, the psychological and pedagogical effects of any medium are more important than its technical features.

The use of video in higher education is considered here in a variety of learning-teaching situations, in a wide variety of subjects, on and off campus, for individualized learning as well as in small and large group teaching. Each chapter is complete within itself and need not be read in sequence. However, the book as a whole is structured and designed to present all aspects of the argument for the use of video in higher education.

The first chapter provides an overall view of video technology in higher education, and the following chapter develops cognitive-based design guidelines and provides a theoretical basis and framework for using video and computer technology in higher education.

The next three chapters provide the reader with an overview of interactive video, video production technology, and the power struggle over video productions (and the control of knowledge) between academics on the one hand and technical producers on the other.

The following six chapters deal with various aspects of 'video self-confrontation': as a stimulus for interpersonal recall (IPR); in staff development; in teacher training; in 'Symmetrical Communication'; in modelling on the behaviours of task group members; and in research on the processes of thinking during teaching and learning tasks.

Following the discussion of video self-confrontation in research the next two chapters discuss video as a research tool: first in presenting stimuli, collecting responses, and providing data; and second in project orientation for developing critical attitudes towards the media, and towards personal as well as public communication.

The subsequent five chapters focus on various ways of students' 'learning to learn': video programs on student study methods; trigger films as a stimulus for affective learning; tutored videotape instruction; and auto-tutorial or individualized learning with videotapes.

The last five chapters discuss the use of video applications in specific areas: in distance education (at the Open University in the UK; the Fernuniversität in West Germany; and at the University of Queensland in Australia); in foreign language teaching; and as resources in the library.

Ortrun Zuber-Skerritt
June, 1983

1. Video Technology in Higher Education: State of the Art?

Dean W Hutton

IT'S MAGIC!

'Television is magic!' That was my considered opinion back in 1956 when, as a 13-year-old youth, I saw it for the first time. I remember the incident vividly. My father had taken me to a demonstration of closed circuit television at the Royal Melbourne Institute of Technology — two years before television broadcasts began in Australia. With more than 200 people we crowded into a small room where a potter was busily working at his wheel. Standing on my toes and peering over shoulders and between heads, I managed to catch a few fleeting glimpses of the clay taking shape. We left the potter at work and pushed into the room next door. There he was, still throwing the pot, high up on the wall in a coarse, flickery, blue-grey picture with round corners behind thick glass, in a shiny mahogany box. It was television! And it really worked!

Part of the magic of television — then and now — is the possibility of *instantaneous distribution*. I saw the pot taking shape as it was taking shape. It took several migrations through the crowds in the two rooms before I was totally convinced of the immediacy of television. But it was happening — picture and sound transmitted from one room to another along a cable — by magic! Another capability of television unfolded to me that night. In the 'television room', I could actually see and learn more about pottery than I could in the 'pottery room'. The television camera with its cumbersome lenses was being manipulated to *control my viewpoint*. For some of the time images were larger than life. Television had magnified reality. Of course, this ability to manipulate size and viewpoint was not unique to television. Still photography and film had been doing it for years, but with television this manipulation was coupled with immediacy and to me this seemed an explosive innovation.

I am quite certain that the pottery program in Melbourne, which provided one of my most vivid visual memories in 30 years, would hold very little popular appeal today. And yet that same marriage of viewpoint control and instantaneous distribution is what makes television such a rivetting medium whenever it transmits 'live'. We have all experienced its power with World Cup soccer, international tennis, the Olympic Games, interviews with prime ministers and presidents, on-the-spot reports from war zones and disaster areas, and, of course, Neil

Armstrong's first step on the moon.

Many people living today cannot remember a world without television. Some, including the writer, heard of television when in infancy but vividly recall their first *actual* encounter with the medium. Others have memories of a time before the concept of television became a popular notion, before the historic demonstration of television in the UK by John Logie Baird in 1926. Baird's demonstration was the first successful realization of a dream which George Carey had 50 years earlier: the dream of transmitting pictures instantaneously from one location to another. Fifty years after Baird, television had become the dominant mass medium in society — transmitting news, forming opinions, arousing, entertaining, soothing, disturbing, hypnotizing. The overbearing nature of television has resulted, at least in part, from its ability to control a viewpoint and distribute that viewpoint immediately to many locations. To most of us, this is still magic!

TV OR NOT TV?

The magic of television reached new heights when the videorecorder was invented. With the quadruplex machine, developed in 1956 by Ampex, it was possible to store both picture and sound on a large spool of two-inch-wide plastic tape coated with iron oxide powder. This was the first really serviceable videorecorder (VTR) for commercial use giving a quality recorded picture which could not be distinguished from 'live' transmission.

Although the VTR was cumbersome and expensive, this machine when added to a television system gave the medium two important new capabilities. The first of these was time manipulation: events could be stored and played back later; rehearsals could be recorded and analysed; mistakes could be corrected; and videotape recording was much faster and more convenient than the use of film for storing events. The second change ushered in by the VTR was an enormous increase in the power of assembly. With 'live' television it had been possible to perform a limited amount of assembly by using two or more cameras and switching between sources during transmission. Now, with the VTR, it was possible to add, to remove, and to insert visual and auditory information from a variety of sources before transmission. Programs could be assembled from a wide range of heterogeneous material into some form of coherent whole.

The videorecorder represented an intervention of the transmission signal and it was this intervention which expanded the communication potential of television systems (see Figure 1). In addition to the VTR, other technologies which can intervene in the transmission process (such as videodisc, computer and satellite) can increase the control of time and program assembly.

Now, of course, the videorecorder is commonplace. In addition to vastly improved, highly sophisticated machines in the broadcasting industry, millions of relatively cheap machines have entered schools, colleges, universities and homes around the world. As this has happened, interesting changes in common usage of the terms 'television' and

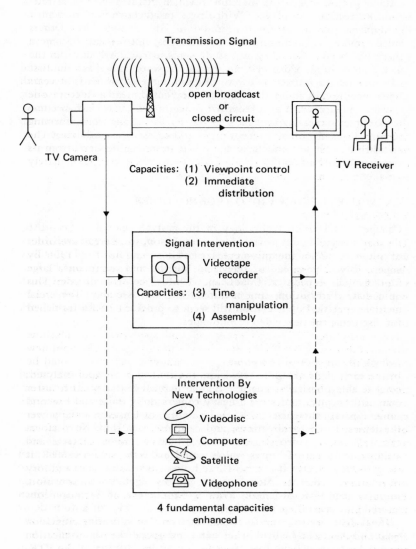

Figure 1. *Fundamental capacities of video technologies*

'video' have developed. The noun 'television' was originally used to describe all aspects of the medium in which pictures were transmitted and electronically displayed. 'Video' was an adjective used to describe equipment used in television production. For example, we speak of: video cameras, video monitors, videorecorders, videocassettes. However, there has been a tendency in recent years, particularly since the proliferation of home video systems, to use the word 'video' as a noun and adjective but to restrict its use to program material which is recorded. When people talk about their 'video' they could mean a videorecorder, a blank videocassette, or a recorded program. On the other hand, there has been an increasing tendency to restrict use of the word 'television' to 'live' transmission and reception — and to use it as both a noun and an adjective. These trends in usage of the terms can be seen in many of the chapters in this book.

CAPACITIES OF NEW VIDEO TECHNOLOGIES

Changes in television technology in the past 15 years have been little short of incredible. Improved picture resolution, widespread availability of colour, reduction in equipment size and cost, and increased reliability have assisted the spread of television but the medium retains its four fundamental capacities (MacLean, 1968): control of viewpoint, immediate distribution, time manipulation, and assembly. The 'fundamental capacities' of television still seem to provide a useful framework for discussing the new video technologies.

Television can control viewpoint

In the early days of studio television, the control of viewpoint required considerable physical strength and great manual dexterity. The cameraman had to push and steer a heavy camera dolly, raise and lower the camera, rotate the turret which held a range of lenses, manually focus the lenses, listen to directions, and compose each shot. Now, anyone can walk into a video store and buy a high technology portable television camera with features which would make the studio cameraman of yesterday green with envy. These home video cameras can produce technically excellent colour images at low light levels, provide an infinite range of focal lengths in a single zoom lens, allow motor driven zooming at several speeds, give the operator a choice of automatic or manual light control, and focus automatically on a moving object. The whole package can be held in the hand and operated with a trigger. It is tempting to conclude that all the important aspects of television camerawork have now been provided automatically for the operator. However, the most important skills in the repertoire of a good camera operator (still, cine or television) have always been more closely allied to the human brain than to optical, mechanical and electronic components. Such skills as choosing appropriate camera angles, framing the subject suitably, composing aesthetically pleasing shots, anticipating the director's requirements, and co-operating with other members of the production crew cannot be bought over the counter. They are craft skills which may depend to a certain extent on flair or intuition but also require serious study and perhaps years of on-the-job practice, frequently in a master-apprentice relationship, for full development.

A high technology television camera does not produce an effective camera operator any more than a 'high tech' fibreglass tennis racquet produces a tennis champion. For some strange reason, we tend to attribute more to the tool than to the craftsman where the newer media are concerned. For example, we tell the photographer, 'Your camera takes excellent pictures', but we don't tell the author 'Your pen wrote a great story'. Perhaps the magic of the media leads us into such errors.

If the control of viewpoint is one of the fundamental capacities of television, it is vitally important to remember, as we are being flooded with new video technologies, that the keys to this control are not in the gleaming, flashing, bleeping, knob-laden boxes we hold in our hands, but rather in the human minds of the camera operator, director, producer and writer.

In the television industry, both formal and informal training in production techniques are valued highly. Unless those of us in education are careful, we may find ourselves believing the slogans aimed at the home video market and expecting craft skills to arrive with the hardware in styrofoam-packed cartons from Japan. Ready availability of sophisticated visual technologies does not remove or reduce the need for careful training in sensitive perception and visual literacy — it increases that need.

Television can distribute picture and sound instantaneously

We witness daily the global distribution capacity of television. Our news broadcasts incorporate overseas satellite feeds, major sporting events are delivered internationally and we nonchalantly watch an interviewer in one city chatting to an interviewee in another.

It is possible that, in the next decade, we could become active participants in global television communication rather than simply passive observers. It is likely that there will be satellite dishes on the roofs of our educational institutions and homes and that we will be able to tune in to program material, 'live' or recorded, from around the world. We may also have the option of sending our own television signals to any destination we choose. The videophone may be as common as today's telephone.

Unfortunately, the arrival of improved video technologies for distributing picture and sound will not guarantee that we will do it any better. Fundamental questions about interest, motivation, sequencing and pacing remain to be answered.

Television can manipulate time

The earliest videorecorders enabled picture and sound to be stored and played back at will, but the emerging video storage technologies provide much more than basic time shifting. Many of the home video-cassette systems currently available can stretch or compress real time.

15

Such features as slow motion, freeze frame, and time lapse are becoming increasingly common on VHS and Beta half-inch domestic video recording systems. And the videocassettes themselves, which are little bigger than a paperback book, can store three hours or more of moving images. Furthermore, by incorporating an accurate tape counter, picture search and memory, many new machines allow surprisingly rapid retrieval of any particular part of the stored material. An educational television producer can use these time controlling features in the new domestic machines to develop interactive programs in which the viewer is told to pause at intervals, consider multiple-choice questions and skip forward or backward as directed. The time manipulation controls allow all the elements of a programmed learning book to be built into a videotape.

Time manipulation reaches its most sophisticated level with the laser optical videodisc system. With this system it is possible to store up to 54,000 still pictures on each side of a shiny, flat 30 cm disc. The stills may be separate pictures, or frames in a motion picture sequence which can be run at normal speed, in slow motion or in rapid scan. But the most remarkable feature of the system is the ease with which information can be retrieved. By simply tapping out the number of the desired frame on the hand control of the videodisc player and pressing the search button, the viewer receives a perfect still image of that frame on the video monitor *within two and a half seconds*! How does it work? Some may talk of silicon chips or microprocessors, others will simply say, 'It's magic!'

Whether our understanding of the laser optical videodisc is clear or fuzzy, some of its educational implications should be very obvious to us. The system allows sophisticated interactive materials to be developed, since access to a large quantity of visual and verbal information is easy and rapid, and it is possible to provide myriad alternative paths through the material. Interactive capabilities of the videodisc are further enhanced when the player is interfaced with a computer. The one serious drawback which the optical videodisc system currently has is the lack of provision for the user to make his or her own discs. Development and mass production of videodiscs are technologically complex and expensive processes and beyond the scope of a portable machine. However, reports of prototypes in Japan suggest that eventually laser optical videodisc machines will emerge with recording capabilities.

Television can assemble heterogeneous material into a coherent whole

The assembly capacity of television is one which it shares with film, still photography and books. With each of these media, it is possible to edit together photographic images, drawings, graphs, charts and verbal information in such a way that the whole is greater than the sum of the parts. Television and film allow the images to be moving or still. In comparison with the other media, television suffers from low picture resolution and relatively small screen size. However, one big advantage which television has over the other media is convenience — it is easier to assemble together still and motion picture sequences, graphic information, speech, music and sound effects. And once these components are combined on videotape, they stay together in perfect synchronization and can be replayed many times with very little loss or degradation. Another point in favour of television as an assembly medium is that the new video technologies are resulting in higher picture resolution and larger, flatter, more brilliant screens.

For schools, colleges and universities, the assembly capacity of television means that it is possible for a group of teachers with sound instructional ideas and relatively modest production facilities to put together ambitious teaching programs to supplement their own face-to-face teaching. This can be particularly important where the subject matter involves events which occur rarely, or contains demonstrations which require elaborate setting up, or includes events which have an element of danger in them.

THE RESPONSE BY EDUCATION

Television and associated video technologies have had a massive influence on society. The medium is responsible for the formation or perpetration of many cultural archetypes and ideologies. Television is a large part of the shared community experience of most industrialized countries. It is the conveyer of news and the purveyor of values. Our children spend more time watching television during their school years than they spend sitting in class (Tindall, Reid & Goodwin, 1977).

Despite the profound effect which television has had on society, it must be admitted that the influence which video technologies have had on education has been peripheral. Certainly video recordings may have replaced 16 mm films as occasional teacher substitutes or 'class minders', but we still tend to use them apologetically, as we did with film. Many teachers and lecturers will videotape and re-run pirated documentaries from broadcast television on a wide range of topics — such as history, geography, biology and literature. But only a small number of teachers and lecturers, relatively speaking, are willing to invest the amount of time and effort required to plan, script, produce and evaluate specific learning materials on videotape for their students.

Of course, television is not alone in its apparent rejection by the majority of educators. Video technology is part of educational technology, and it has been largely rejected along with most of the other means of electronic communication. In fact, if we took a quick trip in a time machine back across the centuries to visit a variety of 'schools' in many countries, we might have to admit that there has been almost no change in education for hundreds and hundreds of years. Certainly, there have been superficial changes in institutions of learning, but the basic ways in which information is imparted, transmitted, discovered or shared have remained constant.

OBSTRUCTIONS TO INNOVATION

In attempting to explain the tendency for educational establishments to reject technological innovation, Hooper (1982) has identified six contributing factors to this resistance:

1. Face-to-face communication is considered by many educators to be the ideal form of communication. Technological substitutes are to be spurned.
2. Technology threatens teaching jobs. Recording and playback; publication and mass production; telecommunications and computing are all perceived as potential means for reducing the need for people.
3. Traditionally, educational institutions have been designed as elitist architectural spaces. Schools and libraries have always had a 'come-and-get-it' attitude to their clients. New communication technologies, and videotapes in particular, threaten this position.
4. Productivity is seen as vulgar and commercial — and productivity is embedded in the language of many of the proponents of new technologies.
5. Education is a monopoly industry. We have state schools and independent schools; we have funding from governments, parents and private foundations; but we are relatively free from the competitive pressures which force change in commerce and industry.
6. In addition to the above factors, it is widely believed that teaching is art and not science and that it is difficult or impossible to specify what you want to do before you do it. This view of teaching and learning does not sit well with the high degree of specificity and planning implied by video technology (see Figure 2).

This is not to suggest that education is immune from the influences of technology. It is simply that for many teachers, the process of teaching is a private and isolated activity (Kerr, 1978). 'Outsiders' are admitted as classroom influences with great reluctance. Wolcott (1977) describes this view, held by teachers all over the world, as a 'subculture' and the intending innovator needs to take account of this perspective and its concerns. It is pointless to offer new technologies and strategies unless they are presented within the framework of classroom practice. Teaching is a practical activity and is often guided best by practice alone. If we attempt to introduce new technologies, but ignore the teacher's viewpoint and dismiss the obstructions to innovation, then we may find ourselves 'scratching where it isn't itching' — offering solutions to non-existent problems!

And we would do well to remind ourselves that awareness of new teaching techniques is no guarantee of their acceptance by teachers. 'Schools filter, slow down, and distort changes in such a way that they are gradually absorbed into existing practices' (Nunan, 1982). We should be prepared for evolutionary change rather than revolutionary change in our schools. But perhaps the tempo of that change is about to increase.

UNFULFILLED PROMISES

For more than a decade extravagant claims have been made for

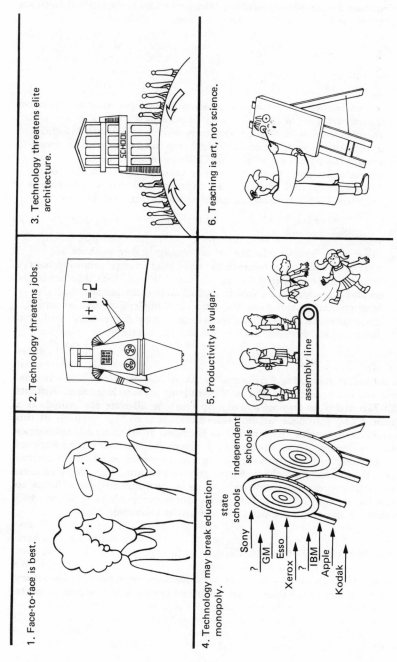

Figure 2. *Education's resistance to technological change*

educational technology, media studies and video technology. Have they fulfilled their promise? Are they legitimate fields of concern? In his fascinating book, *The Concept of Educational Technology: A Dialogue with Yourself*, Richmond (1970) raises many questions which are as relevant today as when they were written. He begins by questioning the need for educational technology and proceeds to argue for its fundamental importance in the theory of teaching and learning.

'In my leisure time I happen to be a bird-watcher. Because I use binoculars, telephoto lenses and computerized flash units — not to mention radar scanning for the study of migration — do I find it necessary to speak of ornithological technology? I do not. Why, then, as an educationist, should I indulge in loose, pretentious talk about educational technology? Why should I go on, as I propose to do, and assert that educational technology is destined to emerge as *the* great central human discipline of the future?' (p. 4)

Unwin (1981) says, bluntly, that he feels the new technologies have not fulfilled their promise:

'The whole field of educational technology has so far been an expensive failure . . . because the term educational technology has implied something that has never been delivered: that is to say it implies an effective application of science to the problems of learning and teaching and the provision of effective ways of solving these problems. It is patently obvious . . . that technology — at least in the sense of *applied science* has been as alien a concept to the fields of educational media and methods as it is to, for example, phrenology or sooth-saying.' (p. 272)

Has video technology delivered what it has promised? Has it been effectively applied to the real problems of teaching and learning? Or has video technology, along with the broader field of educational technology, also been 'an expensive failure'?

After delivering his stinging indictment of educational technology, Unwin does go on to say that he believes that the field of educational technology is on the verge of being able to live up to its claims because recent technological changes have greatly expanded our ability to move information around the world and to process and store it with cheap, reliable devices based on the microprocessor or silicon chip. And, of course, more and more video devices are based on microprocessors.

PROMOTING VIDEO TECHNOLOGIES

Despite the general reluctance of educators to embrace video technologies, the field certainly does have its devotees. Thousands of them! This book is probably preaching to the converted. How can those of us who are convinced of the value of videotape recording and playback in the teaching-learning environment share this enthusiasm with our less enlightened associates and administrators? Stephen (1982) has identified a number of arguments which have been used for this purpose. Some of these are outlined below, with tongue slightly in cheek.

1. *'Money for old rope'*. At the lowest level of video production, the program can consist simply of a videotaped lecture. The experienced, effective teacher can, with a little extra effort, produce a videotaped version of his or her normal classroom presentation. This is not to suggest that such a strategy is ideal. In fact, the chances are that such a program would lose the spontaneity of a live presentation without capitalizing on the special capacities of assembly, time manipulation and control of viewpoint which television can provide when used effectively.
2. *Low financial risk.* If videotape courses are being sold to students, it is possible to require orders to be placed before production begins. It is then possible to tailor the production to the income received. This may sound more like dressmaking than teaching, but the argument may appeal to administrators in times of financial stringency.
3. *Improved quality.* With the threat of a videocamera lurking at the back of the classroom, most academic staff members will do all they can to improve the quality and relevance of their courses. Preparation will be more thorough.
4. *Financial incentive.* Many universities in the United States give an academic who prepares and presents videotape courses a nominal salary incentive, say five per cent. Others work on royalty systems similar to those operated by book publishers. Perhaps educational authorities in primary, secondary and tertiary systems generally could be persuaded to adopt royalty payments in an attempt to improve the quality of instruction.
5. *Variety.* Students may benefit if they can supplement the live presentation on a particular topic which they receive from their own teacher with videotapes made by a range of teachers from all over the world. Different modes of presentation may suit different learning styles. We encourage our libraries to stock a wide range of written opinions, so why not advocate a range of visual presentations as well?
6. *Convenience.* If course material is available on videotape, the student can view it at any time of the day or night (provided he or she has access to a player) and at any place. It can be stopped, started and repeated as many times as required. It may pose a lesser threat to the student ego than a live lesson or lecture.
7. *Distance.* The distance over which an educational institution can exert an influence is limited only by the postman. Videotapes can be mailed as easily as letters and booklets. And students can be encouraged to use other technologies, such as telephone or audiotape recordings to respond to questions and prompts in the video lessons. With widespread use of satellite and cable delivery systems for education, even the postman does not limit the sphere of influence of an institution. Try this one on an aggressive, ambitious administrator!

I am not for a moment suggesting that these ideas should be promoted as justification of available video technologies. I am, however, suggesting that they can be useful in starting a dialogue between teachers and administrators about the potential and the limitations of video communication.

FUTURE SCENARIO

New communication technologies are converging. The television set in the home not only receives open broadcasts, but can also serve as a monitor for the videocassette recorder, the microcomputer and the video games centre. Typewriters and computers are merging. Telephone lines make possible facsimile transmission and computer interaction. Before long we may conduct all our banking, shopping and newspaper reading via computer-linked television sets and telephones.

Where will this all lead? What are the implications for education? One possibility is that we could move towards a society in which formal education, as we know it, is bypassed. Consider the following possible scenario.

The year is 1990. Sam is a qualified, experienced and registered university teacher and he wakes up excitedly to the buzz of a lunar-powered digital alarm clock. Today is Thursday — the only day of the week when Sam is permitted to work at his university.

As he hurries across the university campus towards the main office, Sam admires the tasteful way in which the facades of the old buildings were preserved when they were converted to condominiums. The old library building has become a beautiful recreation centre with ice arena and squash courts. All library and classroom books, paintings, photographs and slides have, of course, gone — recycled for fuel — but not the information they contained. This information has been preserved in the electronic and holographic memory of the gleaming Info-Master, which is the size of a microwave oven and sits in splendour on Sam's desk in a room which used to be the cleaner's storeroom but is now the IMCC (Information Master Control Centre). The desk is shared by the entire university staff — Sam and four others; one day a week each!

New student, Jo, enters the IMCC on schedule to receive an 'information transfusion' from Sam. After admiring Jo's brand new portable paperback-sized, personal, solid state CTVS (computer/TV/VDU/satellite-videophone), Sam connects it to the Info-Master and begins pressing buttons. In a matter of minutes, with a few clicks, bleeps and flashing lights, Sam transfers Jo's entire text, reference and journal requirements for the selected degree course to her CTVS. (This would be equivalent to some 180 books in the days of the now obsolete paper technology.) The transfusion program does, of course, include the automatic phone-in up-date option for periodicals and revised editions.

If Sam has done his work well, Jo may not have to return to the IMC Centre again for the duration of her course. In fact, Jo need not set foot again on the university campus!

If this possible scenario sounds like a nightmarish reality, we should remind ourselves that we can have an influence on the way the educational profession evolves. It is not inevitable that technology will dominate us. We can make a start by putting technology in its place.

TRANSPARENCY OF VIDEO TECHNOLOGIES

Perhaps an important responsibility of those engaged in the video technologies is to work towards making those technologies *transparent* (Hutton, 1979). A bicycle becomes transparent for a cyclist when his mind is filled not with the physics of balance and momentum but with winning the race, getting to the store or enjoying the scenery. To a competent reader, the words on a page are transparent; he looks through the ink patterns and letter shapes to the meaning being conveyed. Pictures are most effective in classroom communication when teachers and learners focus on the meaning created from them. When any communication medium is used effectively, the audience becomes absorbed in the message it carries rather than the medium itself. And so far as the video technologies are concerned, our most effective use of each new device will have to wait until we can look beyond the gleaming, glittering hardware. Information is more important than the technologies which store and transmit it (see Figure 3).

In all aspects of education, we need to strive toward making technology invisible, transparent or at least non-threatening. This is part of the more general need for effective innovation which Nisbet (1981, p. 20) describes: 'The paradox of innovation is that the criterion for successful implementation is when innovation is no longer seen as novel, but is accepted as part of established and accepted practice.'

CHOOSING THE FUTURE

It is difficult to speak of the 'state of the art' of video technology in higher education. There is no 'state'; nothing is static. The only thing constant is 'change'. Electronic technologies change not from year to year, but almost from week to week. The future is being formed today from current decisions. An information revolution is taking place. This, inevitably, influences learning, regardless of the actions of educational decision-makers. But perhaps their role is to make the influence of new technologies on schooling as positive as possible.

Most views on the future of education have been based on what Wills (1972) calls extrapolative technological forecasting. This is a logical system involving the projection of existing trends to predict the direction and time scale of future events. Many people have analysed current trends and attempted to see where technology is taking us — and to prepare schooling for that destiny. For example, Papert (1982, p. 89), in describing his computer-dominated 'School of the Future' in New York, says: 'What we're trying to do in this school is to create an environment that will move children from the present day in the *direction* of what schools of the future will be.'

Educators, information professionals and concerned members of society, need not wait passively for 'experts' to extrapolate and predict the future. We could be more active. If we abdicate responsibility and retreat from opportunity, the day may come when the new communication technologies, with their awesome potential for extending informational services to every home, actually bypass

23

Figure 3. *Transparency of technology*

schools, universities, teachers and educational administrators. And these technologies are being driven by powerful market forces.

Perhaps visually literate information professionals should be taking a leadership role in what Wills (1972) identifies as normative technology forecasting. That is, forecasting, which first assesses future values, goals, needs and desires — and then works out the best way to achieve them. Jones (1982, p. 256) stresses that 'we must assert the right to choose appropriate types of technology at our own pace, and to express a preference for those which enhance and extend human capacity, dignity, diversity and understanding.'

We have entered a new Video Age. The power of the visual is not only taking new forms but is also becoming more accessible to more people. Technology can give society almost anything it wants. Let's work out what we want.

REFERENCES

Hooper, R (May 1982) 'Telecommunications in education', Keynote Address, Australian Society of Educational Technology Annual Conference, Sydney.

Hutton, D W (1979) 'Visual education: Theory and practice', *Proceedings of the 11th Annual Conference on Visual Literacy*, Anaheim, California: International Visual Literacy Association.

Jones, B (1982) *Sleepers, wake! Technology and the Future of Work.* Oxford University Press, Melbourne.

Kerr, S T (1978) 'Change in education and the future role of the educational communications consultant', *Educational Communication and Technology Journal*, **26**, 2, 153-64.

MacLean, R (1968) *Television in Education*, Methuen, London.

Nisbet, J (1981) 'Educational technology: Its current impact', in Percival, F & Ellington, H (eds) *Aspects of Educational Technology*, **XV**, *Distance Learning and Evaluation*, Kogan Page, London.

Nunan, T (1982) 'New technologies and schooling', *Education News*.

Papert, S (1982) 'Computers are objects to think with', *Instructor*, **7**, 86-89.

Richmond, W K (1970) *The Concept of Educational Technology: A Dialogue with Yourself*, Weidenfeld and Nicolson, London.

Stephen, K D (1982) 'Video-tape courses — Open/distance learning: Information technology here and now', *Journal of Educational Television*, **8**, 1, 55-64.

Tindall, K, Reid, D & Goodwin, J (1977) *Television: 20th Century Cyclops*, Sydney Teachers College, Sydney.

Unwin, D (1981) 'The future direction of educational technology', *Programmed Learning and Educational Technology*, **18**, 4, 271-73.

Wills, G (1972) *Technology Forecasting*, Penguin, Harmondsworth, England.

Wolcott, H F (1977) *Teachers versus Technocrats: An Educational Innovation in Anthropological Perspective*, Centre for Educational Policy and Management, Oregon.

2. Cognitive-Based Design Guidelines for Using Video and Computer Technology in Course Development

Robert D Tennyson and
Klaus Breuer

SUMMARY

This chapter presents a method for media application in higher education based on a two-staged process of course analysis and media selection. Using recent research findings in cognitive psychology, the first stage consists of a profile analysis procedure involving an assessment of a course in terms of its content, students, learning requirements and instructional methods. The second stage, selection of media, matches the profile analysis interpretation with the specific attributes uniquely represented in each media form. Advancements in the field of microelectronics and media research provide the basis of the selection process, offering educators direct, cost-effective use of computer and video technology in instruction.[1]

INTRODUCTION

Use of educational technology in the conventional higher education classroom system has not been as widespread as in some of the alternative higher education systems (such as the Open University in Great Britain and the Empire State University in New York state). Attempts to use video technology in college instruction was experimented with in a number of larger institutions during the 1960s and 1970s, but given the relatively poor and conflicting results of those trial courses, video usage is currently severely limited to continuing, heavily financed prototype courses. A few notable successes in video-based courses can be found, but the failures continue to hamper real growth in the use of video technology in higher education. And, with colleges and universities worldwide facing extreme budgetary problems, the prospects for future use of educational technology look bleak indeed. The purpose of this chapter is to present a set of instructional design guidelines for the selection of video and computer technology for use in higher education with reference to the above-defined problems of (a) the mixed findings on the use of educational technology in both experimental studies and field applications, and (b) the tight budgetary situation in colleges and universities.

The instructional design guidelines for video and computer technology use that we are presenting are framed within two design categories associated with recent developments in both electronics and psychology (Tennyson, 1982). These new developments offer new and direct contrasts to previous methods of media application. First, in the field of electronics there have been phenomenal changes since the mid-1970s in both video and computer technology. In higher education, the changes are in the form of less expensive hardware and the simultaneous improvement of more direct user applicability. While inflation has increased the costs of all forms of higher education expenditure, video and computer technology costs have stayed basically at the mid-1970s level. This stable price condition indicates not that electronic equipment is 'cheap', but that it is 'reasonable' when compared to other more conventional methods of instruction. In other words, with appropriate application, video and computer technology could be more cost-effective than traditional forms of instruction in terms of real expenses and performance levels of student learning. One consistent finding in educational technology research has been the stability of student performance. For example, computer-assisted instruction has rarely resulted in poorer student performance as compared with conventional instructional methods (Breuer, 1982). In this regard, it is our proposal that the application of cognitive-based instructional design guidelines as discussed below would provide improved student performance, thereby creating situations where video and computer technology would be favourable in cost-effectiveness terms for higher education.

Educational practice for the past three decades has been directly influenced by the behavioural approach to instruction. That is, an approach to the design of instruction that focuses only on subject matter (as externally represented), with student learning manipulated by external sources of reinforcement and tested by observable performance outcomes — never directly dealing with the process of why and how humans actually acquire, store and use information. Needless to say, the behavioural approach to learning has influenced other areas of our society also; for example, in business there is 'management-by-objectives', in clinical psychology there is 'behaviour modification', and in daily life, the individual is encouraged to define and plan what he or she will be doing in five years' time (with no real definition of how he or she is to get there).

The behavioural theories of learning are basically defined around the concept of 'reinforcement' (Skinner, 1958). That is, reinforcing in a positive way a response generated from a given stimulus. Although this behavioural phenomenon has been replicated successfully in animal laboratories with mice and other animals, it has never been significantly tested in higher order human learning situations. Noted American psychologists started citing the failure of the behavioural approach to classroom learning in the early 1970s (for example, McKeachie, 1972; Jenkins, 1974). By that time, proponents of the behavioural approach to instructional design had already developed well established design systems for producing behaviourally controlled learning environments. By the mid-1970s, however, the resurgence of cognitive psychology, especially in the United States, brought forth new ideas of human learning. These ideas implied that instruction should first understand why and how the human mind works when learning new information, not when ignoring it (as in the behavioural approach, which is only concerned with overt behaviour).

Research evidence now clearly shows that many aspects of the behavioural methods of instruction actually interfere with student learning (Rohwer, 1980). Such things as immediate feedback, cueing and promoting, and many forms of reinforcement have been found to inhibit human learning. The linear, step-by-step method of programmed instruction seems to be fine for short, rote memory tasks but not for higher order mental processes (like problem-solving and creativity) (LaBerge, 1976). The cognitive approach to learning attempts to explain and understand the basic functions of the human mind and thus prove the means for designing instruction accordingly (Glaser, 1977). Instructional design strategies from a cognitive theoretical view can be as prescriptive as the behavioural, the difference between the two being the focus of the manipulation of the stimuli. In the former it is on the coding and retrieval of information in the memory; in the latter it is on the control of the stimuli and reinforcement of desired responses.

Before proceeding with the instructional design guidelines, we would first like to present a brief overview of a basic cognitive model of human learning and thinking. It is hoped that this will assist the reader without a good background in cognitive learning theory to achieve a proper understanding and appreciation of the guidelines. Following this brief overview then, we will proceed directly with the instructional design guidelines for the selection of video and computer technology for use in the college or university classroom.

A BASIC MODEL OF HUMAN LEARNING AND THINKING

In designing courses of instruction for higher education, educators should have some type of theoretical assumption of how adults learn and think. Ideas of learning and thinking are very often not clearly understood by the educator; many educators confuse ideas from various conflicting theories of adult learning and thinking. The scope of this chapter does not allow us to review and discuss the various models and ideas about adult learning, but we consider it important that we discuss a basic model of the cognitive approach to learning.

It might be helpful to start with definitions of the terms 'learning' and 'thinking'. Both of these terms are abstract concepts that vary in definition according to the context in which they are used. The way in which we are defining them is in reference to the college classroom environment and to the highest order of mental processing desired by higher education problem-solving and creativity. That is, the primary learning outcome of higher education is the development of an individual who can successfully solve problems and advance knowledge after the termination of formal learning, not just someone who has only acquired facts and responses to a set of certain limited classroom-related stimuli. Basically, learning is the acquisition of information and the process of using that information (Lindsay & Norman, 1977). In formal terms, it is the encoding and storage of information into the memory.

For instructional purposes, learning can be viewed as consisting of three aspects. The first is the coding of information from external sources. Usually, this is thought of as direct storage of information as represented in the external environment — often referred to as episodic (Tulving, 1972). Variations in individual perceptions (Gibson, 1969), current knowledge (Tobias, 1976), and certain biological factors (Kieffer & Tennyson, 1973) account for differences in the coding process for individual students. The second aspect is the generation of skills or strategies in memory for using coded information. This aspect of learning is the most challenging but the most disregarded in instruction. In cognitive terms, what the student learns here are semantic processes for understanding given situations and retrieving information directly related to specific situations. Associated with the generated retrieval strategy are the criteria by which a given semantic process evaluates possible solutions or outcomes. At this point, then, learning can be viewed as a multidimensional process involving the acquisition of information followed by generation of internally derived retrieval skills or strategies within a framework of solution criteria (Perlmutter, Harsip & Myers, 1976; Schroder, Driver & Streufert, 1967; Streufert & Streufert, 1978). This second aspect of learning implies student ability to make quality judgements when solving or proposing problems. Thirdly, as students acquire more specific information along with generated semantic processes, they begin to develop a means for governing this vast array of knowledge. The governing mechanisms of the memory are often labelled schemata by psychologists (Piaget, 1972). This third aspect of learning is an important concept to remember when designing instruction because it is the aspect most influenced by each student's cognitive system (that is, the total of the information, semantic processes and schemata elaborated within an individual). Every student exhibits these aspects of learning in a different way, and possible differences should be considered when designing a course of instruction. (We will refer back to these aspects when presenting the instructional design guidelines.)

'Thinking' is a term which labels the mental process of applying a cognitive structure in some way (such as writing a book, driving a car or talking). To illustrate the phenomenon of thinking we will present seven general variants of thinking from which other combinations can be defined for specific situations. We are not trying to reduce the possible complexity of thinking, but only attempting to clarify the concept of thinking before introducing our guidelines on selection of video and computer technology. The basic aspects of thinking include, as a minimum, the following:

☐ recognition of a previously learned task and the application of the appropriate solution;
☐ recognition of a previously learned task, but when given a different situation, creation of a new solution using appropriate criteria;
☐ recognition of a new problem and creation of a new solution using appropriate criteria;
☐ recognition of a new problem and creation of a new solution using new criteria;
☐ creation of a new problem followed by creation of a solution using

appropriate criteria;
☐ creation of a new problem followed by creation of a solution using new criteria.

All of these conditions conclude with a solution, but thinking is occurring throughout each phase. Thinking at the higher levels of the above problem conditions shows increasing forms of creativity.

An underlining educational principle for the model of learning and thinking presented below is that the purpose of instruction is to facilitate — not to interfere with — acquisition of instructional goals and objectives. Instruction should enhance learning, making it both effective and efficient. As stated earlier, research findings on learning and instruction show that standard instructional methods can interfere with and actually inhibit learning, and that the students who are most successful are those who have the intellectual capacity to ignore conventionally designed instruction and learn independently of the instructor or program of instruction. A good understanding of how adult learning and thinking take place is essential in the design of college and university courses; conscious reference to that understanding should be made while manipulating instructional design variables and conditions.

Our model of learning and thinking is heavily influenced by cognitive learning theories, which explain the function of learning in the following way: within the human memory, an internal system receives information and, depending on the purpose or purposes for which the information is to be put to use, the system processes the information and may or may not provide an observable output. The internal memory system has various components or routines that can (a) store the new information, (b) use newly received information with previously stored information, and (c) when necessary, create new routines from either new information or from a combination of new information and previously stored information. Of course, cognitive learning models, such as Anderson's (1976; one memory theory), Tulving's (1972; two memory theory); and Doerner's (1976; problem-solving theory) differ in detail and emphasis according to the individual interests of the psychologist. This chapter is concerned with adult learning and thinking and the use of video and computer technology in higher education; our model therefore focuses on the thinking process in relation to defined learning goals and objectives of a college or university classroom.

In presenting our learning and thinking model, three major processes within the cognitive system are defined and separately identified (Figure 1). The first, cognitive strategy, is the main controlling component of the cognitive system in reference to both learning and thinking (that is, the schemata). In the cognitive strategy are the means — both learned and genetic — by which the individual controls the various mental operations that humans perform, for example, habits, skills, problem-solving and creativity (Wickelgren, 1977). The second component, memory structure, is where information (content and semantic networks) is stored. In the memory structure are the strategies for coding newly acquired information (encoding) and retrieving information (decoding) when required (Baddeley, 1974). The memory structure is actually a storehouse (library) with an elaborate management system that functions to encode information in such a way that it can be economically used later. Instruction that helps in this process of properly encoding information would certainly help a student use that information later.

The terms 'short-term' and 'long-term' memory are often used to describe what is learned; much of formal classroom learning only resides in short-term memory and is soon forgotten — especially after the final test. For example, students typically show 80-90 per cent test reductions only two weeks after the final examination (Tennyson, 1981a). This forgetting phenomenon does not happen because information is kept in short-term memory but because the coding process into long-term memory ends after the first aspect of learning, and the second and third aspects (semantic and schemata) are never learned. This usually occurs because the content is presented in such a way that the coding process occurs in a random fashion and information is, thus, seldom linked into a semantic network for useful retrieval. Short-term memory implies a temporary coding process in which information is not consciously linked into the memory's information retrieval strategy. Long-term memory implies storage of information (content and semantic) and can comprise its linkage to memory structure (second form of learning) and to appropriate schemata (third form of learning).

The third component of the model is the learning strategy. Putting information into the memory structure implies a means by which the individual selects what information to attend to and what information to organize for storage. This twofold process of selection and organization in the learning strategy governs what needed information goes into the memory structure. Information and mental processes vary in how they can be stored in the memory structure and used in the cognitive strategy operating system; good learning strategies adapt to these differences and provide an effective means for coding and retrieval. Given this cognitive model of learning, it is necessary for classroom instruction to provide students with both content (subject matter) and cognitive processes (Schroder, Karlins & Phares, 1973). That is, along with teaching content, educators need to be aware of the mental processes for a given content and work towards student acquisition of appropriate learning strategies as well. Without an appropriate learning strategy for a given content, students will fall back on learning strategies that can actually be counter-productive. A strategy for learning, say, history may not be useful as a strategy for learning zoology (history requires a learning strategy for written information while zoology requires a strategy for learning visual information).

In summary, the cognitive strategy component of the human cognitive system contains the operating or governing strategy of the learning and thinking process. The term 'strategy' is appropriate here because it implies a plan for accomplishing a defined goal. In the memory structure component, coding strategies store and retrieve information (content and semantic networks are both externally provided). In the learning strategy component are the means by which

31

the individual selects and organizes external resources needed for some perceived goal or objective — either extrinsic or intrinsic.

The functioning of the above model of learning and thinking can be described briefly in three stages:

1. The first stage involves a mental process that assesses directly a task or problem within the cognitive strategy. This process simultaneously includes both the perception of the situation and the cognition of it. Perception is a necessary prerequisite assessment to the cognition assessment, using the following three primary values: (a) assessment of the perceived relevancy of the immediate situation to one's own learning and thinking needs; (b) assessment of one's view of the situation's level of difficulty within one's range of perceived ability (that is, not too easy or not too difficult); and, (c) assessment of one's perceived attitude towards the situation in terms of future learning and thinking needs (Tulodziecki & Breuer, in press). If the perception assessment is positive, the cognition assessment, which is actually processing simultaneously, continues assessing the nature of the task or problem to determine if a possible solution is currently part of the cognitive strategy. If it is, the individual can proceed with the solution. However, if an appropriate solution is not readily available, the cognitive strategy proceeds to the memory structure, Stage 2.

2. In the memory structure, the retrieval strategy either decodes previously stored information or decodes other information that the

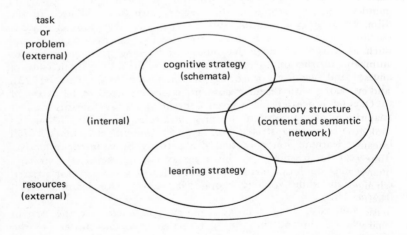

Figure 1. *Basic components of the cognitive system*

cognitive strategy component can then use to organize a solution more suitable to the given task or problem. In this latter process, there is direct movement of information (both content and semantic) between the cognitive strategy and the memory structure components. If, in this mental process of search and solution formulation, a solution is not adequately achieved, the cognitive strategy activates the learning strategy component, Stage 3.

3. To acquire new information to solve a given task or problem, the individual uses a learning strategy that most appropriately interacts with the perceived needs of the situation and all possible external resources. In certain situations, the student may need to adapt a current learning strategy or acquire new ones before proceeding in the acquisition of information needed for an acceptable solution. Once the appropriate resources are acquired, the newly obtained information can be coded into the memory structure and, finally, the cognitive strategy can form a solution to the given task or problem.

Although the above cognitive system model of learning and thinking may seem over-simplified from a psychological point of view, it does form a sufficient basis for our video and computer selection guidelines and shows that media application should not be viewed as an arbitrary factor in instructional design. Simply putting a course on videotape will not in itself result in improved learning or, in fact, any learning. Educational technology, when applied in reference to human learning, can facilitate classroom learning. The above discussion on cognitive psychology of learning may serve as the theoretical foundation for the design guidelines discussed below.

INSTRUCTIONAL DESIGN GUIDELINES

The above discussion on human learning and thinking emphasizes that student encoding of information in the classroom directly involves three main factors. The first factor is the way information is represented in the external world. This form of representation will in large part determine what information can be encoded in the memory. That is, if the instruction is rich in information, the student has more potential information to encode. Thus, learning environments that provide an abundance of resources (both relevant and irrelevant information) increase the probability that learning will occur. The other two factors involve the individual student's cognitive system; these include the form and type of previously coded information and perceptions. In our description of human mental processing, we stated that in learning new information, the individual first searches through the memory to see if he or she already has that information and, if not, to determine a coding scheme for that new information either by extending a given coding scheme (for example, in mathematics, adding algebra to basic mathematics) or establishing a new coding scheme.

This latter activity takes much more time and explains in part why adults learn faster than children: adults have a larger repertoire of existing coding schemes which can be extended with newly presented information. On the other hand, children seem to have more mental energy with which to establish new coding schemes. Perception is a cognitive factor that controls the intensity of the encoding process (Johanson & Tennyson, in press).

Students tend to approach higher education learning activities with either high intensity or neutral intensity, but instructional presentations can unfortunately reverse this natural order of processing into a negative perception. Negative perception makes learning more difficult and other personality variables such as anxiety can interfere with and actually inhibit learning (Tennyson & Boutwell, 1974). Our instructional design guidelines take into account the need to address the human cognitive system when preparing instruction for the classroom.

The guidelines for use of video and computer technology in higher education are organized in two stages of instructional design. The term 'design' here refers to establishing the specifications for course development, not the production. Quality of production does influence the acquisition of information and directly influences student perception of a course, but we consider the specifications of course design to be the primary function in development of instruction. Stage 1 of the design process involves developing a description of a given course such that a media profile of the course can be specified. In Stage 2, that profile can be used to select the medium or media of the lessons within a course. Completion of the specifications leads directly to the development and production of the course.

Before setting out the instructional design guidelines, we would remind the reader that their use is under your direct control and that they should therefore be creatively applied to individual courses and lessons. For a complete understanding of the three aspects of learning with which this chapter is mainly concerned, the reader may need to view a complete lesson developed with the guidelines; these lessons are available from the authors upon request.

The purpose of instruction is to present information to a student so that the desired learning can occur. Each of the three aspects of learning should be addressed in the course specification profile:

Aspect 1: Acquisition of content
Aspect 2: Formation of semantic networks
Aspect 3: Development of schemata.

To facilitate the learning of information, it is important to use instructional methods that contribute to each aspect; three basic types of instruction that we include in the profile analysis are as follows:

Type 1: Presentation of information
Type 2: Demonstration of information
Type 3: Practice of information.

These types of instruction are well known to all educators: what is less well understood is how to manipulate types 1 and 2 in course presentations. Educators tend to use the simple lecture method of instruction to present all aspects of learning; only occasionally do they use the demonstration type — and then usually in the wrong place. The lecture method (narrative presentation) of presenting information limits all three aspects of learning and, although useful in presenting some varieties of information, it is inadequate for most learning situations, even with regard to acquisition of content (aspect 1). The reason for this inadequacy is associated with the concept of 'transmediation'. Transmediation is a commonly used concept in literary criticism, in which an original form of expression is transferred from that medium to another; for example, when a novel is made into a movie or a painting is reduced to a photograph and put into a book. There is an inevitable loss, not necessarily of relevant information but of irrelevant information, and this makes the new representation much less than the original. The goal of good instruction should be to minimize the loss of original information (both relevant and irrelevant). It is the educator's primary responsibility to control the negative effects of transmediation. These negative effects are most clearly seen in types 1 and 2 of conventional higher education instruction. Educators seem to rely too heavily on students' previously coded information and positive perceptions to overcome inadequate presentation of the information (Bruner, 1971).

The ideal instruction minimizes loss of information so that what students encode in their memories is, as much as possible, the information in its original form. If the means of presentation distorts the information only minimally, then encoding effectiveness is adequate; if the means unduly distorts the information, student learning is hampered (Jassal & Tennyson, 1982).

It is clear that selecting a delivery system involves understanding variables in the students as well as certain characteristics of the information to be learned. In Stage 1, then, the profile of the information comes from an analysis of both the content and the students. This analysis is accomplished in four steps; the final outcome of each step is a quantitative judgement based on a five-point scale. These scales will be used to construct the profile analysis for media specification and then selection. (The reader may refer to the 'List of Stages and Steps in the Instructional Design Guidelines' in the Appendix — see p. 62.)

Stage 1: Course specification profile analysis

Step 1: Content analysis
It has been stated earlier that adults often have a large repertoire of stored information that can contribute positively to the learning of new content. This, however, cannot compensate for lack of relevant information in instruction: students can learn from a course only what is available. For instruction, that means that students can develop misconceptions not through their own fault (or lack of work) but from poorly presented forms of information (Tennyson & Park, 1980). For example, a curriculum in art history that consists entirely of picture books and slides, without direct visits to the great museums, would certainly result in many misconceptions about art (regarding size, colour intensity, texture, and so on). For learning to be complete, information should be encoded in the memory from the original or from a form as nearly like the original as possible. Instruction should

minimize the loss of what is called irrelevant information because, in learning, the irrelevant information provides much of the linkage codes between forms of relevant information (Herrman & Harwood, 1980).

The analysis of the content of a course should focus in part on the concept of transmediation — in this case, the transfer of information from its original form into an instructional presentation form. In the example of art history used above, because it is not possible to bring together in one instructional location all the appropriate art works, they are reproduced for presentation either in book or in slide form. The basic relevant characteristics of the art can usually be transferred but, as stated above, many of the irrelevant characteristics are lost (through photo-processing distortion), and the emotional feeling generated by the original work and its surroundings is diminished. Selection of a medium for information presentation should consider first, of course, loss of relevant information in the transmediation but also the loss of irrelevant information. In this first step, there are three factors to consider in developing the media specification profile: analysis of the information in terms of its original form, imagery capability, and manipulative aspects.

A. Original form. Content within most disciplines takes a variety of original forms. There are a few disciplines that are almost exclusively verbal (such as literature and language), while others seem to be highly visual (such as zoology or anatomy). It is helpful to use a rating scale to determine the basic original form of the content to be learned. (The scale below only provides a numerical symbol for the media specification profile and not a quantitative indicator. The middle range indicates the mix of the two dichotomous original forms of a given content.)

1	2	3	4	5
Highly verbal	Verbal	Verbal/ visual	Visual	Highly visual

Analysis of the original form is especially important for disciplines with visual forms of content because it is here that transmediation can result in the greatest loss of relevant and irrelevant information. There have been successful attempts at transferring verbal content to visual form (for example, books into movies) but visual-to-verbal transfer has been largely unsuccessful. The main problem is that verbal information is usually linear in form while visual information is spatial; it is more difficult to reduce spatial information to a linear form than *vice versa*. If loss of the original form of the content is unavoidable, an alternative form of representation selected must minimize loss of the original characteristics. For example, if the art history instructor cannot use originals then slides may be a better form of representation than a book.

One final comment on the coding and storage of information. Research clearly shows that if information is coded in the memory from its original form it will have a better code (storage) and be better used (retrieved) than if coded from an alternative (transmediated) form (Tennyson, 1978). This occurs in large part because the memory can store information simultaneously as both verbal and visual (Moscovitch

& Klein, 1980), but when the memory has to code instructional information that is altered or incomplete (for example, visual content as verbal), that altered information may (a) not provide the additional needed meaningful features or dimensions of the information (thus the content becomes basically useless information — random facts) or (b) not provide elaborations from and/or linkages to previously coded information. In this latter instructional situation, the major in a discipline certainly has an advantage over the non-major because the major has the previously coded information with which to fill in the gaps and the aptitude to generate (in the memory) the necessary missing information.

B. Imagery capability. Within cognitive learning theory there are some research studies on the processing of verbal information in situations when either the content is being associated with a visual image or the learner is directed to conjure up an image that is directly associated with verbal information (Rosenberg, 1980). This dual processing theory states that information that is coded correctly both as verbal and visual will be better stored and retrieved than single processing (Rasco, Tennyson & Boutwell, 1975). Instruction whose content is verbal does not need to have visuals added, but students must be directed in the presentation to conjure up visual representations so that the dual processing occurs (Tennyson, 1978). For information that is low in imagery, visuals are recommended so that the student has both forms of the information to facilitate coding. One can analyse the content to determine its imagery-evoking power. Content with high imagery potential (such as literature) would not necessarily require visuals in the learning environment, in contrast to content areas with minimal imagery-evoking power (such as physics), which would benefit from visuals. The analysis should test whether or not a dual processing of the content would occur from either (a) verbal information and the student conjuring up in his/her memory the visual, or (b) verbal *and* visual information. If the former condition exists, the content has high imagery; if the latter condition exists, then the content has low imagery.

1	2	- 3	4	5
Very high	High	Medium	Low	Very low

Note that 'very high' imagery is rated a 1 and 'very low' a 5. This is done for purposes of the media specification profile and not as a value for use of visuals in instruction.

C. Manipulative aspects. Certain disciplines require physical manipulation of objects in the course of learning and performing. For example, in biology it is necessary to dissect various life forms; in anatomy students have to dissect first a monkey and, later on, human cadavers; and chemistry requires the manipulation of dangerous substances. In these disciplines, instructors often seek indirect methods for student introductory learning because of possible attitudinal problems, physical danger, high expense and so on. For example, in medical pathology it is often useful to introduce students to an autopsy by indirect visual instruction such as by a film or videotape. The transmediation effect here is to preserve some of the relevant information while delaying for live instructions other relevant and irrelevant information. The analysis here should consider only whether or not manipulation is part of the course or lesson learning environment. In the comment section of the media specification profile it can be noted whether or not an indirect method of instruction would be desirable. This scale runs from 'none' to 'very high', at which latter point manipulation is an integral part of the course and cannot be eliminated if learning is to occur.

1	2	3	4	5
None	Low	Some	High	Very high

Manipulative activities can also be used in certain learning situations in which students can generate visual stimuli to help encode information. For example, in foreign language learning, students with a strong visual aptitude are directly aided in learning if they write out words and sentences, while students with a strong verbal aptitude only require listening instruction.

Step 2: Student analysis
We have repeatedly stated that students primarily encode information as represented to them in the external world. We have also stated that this processing is influenced directly by the students' prior knowledge and perception of the information to be learned. Students with high levels of prior knowledge and good perceptions require minimal instructional support from the learning environment. From a cognitive point of view, formal instruction for such situations would probably be interfering, especially if such students have adequate learning strategies for acquiring the needed missing information. However, students with these characteristics are usually the final product of higher education; thus there is the continuing need to provide good instruction until students reach that end-of-school level of knowledge. The purpose of this second analysis in the media specification profile is to determine the characteristics of students enrolled in a given course. Our assumption is that the learning of information by adults in higher education is directly affected by three basic variables: (a) the students' aptitude in reference to specific content areas; (b) prior knowledge students may have that would influence learning of the content; and (c) the students' perception of the course content.

A. Aptitude. One assumption that can be made for most students in higher education is that they have a higher-than-average intelligence. Of course, this varies among institutions such that the better colleges and universities have a more homogeneous student body with higher intelligence than lower rated institutions. Intelligence of the students is not analysed because it does not seem to enter directly into the application of video and computer technology in higher education. However, *aptitude* does seem to be an important factor because students with a low aptitude for a specific content would profit from an instructional program which deals with their low aptitude without handicapping the high-aptitude students (Snow, 1980). For example, students majoring in psychology usually have an excellent verbal aptitude but a low quantitative aptitude and need special attention or help in statistics and measurement courses; students with a good mathematics aptitude usually have no difficulty with psychology-based statistics. Rating students' aptitude for a general course may not be difficult: the nature of the course may ensure a wide range of aptitude. Similarly, it may be easy on advanced courses where the nature of the course would produce a minimal range of high aptitude students. But it may be more difficult on an introductory course or on a course for majors with some content outside the discipline (for example, a psychology course for pre-med majors). The point is not to assume automatically a common aptitude for all students in all courses. Courses for students with a wide range of aptitudes could profit directly from video and computer technology. This does not mean that where there is a narrow range of aptitudes courses would not profit from this technology, but that the unique attributes of video and computer technology are highly suited to dealing with individual and personal differences. It is therefore desirable to develop courses for students with a wide range of aptitudes before developing courses that do not necessarily have to account for such a range.

In using this aptitude scale, consider as 'very wide' courses in which at least 70 per cent of the students have a low aptitude for the content and as 'very narrow' courses for which 80 per cent or more of the students have high aptitude. These numbers are somewhat arbitrary, so use professional judgement and perhaps consultation with colleagues.

1	2	3	4	5
Very narrow	Narrow	Equal	Wide	Very wide

Remember not to confuse aptitude with intelligence. That is, highly intelligent students may have certain difficulties in specific content areas and would require appropriate instructional support (Burns, 1980).

B. Prior knowledge. This factor may be difficult to analyse because of the usual uncertainty among instructors about what specific prerequisites are necessary for a given course. Research on learning sequence shows that random ordering of information is as effective in post-test performance as some logical ordering (Tennyson, 1972). What is known on the topic of prior knowledge shows that information stored in the memory can influence the acquisition of information to be learned. The influence seems to be in the development of the coding scheme. Students with large amounts of prior knowledge directly related to the information to be learned in a course can easily extend their existing coding scheme, building rapidly an expanding network of information. In contrast, students without prior knowledge have the additional problem when learning new information of establishing an effective coding scheme. Also, specific learning strategies may need development. Educational technology may offer help to the student in these two problem areas. On this rating scale, 'very high' would apply to students with prior experience in the content area and the appropriate learning strategy; 'none' would apply to students satisfying neither of these conditions.

1	2	3	4	5
Very high	High	Some	Low	None

Again, we favour the use of technology in situations where its unique attributes can be applied to facilitate possible learning problems rather than just the acquisition of knowledge.

C. Perception. The factor of perception in the context of course design is defined as the students' initial view toward a given content area. During the course of instruction, their perception may or may not change. If it is initially low then it will interfere with learning unless this is taken into account when designing the course. Perception of information determines the intensity applied by the student in the coding process (Johansen & Tennyson, in press). For example, if perception is low, students may obtain an excellent mark in a course, but they will not necessarily apply the intensity in the coding process so that the information can become useful later on. Research findings on the phenomenon of forgetting show that, without positive perception, even the top students do poorly on retention tests. Educational research on technology consistently indicates that students have more positive attitudes toward general courses taught with some form of technology than when taught in a conventional manner (Tennyson & Boutwell, 1974). This probably occurs not just because of the technology but also because of the other factors associated with good course design when developing media-based instruction. If student perception is low, educational technology, all other things being equal, seems to produce an initial improvement in attitude which is maintained throughout the course.

Rate perception as 'very good' when students enter the course in a non-coercive manner and 'very poor' when previous evidence indicates high drop-out and/or absenteeism.

1	2	3	4	5
Very good	Good	Neutral	Poor	Very poor

A rating of 'good' and 'very good' usually indicates disciplines with good maintenance in instructional practice. A 'good' rating should not exclude the use of video and computer technology; for it may be useful for other recognized purposes.

Step 3: Learning analysis
In our discussion on learning and thinking we mentioned that both the information and mental processing should be defined in course design. The third step in the course specification profile analysis is to clarify the aspects of learning that are desired in the course to be developed.

A. Acquisition of content. At college level, acquisition of content is obviously a primary outcome of most instruction. We include this factor in the analysis, although we anticipate a fairly high, constant rating. Before automatically scaling this factor high, consider the depth of content to be learned: majors in a discipline would require a higher degree of recall of content than non-majors. A lower marking does not necessarily imply weaker standards but a lower level of detail in content recall. Also, higher markings imply increased effort on the instructor's part as well as on the students'.

1	2	3	4	5
Very low	Low	Medium	High	Very high

B. Formation of semantic networks. This form of learning implies the ability to create skills or strategies with which to use learned content in newly encountered situations. That is, the students learn to use information for solving tasks or problems in a defined context (Scandura, 1977). In certain disciplines, this also implies transfer of the information to help in solving problems not in the defined context, such as using certain principles of psychology in dealing with the ethics of a professional position. This scale represents difficulty of application from 'very concrete' situations in which problems resemble directly the context of the learned skills or strategies (and thus can be called tasks; Doerner, 1976) to 'very abstract', in which problems constantly require generation of new skills or strategies. Again, majors within a discipline should exhibit problem-solving strategies at a much higher level of difficulty than non-majors. For instruction, the *higher* the marking, the *more directly* related to the actual real-life context the learning environment should be.

1	2	3	4	5
Very concrete	Concrete	Middle	Abstract	Very abstract

The two extreme reference points define the semantic context such that 'very concrete' allows the student to solve tasks (of a known type) using known solutions, while 'very abstract' allows the student to create both problems and solutions. The 'middle' point implies a category of semantic context associated with general problem-solving skills or strategies that can be applied to new situations. (Refer back to our discussion on thinking.)

C. Development of schemata. This aspect of learning is the most complex because it is the governing mechanism of the memory. That is, the schemata govern the thinking processes and are closely referenced in education to student responsibility in learning. Associated with this form of learning is motivation (Scarr, 1981), but setting that aside, this scale focuses on the amount of instructional time in a course that is devoted to direct learner responsibility in developing schemata. Aspect 3 learning in higher education is mainly limited to majors of a discipline, although this does not entirely eliminate it from certain courses serving only non-majors (especially advanced non-major courses).

This scale indicates a range from complete instructor control of the instruction to complete student control. A rating of 2 implies instructor control with some student control in decision making while a rating of 4 implies minimal control by the instructor.

1	2	3	4	5
Complete instructor control	Some student control	Joint control	Some instructor control	Complete student control

In analysing this scale, consider whether or not the students will directly use the information presented in their intended post-college career. A course should give majors a direct opportunity to develop schemata, and if it does not, the total curriculum should be reviewed to see where it is developed. Since this aspect of learning can be completely individual, it should be carefully analysed to see if the course could or should provide student control.

Step 4: Instruction analysis
In the introduction to this chapter, we stated that information consists of both content and semantic networks and that the memory governs information usage by schemata. Instructional methods in a curriculum are intended to facilitate the learning of information; other activities in the curriculum, usually non-instructional but planned, are intended for the development of schemata. The analysis of instruction, then, focuses almost entirely on the learning of information (that is, content and semantic networks) and should not be viewed as being directly associated with the three aspects of learning. The analysis of instruction is based on group size and efficiency of instruction in reference to the course objectives.

For example, when presenting new content (Aspect 1) a large-group format may be more appropriate than presenting the same information to each individual student. A lecture method of instruction can be more useful than a mediated form of instruction, especially if the instructor puts some sort of emotion into the presentation (Tennyson, 1981a). The rating scale in this section does not put a qualitative value on the scores; it serves only to help establish the specification profile for decision-making in applying video and computer technology. In other words, all instruction, whether of large groups, small groups or individuals, is valuable, provided the method used is selected carefully by analysis and not adopted through convention or default.

A. Presentation of information. The first analysis of the instructional method concerns rating the efficiency of the presentation in reference both to the aspects of learning and to the content. For example, where the student group is known to have medium prior knowledge of a discipline and the information as organized for the course or lesson is not available in any other form, then large group presentations may be the most efficient method of instruction regardless of the aspect of learning. Also, if course objectives include attitudinal and/or emotional outcomes, then a live presentation may be the only means of accomplishing them. On the other hand, if the range of prior knowledge and/or aptitude is known to be large, individualized instruction would be a more efficient method of instruction — especially if some form of adaptive instruction is used (Tennyson & Rothen, 1977). Obviously, the higher aspects of learning require smaller units of students to balance the expenditure of instructional time with the higher learning outcomes. Efficiency of the presentation of information should be rated with reference to course objectives.

1	2	3	4	5
Large	Medium large	Medium	Small	Individual

Consider 10-15 students as 'small', 15-30 as 'medium', 30-70 as 'medium-large', and anything higher than 80 as 'large'.

B. Demonstration of information. Briefly, this type of instruction is used to show students how the information to be learned is applied in a 'real world' context. Rarely is this method of instruction used with non-majors in higher education. This type of instruction actually shows the usefulness of a given discipline but, unfortunately, is usually reserved for advanced majors. For example, in most college general physics courses, non-majors finish the course without really knowing what physicists do and/or how physics is useful. This can also be said for history courses, English courses, and so on; all that is usually done at the introductory levels is the presentation of information at the Aspect 1 level of learning (acquisition of content). In analysing this second type of instruction, first consider your rating on the need for learning semantic networks (Aspect 2 in Step 3). If that aspect is highly rated, then proceed to determine the efficiency of presentation for the demonstration of information. Again, we use the group size as the variable to analyse this method of instruction. If the demonstration of an example can be easily presented to a large group then it should be (especially for introductory courses), leaving individual presentations to those more advanced learning situations where parts of the instruction are individualized.

1	2	3	4	5
Large	Medium large	Medium	Small	Individual

Use the same group-size values as above.

C. Practice of information. In the next stage of instruction the students obtain practice in using the information of a discipline or field of study to solve problems. This scale differs from the above two in that group size is based not on efficiency of presentation but on how the information learned is applied in productive thinking (that is, problem-solving and creativity). In certain content areas, groups are the basic means for solving problems; in others, problems are solved only individually, and in certain circumstances group and individual work are combined. Rate this third type of instruction with reference to the needs for formation of semantic networks (Aspect 2 in Step 3) and the development of schemata (Aspect 3).

1	2	3	4	5
Group	Group/ individual	Equal	Individual/ group	Individual

Step 5: Interpretation of profile

This step involves an interpretation of Steps 1-4 (*cf* Appendix pp 62-3). As a practical application, an example of media specification profile analysis (following Steps 1-5) is given. Putting together the specification profile analysis involves creative judgement. None of the steps described above is completely independent of the other steps so the results of this final analysis and interpretation are not absolute but are on a continuum, ranging between the two absolutes of 'yes' and 'no' concerning the application of video and computer technology. Proceed in the analysis as follows:

a) Add together the ratings for each step and put the total score on the specification profile analysis chart (Figure 2).

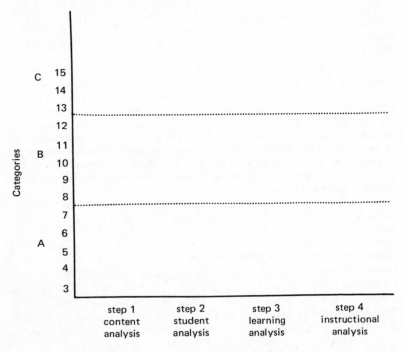

Figure 2. *Step 5: media specifications profile analysis chart*

b) For each step there are three basic decision categories (dotted lines in Figure 2); Category A, scores 3-7; Category B, scores 8-12; and Category C, scores 13-15. Interpret the decision categories per step as follows:

Step 1: Content analysis

Category A. A rating score in this low range indicates that the content of the course is probably very verbal, non-manipulative, and perhaps has high imagery. Where possible, use of alternative media sources should be avoided. Any media used should be carefully checked for effects of transmediation. Use of media may be helpful only if there is a low rating score in Step 4. That is, in large-group instruction, media of some sort may provide improved attention and interest (check for a Category C rating in Step 2). Conventional instruction may be the most cost-effective here if there is a Category A rating for Step 3. Other forms of instructional support, such as handouts, lecture notes, overhead projectors and so on are valuable in this category.

Category B. A middle rating score probably identifies the majority of courses in higher education. A course with this content rating would benefit from the use of educational technology no matter what the rating scores on the other steps. The important decision is which media to use and for what purpose. If, for example, the course is a Category C in Step 2, then a highly sophisticated adaptive instructional system would seem necessary to cope with the wide variances in the student population — this is true regardless of the instructional rating score in Step 4.

Category C. A rating score at this highest level may at first glance not seem possible, but it does fit nicely for many science courses that are highly visual and manipulative but which have contents that are actually low or marginal for evoking imagery (that is, many concepts in science are labelled by the scientists' name rather than by logical symbols, or the phenomena cannot be easily reduced to verbal presentation — as in a printed textbook). With student learning of information in science, imagery ratings may increase, so this rating may fall back to a Category B rating part way through a course. Instruction here would seem to dictate the use of visuals and provide opportunity for direct student manipulation. Media selection should provide visual support but caution is needed for the effect of transmediation. For example, in an astronomy course on weather and climate, slides on clouds could not be as effective as large screen video demonstrations where movement can be observed. Care should be taken in laboratory courses where real objects may be thought of as the original form if taken out of context. An example of this is lab work in geology, where small rocks are studied in isolation from their source; a student may recognize the lab specimen in the laboratory but fail to recognize it in the real world.

Step 2: Student analysis

Category A. A low rating on this step would probably be found in advanced undergraduate and graduate school courses. Selection of media would certainly depend on the rating score for Step 1. Rarely would a course be found with a Category A here and Category A for Steps 3 and 4. At this intellectual level, the students in a Category A course would probably be manipulating the media themselves. Media usage would probably be beneficial if it were a direct part of the discipline. Other components of good course design should, of course, be followed.

Category B. A middle-range rating score implies diversity in the students, and media selection should be based on the greatest cause of diversity. If diversity is in prior knowledge, then adequate initial assessment is required for each student's introductory form of instruction. Speed in assessment is essential. If diversity is in aptitude, then continuous assessment may be necessary to provide adequate instructional support throughout the course. One of the primary benefits of using educational technology concerns problems in student perception. Media, other than the conventional methods of instruction, seem to provide students with needed changes in initial course perception. Caution is needed, especially if Steps 3 and 4 have rating scores in Category A.

Category C. A rating score in this high range indicates courses which are probably the most difficult to teach and design. Educational technology, in both video and computer forms, can be of almost guaranteed success if applied here. Research findings in educational technology on subject populations with this category rating are entirely positive. If a course has a Category C rating on Step 2, mediate it immediately.

Step 3: Learning analysis

Category A. A rating score here indicates a focus on the learning of information requiring minimal higher-order mental processing. Selection of media should be based on efficiency of presentation and cost benefit; that is, the least costly method of instruction which allows learning objectives to be met within the shortest time.

Category B. A rating score in the middle range would assume fairly high learning objectives for the course. Instruction should provide for direct demonstration and perhaps some minimal practice in application. Media selection would necessarily include a variety of forms, especially if there was a high rating score in Step 1.

Category C. A rating score in this range would require a highly designed course because the students would be involved in all three aspects of learning. Opportunity to learn semantic networks and schemata should imply a variety of activities in the learning environment, and only the most verbal of content areas would not benefit from use of video and computer technology.

Step 4: Instruction analysis

Category A. A rating score should correspond to an equally low score in Step 3. The type of instructional method could follow conventional forms, but with large groups of students it may be possible to use alternative methods to maintain the quality and consistency of information presented. Mode of instruction should provide for individual learning needs while maintaining cost-effectiveness (that is, adequate student performance at minimal instructional cost).

Category B. A middle rating score shows increased instructional need for small-group learning environments. Such small groups occur mostly in disciplines in which direct demonstrations and practice are part of the content structure. Check with Step 3 to determine which aspects of learning are emphasized; a low score in Step 3 and a medium score here means the objectives of the course are for acquisition of content but much of the learning demands small-group participation. Media selection would follow Category A, Step 3. However, a Category B rating in Step 3, along with the same rating score here, implies the instructional need for various forms of media; check with Step 1 on imagery of the content.

Category C. A high rating score on instruction here implies a need to design high quality, individualized programs of instruction. Media selection should include not only concern for instruction but also for a means of continuous student assessment throughout the course. Students should be continuously advised on their individual learning progress and have sufficient assessment checks to be able to make instructional decisions on learning needs. Media selection should also provide adequate adaptation of the instruction, especially if there was a high rating score for Step 2.

At this point, the media specification profile is ready and Stage 1 is completed. Stage 2 involves matching the profile with the attributes of the various media to determine which technology or technologies to apply in a given course and lesson. Before presenting Stage 2, we give an example of an actual course analysis.

EXAMPLE OF A MEDIA SPECIFICATIONS PROFILE ANALYSIS

Application of the profile analysis to the design of a specific course in higher education will be illustrated in the field of teacher education within the West German university curriculum. A typical program of study for a college student includes work in two major disciplines (for example, mathematics, physics, geography, biology, German, English, physical education, and so on). For students in teacher education, these disciplines become the subjects they will be certified to teach after graduation. For teacher certification, students are required to take courses in the field of teacher education. Students do not have prior experience in teaching when they enter the teacher education program; therefore, they have to start their program with an introductory course in the 'analysis and planning of teaching'. Within such a course at the University of Paderborn, two major objectives have been defined:

☐ The knowledge for understanding the analysis and planning
   categories of instruction

☐ The capability and readiness for planning, performing, and analysing simulated teaching lessons.

In achieving these objectives the students are set four interrelated tasks:

☐ Learning of relevant categories for planning and analysing lessons
☐ Applying the categories in the development of a concept learning lesson using a content from one of the student's two disciplines
☐ Practical performance of the concept lesson within a simulated classroom situation
☐ Participating in an analysis of the teaching performance of the other students in the class.

Because of the possible stress from the practice teaching, the faculty have limited the number of participants within each introductory course to 15 students.

With this background information, we shall proceed with our example.

Example Step 1: Content analysis

A. Original form. The planning and analysis categories (or didactic theories) are primarily presented in book form and are highly verbal. In contrast, the process of instruction as a real event is highly visual. Therefore, on this scale we rate original form as a mix of the two, using a mark of 3.

B. Imagery capability. In judging the imagery potential of the content one should pay special attention to its critical components. Our conclusion here is that the literature on instructional theories has little imagery-evoking power for novices because of their lack of personal teaching experience. We, therefore, mark this factor as a 5.

C. Manipulative aspects. Personal action, in the form of gaining one's first experiences in teaching, is obviously the aim of this course, thus we rate this factor as a 5.

Example Step 2: Student analysis

A. Aptitude. There are at least two primary aptitudes required for this course. First, the capability for text analysis and comprehension, and, second, skill in interpersonal communications. There is little empirical evidence of overall high aptitude in both respects. So a judgement of a wide range is made, and a 4 seems reasonable.

B. Prior knowledge. Prior knowledge is rather easy to judge in this case. Students are beginners in teacher education with little or no knowledge from previous courses. Additionally, their main study efforts refer to other subjects. This is most critical when the subjects are very different from education. Some students have chosen mechanical engineering and mathematics, for example, and thus will have developed learning strategies which are not very appropriate to education. Considering this, the assumption of no prior knowledge is made; a rating of 5 is realistic.

C. Perception. All the students have decided to become teachers and will see the problems of instructional design as a central part of their future jobs. The development of a first concept learning lesson and its performance within a simulated class should not evoke as much stress as giving a first lesson in a real class. Failing in the simulated situation does not include a loss of personal authority and can be seen as being fairly free of personal consequences. Also, students can choose among courses offered by different faculty members. Thus there is no reason to expect a poor perception; a rating of at least 3 seems valid.

Example Step 3: Learning analysis

A. Acquisition of content. From the character of the course it is obvious that it can follow introductory aims in respect to content learning only. The course content has to concentrate on basic planning categories and to avoid too much confusing detail. So the desired level of recall has to be kept low; a mark of 2 is made.

B. Formation of semantic networks. The basic knowledge of the content, however, is to be applied by the students directly in the analysis and the design of concept learning lessons. Looking at different lessons and subjects taught leads to requirements in information processing which demand the recognition of a new problem and the creation of a new solution by using new criteria. Considering the reduction from in-school lessons to simulated ones, a rating of abstract, that is, a score of 4, seems appropriate.

C. Development of schemata. That schemata have to be built up by the students has been argued before. As there are no prior experiences available for most students, it does not seem helpful to allow total student control of instruction. Therefore, a joint control rating of 3 is the choice.

Example Step 4: Instruction analysis

The instruction analysis in our example can start from the known limitation of 15 participants within the course. The two aspects of demonstration of information — firstly, students visiting real school lessons, and secondly, students developing and performing a first concept lesson in the simulated teaching — have already led to a small-group organization for the course. (The reader should note that using our profile criteria would have led to a similar approach being adopted.)

A. Presentation of information. The presentation of instructional theories might as well take place in a group of large or medium size. Therefore, a mark of 2 can be made.

B. Demonstration of information. The demonstration of teaching in a real classroom obviously limits the possible number of participants, thus a rating of 4 is given.

C. Practice of information. Since teaching is primarily an individual activity, a mark of 5 indicates individual practice.

Example Step 5: Interpretation of profile

This step of the analysis leads to an overall view of the categories judged in the prior four steps. The ratings for Steps 1-4 total 13, 12, 9 and 11 respectively. That is, we find a category C in Step 1 and B categories in the others. The result indicates that media usage should be profitable within this course.

The main demand for the use of media comes from the content analysis. Media should compensate for the lack of imagery in the instructional theories and should complement individual teaching. Analysis shows that heterogeneity in aptitude and lack of prior knowledge can be expected. The learning analysis points to difficulties in the application of instructional categories, and the instruction analysis asks for demonstration and practice. The attempt to cope with this requirement leads to three main media applications:

1. The necessary information on instructional categories should be given to the students by means of a printed handout. It can be studied individually, text comprehension can be enhanced by systematic discussion in the class, and it can be referred to during the planning and analysis of the simulated lessons.
2. Instructional categories can be visualized by means of video recordings from lessons. Explanations and comments can be provided for the application of the categories within the recorded lessons.
3. The performance of the students in their simulated teaching can be recorded by video. This allows for the repetition of the actual behaviour, its systematic evaluation in the course, and a visual feedback to the student.

The suitability of this decision will become more obvious to the reader after a closer look at the attributes of video and computer technology.

Stage 2: Media selection
In the introduction we stated that the application of educational technology was becoming more feasible in higher education because of the new developments in both the instructional design process (that is, growth of cognitive psychology in application for instruction) and the cost factor in electronic equipment (especially for computers and video). In Stage 1, the first of these new developments was incorporated in the course analysis procedures by creating a specification profile for purposes of media selection. The profile analysis procedures are fundamentally based on a cognitive approach to learning as described in the first part of this chapter. We can now proceed with the decision making on media selection, using the new developments in educational technology. We discuss first the attributes of video and computer technologies in instruction. Then we describe the procedures for matching the specification profile with the media attributes.

Video technology
Technology has contributed to the dissemination of information since

Gutenberg's invention of the printing press in the fifteenth century. Since then we have had telephone broadcasting, audio disc and tape recordings, photography, motion pictures and sound pictures. Video technology may, at first glance, seem to offer little beyond what is achievable by sound pictures. But in fact video presents several new opportunities. For example:

☐ We can watch the World Cup Final thousands of miles away without any time delay

☐ The soccer fan can simultaneously make a personal copy of the event and replay all or part of the action at any time and as often as he or she wants to

☐ The coaches of the teams involved can tape the game, and play it back in slow motion to analyse the strengths and the weaknesses at half-time and after the game

☐ The engineer in an atomic power plant can control the actions of a robot in a non-accessible area via a video screen display.

All of these possibilities exist because:

a) the video camera converts a given audio-visual event into a sequence of electric signals that can be transmitted to a remote place and reproduced on a video screen

b) the videorecorder allows for storage of signals

c) it allows for the retrieval of a visual (and audio) representation of the original event subsequently and repeatedly.

Several ways of using video technology have been developed in higher education. First, broadcasts from commercial and public television stations can be taped for classroom use at times and places which suit class timetables and teacher needs. Teachers are no longer forced to adjust the sequence of lessons to the dates and hours determined by a broadcaster. Furthermore, they can select a single program from a series to suit their own educational aims; for example, to review a topic already taught, to demonstrate the importance of a content by a real-life example, or to help the students solve a particular problem. This use of video is not, of course, limited to educational programs. Those produced for general public viewing can very well be integrated into a lesson; for example, a professor of German literature could find useful a videotape of a televised performance of Goethe's *Faust*; a biology teacher might find important information on the changing living conditions of whales given most effectively in a televised news report; news reports on water pollution caused by cellulose factories could be used to stimulate discussion in a political science class. The enormous possibilities offered by video along these lines are limited mainly because of lack of experience in instructors and shortage of necessary equipment.

Another common educational video use is the transmission of scientific experiments. A professor can demonstrate a chemical or physical process via videoscreens to a large audience, whereas without the aid of a video camera, all the important details would be visible only to a small group of students. Even microscopic processes can be enlarged and viewed by students. As the experiment is recorded, it can be demonstrated again and again. This can be very cost-effective when the material and effort required to set up a repetition of the original experiment are considered (and it is certainly cheaper than film making). It can become the only way to give students an audio-visual demonstration of an experiment which has to be conducted in the laboratory because of the equipment, danger or length of time involved.

A third example of video use is the recording of performances by students. In role playing, recitations, skill training, lecturing or sports exercises the behaviour of the students can be taped. Student and instructor can then analyse the student's actions and discuss problems by referring to the recording of the actual process. Misconceptions can be straightened out and, most important, students can get an impression of their own behaviour from the viewpoint of an observer. Such visual and audio feedback can be helpful in developing a realistic self-concept.

Further uses of video technology are described elsewhere in this book or see, for example, Fahry and Palme (1980). What is more important here is to relate the instructional design variables developed from the model of learning and thinking to aspects of video technology, especially addressing the forms of learning explained earlier in this chapter: for learning, video may be used to present content in an audio-visual mode. The video presentations used must correspond to the depth of learning planned. For this reason public programs especially must be used with care. In news, interviews and magazine entertainment brilliant pictures often dominate the structured presentation of content, and, not surprisingly, recall rates for such programs are generally not high.

Any increase in the level of information processing can be obtained by two basic approaches:

1. In student-controlled situations, students can review the whole program or 'difficult' sequences until the desired precision of encoding is reached. Such study can be supported by additional printed handouts giving summaries and mnemonics.
2. In more instructor-controlled approaches, the lesson can include additional practice, discussions, or problems on the new content.

This second possibility leads to the learning of semantic networks. That is, content-element interrelations become established and provide the basis for problem-solving processes. On the more concrete level, video applications can contribute to the development of semantic networks in two respects. First, new problems can be introduced to students; their importance and their basic components can be explained so that students can build up an initial orientation to the new situation. The illustrative potentials of an audio-visual presentation here can especially motivate students to cope with the given problem. Second, the path to a solution for a given problem — the corresponding algorithm or strategy — can be demonstrated. The demonstration method can furthermore be taken over by students via practice with problems of the same type following the instructor-presented demonstration. Starting with such a demonstration can avoid the elaboration of wrong strategies by students, which often happens when there is no appropriate model.

In complex content areas, video applications can contribute to learning by the direct presentation of real-life situations. The situations can first be viewed and then specific problems and solutions can be analysed. In a business management class, for example, the flow of material in a production line could be demonstrated by a video tape; students would observe the 'bottle-necks' that limit productivity and then work out proposals for improvement with a view to safety, working conditions, costs and so on.

In analysing a complex situation as in the above example, the student has the opportunity, more or less consciously, to develop a corresponding schema. Video applications in the development of schemata may not seem to be possible. However, thinking of such schemata (which regulate social or communicative behaviours) hints at video uses — for example, for feedback on student performances as mentioned above. Role-playing or teaching-skill tasks can be re-analysed in respect to the schemata that may have been applied by the actors. Possible aspects for such an analysis could be in regard to the amount of information used in an interpretation, the flexibility in reactions to changes in the given body of information, or the possible set of alternatives for the interpretation of some body of information.

Just a hint on a last type of video use in regard to the development of schemata may be given toward the active video production by students. Producing a video tape on a topic in this respect means to elaborate an interpretation of it. In other words, this can be said to be part of the development of a schema to an aspect of a person's environment.

Computer technology

Computer technology has for many years offered educators a medium by which individualized learning could be implemented in a variety of instructional formats, for instance, complete computerized systems (computer-assisted instruction, CAI), use of the computer for management and assessment (computer-managed instruction), simulations, and educational games (Breuer, 1981; Tennyson, 1974). Recent advancements in microelectronics provide educators with even further hardware and software capabilities for designing truly sophisticated computer-based instructional (CBI) learning environments (Tennyson, 1981a). However, higher education faculty have not fully applied the attributes of computer technology to their fields of specialization. Selecting appropriate uses of computer technology for individual course specifications, we present a brief overview of the four primary instructional uses of computer technology: CAI, CMI, simulations and games.

Computer-assisted instruction (CAI) is a means of instruction by which the primary learning materials are presented directly to the student via the computer. CAI performs three functions: instruction, assessment and management. The critical feature of a good CAI lesson is that it is adaptive to the individual student (Rothen & Tennyson, 1978). An adaptive system provides a CAI lesson that can modify the instruction in some meaningful way and we can have a management system that is both diagnostic and prescriptive. An adaptive management system modifies the instruction by constantly updating its data base while the student is learning. This iterative process accounts for both the amount of instruction presented as well as the sequence of the instruction. Information is collected during on-task learning so that students receive only the instruction needed to achieve the mastery criterion of a given unit of instruction. This form of instructional management is based on cognitive principles of learning and is put into operation as computer programmed decision rules, not the branching technique favoured by educators in designing programmed instruction. (For more detailed discussion of this approach see Breuer & Keller, 1977; Tennyson & Rothen, 1979; Tennyson, 1981b.)

CAI lessons vary in length for each instructional unit, usually according to individual student learning time. Obviously, using computers in this mode of instruction requires a learning environment in which computers are easily available in sufficient numbers to accommodate the students without the inconvenience of waiting in line, restricted hours or scattered locations. One computer terminal, in a typical learning environment, can handle approximately five hours of instruction per day. In other words, given a 30-minute instructional lesson, it would be possible to schedule ten students per terminal each day.

Computer-managed instruction (CMI) refers to use of the computer to manage the progress of students through a particular instructional program. With CMI, the instruction is usually delivered to the students via other media. CMI management functions include record keeping (for example, student course and/or assignment schedule, performance records), reporting (for example, output summaries according to course needs), and advising (for example, informing teachers and/or students on current performance status, informing both of future instructional needs, and so on). Many CMI system software programs for microcomputers are available for purchase from commercial sources.

Simulation refers to learning situations in which a real event or phenomenon can be replicated. Computer simulations are useful in training for specific semantic networks or in learning complex schemata, where practice in certain situations is necessary to learn appropriate, rather than specific, solutions. Since simulations replicate real-world situations, each simulation design is unique and must be evaluated according to how close it replicates both the critical and irrelevant features of the real situation. Simulation can be appropriate in several situations, including: (a) where the event or phenomenon is too dangerous to use in learning, (b) where the event or phenomenon cannot occur or rarely occurs in a learning environment, (c) where practice is necessary but costly, (d) where a simulation as part of the situation can act as a screening device for candidates, and (e) where other variables or conditions make a simulation more cost-effective than the real event or phenomenon.

Simulations may also be useful in courses directed towards learning cognitive processes — especially in a practice format where students learn techniques in solving problems using variations in assessment criteria. In such simulations the educator or the program could adjust certain critical parameters of the situation and then view the students' process in dealing with the changes. In many situations with numerous and/or complex systems of parameters, a computer program could provide an infinite number of simulations. Simulations that contain a finite number of rules and outcomes do not seem of particular value other than perhaps as motivation or as an introduction to computers; such simulations often get close or actually turn into games.

Educational games are mental competitions conducted according to rules, and they should be directly linked to an educational goal or objective defined in the curricular plan or course. Confusion between simulations and games occurs when educators use some real situation (for example, the American Civil War or the Western movement in America during the nineteenth century) in a game format. In a game, unlike a simulation, specific rules are used, player choices are made in the context of the rules and, being a competition, one either wins or loses as the end product. Games are valuable in education when they fulfil some indirect learning goal or objective. That is, games themselves do not result in acquisition of knowledge or cognitive processes that are adequate for reality. If the educator is not careful in labelling a computer game as such, the student may erroneously encode the game as factual knowledge. Games can be a means of assessing certain psychological factors, and thus be valuable in a selection process or in diagnosing mental problems (Tennyson & Tennyson, 1982). In making decisions on possible use of games it is important to consider the following: (a) games should not be a means of providing directly the content of a course; (b) games can be part of a motivational program; (c) games can be used as assessment devices when direct assessment is not possible or desirable.

During the 1970s, most educational computing centered on the development of games and instructional programs either of a one-session format or of a drill-and-practice nature using only the simplest of criterion (that is, percentage correct out of a specific set number). In these uses, computers proved to be quite costly, and not widely accepted by educators for use in programs of instruction. However, by analysing the attributes described here, it may be possible to introduce computer technology into the main instructional programs of higher education.

Attributes of video and computer technology
Selection of video and computer technology for application in higher education instruction is based on evaluating four primary evaluation attributes in reference to the media specification profile analysis (see Figure 2) of a given course. These attributes are visual, audio, calculation and sequence.

Visual
Video is a recording device for replicating directly the relevant and irrelevant features of any visually-based object or event. Computers, on the other hand, can only provide programmed visuals, usually with

omission of irrelevant features. Such omissions may not be a serious problem in certain learning situations where imagery rating of the content is high. Video is, of course, the current most cost-effective means for recording and displaying visual information. Film is much too expensive for educational applications, except for commercial projects that seek wide distribution. With the growing number of video playback recorders in private use, high-quality video-based instruction in the home has become increasingly possible. Even on conventional campuses, private video systems are so readily available that students can borrow video-based course materials for use in their places of residence.

With video-based instruction, the conventional campus can expand its form of instruction without changing its present administrative structure; students can actually assume part of the equipment and operation costs. Video-based visuals offer still pictures, motion, black and white, colour, and repetition of specific sections (when appropriately indexed). Computer-based visuals offer motion (but here it is definitely a simulation and extremely limited in presentation of irrelevant features), certain models offer colour, and repetition is possible but usually more complex in operation than video (that is, directions for finding specific displays are often not available). Selection of media for visual needs should include an analysis of these attributes:

Video	*Computer*
Linear motion	Animated graphics
Still frames	Loss of irrelevant information
Minimal loss of irrelevant	not important
information	Dynamic display of visuals
Information retrieval	

Audio

Both video and computer technology offer audio; but there are distinct differences. Video-based tapes offer audio simultaneous with visuals in a rich mix of the two. Computer audio, like computer visuals, is limited in irrelevant information. A single voice is of course available on computers, but the sound is limited in contrast to video technology; however, in certain applications (for example, language development) the computer audio is more flexible because of its random access retrieval capability and dynamic nature to create infinite sound productions. For example, computer audio is flexible in sound generation for study or assessment of music production. Video-based audio should be viewed as a pre-recorded attribute that provides almost complete reproduction of live sound; computer-audio, on the other hand, should be viewed as providing instantaneous, dynamic sound.

Calculation

This attribute is the prime purpose and function of computers; video technology does not have a calculation capability. Calculation capability offers a number of possibilities for providing direct, individualized instruction. Most of the unique features of the four types of computer-based instruction described above are based on this attribute. These include such things as immediate assessment for diagnosis and prescription of instruction, moment-to-moment (micro) updates of learning needs, ready access to student cumulative instructional records, flexibility in simulation and game parameter figures, speed in presenting decision-making information, creative forms of student control and decision-making, and other spontaneous instructional and learning conditions only previously available in one-to-one, tutor-to-student learning situations. For example, the calculation attribute can be used for adjusting the instructional display time according to specific periods in the learning process (Tennyson & Park, in press a). That is, when encoding information, increased amounts of content are initially needed per learning period while in later learning of semantic networks and schemata less content and more processing time are required per period. Determination of this display time interval is calculated from preassessment data, error pattern, time expended on previous displays, and current learning time.

Sequence

Conventionally presented instruction can be characterized as sequencing information in a linear manner. Video by itself is also basically a means of presenting information in a linear manner and is usually very efficient at it. It can be interrupted for review and exact replication — unlike a lecturer or live presentation. Computers, on the other hand, provide maximum flexibility in sequencing. The lowest form of program-controlled sequencing is the branching technique (Crowder, 1960), but now sophisticated computer-based management systems provide for adaptive and intelligent sequencing based on parameters of performance, learning, time, response patterns, period of learning, and structure of the content to be learned (Park & Tennyson, 1980; Tennyson & Park, in press b).

Video and computer technology will eventually provide effective computer controlled sequencing of video-based lessons (for example, video discs), providing video technology with flexibility in sequencing. But this remains a prospect for the future, although certain development projects have already produced computer controlled video-based instruction. These joint video/computer development projects have been very expensive and limited in dissemination because of the hardware requirements for such a joint instructional station (that is, video monitor, playback recorder, computer and connections).

Matching profile analysis with video and computer attributes

The second stage of media selection involves two steps: firstly, defining the media specifications for a course and, secondly, selecting media usage for course lessons. This deductive approach to course development provides the means for applying video and computer technology at the lesson level by passing through a macro to a micro process of decision-making.

Step 1

The matching process in this first step of macro analysis involves the following:

1. Do the media specifications profile analysis.
2. Check for any scores in the four analysis steps that are 4 or 5 (see Figure 2). Any such score would indicate a need for some sort of course mediation.
3. Obtain the total score for each step and identify each corresponding category. Using the descriptions provided in this chapter, make an interpretation of the analysis. Include Item B above in this interpretation.
4. From the interpretation, specify the media needs for the course.

It is necessary next to analyse the individual lessons of the course. This micro analysis is rarely done, and instructors attempt instead to fit a given medium to all lessons regardless of the different media needs of each.

Step 2

The matching process in this second step (micro analysis) involves the following:

1. Identify the content and activities of each lesson within a course.
2. Using this chapter and others in this book, to make yourself familiar with the possible applications of each medium.
3. Within each lesson, compare the content and desired objectives with those of the course media specifications profile; clarify any possible differences. From this lesson analysis, check the desired instructional needs of the content with the four media attributes: visual, audio, sequence and calculation.
4. For each lesson, identify the desired medium or media and integrate each lesson into the total structure of the course. For example, if the course is to use some form of computer-managed system, would individual lessons use the computer, and if so, would the lesson's management system be adaptive? Also, some courses may be entirely individualized but the lessons may exhibit a variety of media depending on the content and objectives of the specific lesson. On the other hand, some courses may use the same media in every lesson because the content and objectives remain constant.

In summary, the selection of media for a course should proceed in a deductive logical approach allowing for the tracing of each learning activity in a lesson back to the most general analysis of the course. The Stage 1 analysis provides for those general specifications of a course while Stage 2 moves the specifications to the lesson level. Associated with Stage 2 is the understanding of video and computer usage in learning environments and the selection of each technology based on matching the content and objective needs of the lesson with the media attributes.

The need for creativity in course and lesson design should be emphasized. When trying to use a new medium, users often try to apply the same method and/or format they used in the conventional medium. For example, when video technology was first introduced in higher education, it was almost entirely for the videotaping of a professor giving a lecture. So the students, instead of listening to a live lecture, listened to a videotaped lecture — hardly a creative use of video. The same is true of computer technology, where initial uses were simply mini-lessons using a programmed instruction (PI) format of single-framed, linear presentations (with branching based on a given response without taking into consideration previous history or patterns of responses). Naturally, once a deductive approach has been developed, it is possible to review and evaluate the course system by an inductive approach. This allows for further refinements in the decision-making on media application.

CONCLUSION

In this chapter we have introduced a means for media selection according to a cognitive theoretical approach to learning. Cognitive psychological theory focuses on the higher order thinking processes because it is concerned with how and why people process information in the memory. Because of this philosophy toward its theory base, the cognitive approach to learning makes it possible to use more thoroughly the powerful attributes of both video and computer technology. Cognitive psychology is directly concerned with the processing of information through the three aspects of learning defined in this chapter. Creative application of the attributes of video and computer technology can allow for learning, and eventually thinking, within the classroom at the highest levels. Instructors can then view the classroom as more than a place for just disseminating content; they can also see it as an environment in which semantic networks can be learned and provide for the development of schemata in the higher education curriculum. Video and computer technology, with increased availability, can facilitate directly student learning at both the semantic and schemata levels while attending to the acquisition of content.

This chapter provides the initial process in the design analysis of a course in reference to its content, students, learning outcomes, and instructional methods. It further extends that process by deductively selecting media needs at the basic unit of learning — the lesson. To make this process efficient, we have attempted to put the total procedure into a series of steps, assuming that after going through the chapter a reader will be able to effectively use the steps without expending undue time. Also, we expect each user to adjust the process according to his or her individual situation and update iteratively the process for improving it. What we have presented are guidelines, allowing each reader the opportunity to adjust and modify according to his or her situation.

Notes

1. Funding for this chapter was provided in part by the Educational Systems Research and Development Division of Control Data Corporation, Minneapolis, Minnesota (#82T101).

REFERENCES

Anderson, J R (1976) *Language, Memory and Thought*, Erlbaum, Hillsdale, NJ.

Baddeley, A (1974) *The Psychology of Memory*, Basic Books, New York.

Breuer, K (1981) *Computerunterstuetztes Lernen auf der Basis eines Informationsprogramms*, Arbeitsgemeinschaft fuer Hochschuldidaktik, Hamburg.

Breuer, K (1982) 'Zur Lehr-lerntheoretischen Grundlegung der Computerunterstuetzten Unterweisung', *Log In*, 2, 3, 11-14.

Breuer, K & Keller, W (1977) 'Realisationsformen der Lernersteuerung im Computerunterstuetzten Unterricht (CUU): Das Modell TICCIT und das Aachener Modell', *Zeitschrift fuer Erziehungswissenschaftlichte Forschung*, 11, 191-207.

Bruner, J S (1971) *Studien zur kognitiven Entwicklung*, Klett, Stuttgart.

Burns, R B (1980) 'Relation of aptitudes to learning at different points in time during instruction', *Journal of Educational Psychology*, 72, 785-95.

Crowder, N A (1960) 'Automatic tutoring by intrinsic programming', in Lumsdaine, A A & Glaser, R (eds), *Teaching Machines and Programmed Learning: A Source Book*, National Educational Association Department of Audio-Visual Instruction, Washington.

Doerner, D (1976) *Problemloesen als Informationsverarbeitung*, Kohlhammer, Stuttgart.

Fahry, D & Palme, K (1980) *Video Technik: Handbuch 1, Grundlagen, Anwendungen*, Oldenburg, Muenchen.

Gibson, E J (1969) *Principles of Perceptual Learning and Development*, Appleton-Century-Crofts, New York.

Glaser, R (1977) *Adaptive Education: Individual Diversity and Learning*, Holt, Rinehart & Winston, New York.

Greeno, J G (1980) 'Some examples of cognitive task analysis with instructional implications', in Snow, R E, Federico, P A & Montague, W E (eds), *Aptitude, Learning, and Instruction, 2: Cognitive Process Analyses of Learning and Problem Solving*, Erlbaum, Hillsdale, NJ.

Herrmann, D J & Harwood, J R (1980) 'More evidence for the existence of separate semantic and episodic stores in long-term memory', *Journal of Experimental Psychology: Human Learning and Memory*, 6, 467-78.

Jassal, R S & Tennyson, R D (1982) 'Application of concept learning research in design of instructional systems', *International Journal of Instructional Media*, 9, 185-205.

Jenkins, J J (1974) 'Remember that old theory of memory? Well forget it!' *American Psychologist*, 29, 785-95.

Johansen, K J & Tennyson, R D (in press) 'Effect of adaptive advisement on perception in learner controlled, computer-based instruction using a rule-learning task', *Educational Communication and Technology Journal*.

Kieffer, L & Tennyson, R D (1973) 'Effects of concurrent negative feedback on performance of two motor tasks', *Journal of Motor Behavior*, 5, 241-48.

LaBerge, D (1976) 'Perceptual learning and attention', in Estes, W K (ed), *Handbook of Learning and Cognitive Processes, 4, Attention and Memory*, Erlbaum, Hillsdale, NJ.

Lindsay, P & Norman, D (1977) *Human Information Processing*, Academic Press, New York.

McKeachie, W J (1972) 'Instructional psychology', in *Annual Review of Psychology*, **25**, Annual Reviews, Inc, Palo Alto, CA.

Moscovitch, M & Klein, D (1980) 'Material-specific perceptual interference for visual words and faces: Implications for models of capacity limitations attention, and laterality', *Journal of Experimental Psychology: Human Perception and Performance*, **6**, 590-604.

Park, O & Tennyson, R D (1980) 'Adaptive design strategies for selecting number and presentation order of examples in coordinate concept acquisition', *Journal of Educational Psychology*, **72**, 362-71.

Perlmutter, J, Harsip, J & Myers, J L (1976) 'The role of semantic knowledge in retrieval from episodic long-term memory: Implications for a model of retrieval', *Memory and Cognition*, **4**, 361-68.

Piaget, J (1972) *Psychologie der Intelligenz*, Walter, Olten, Freiburg.

Rasco, R W, Tennyson, R D & Boutwell, R C (1975) 'Imagery instructions and drawings in learning prose', *Journal of Educational Psychology*, **67**, 188-92.

Rohwer, W (1980) 'How the smart get smarter', *Educational Psychologist*, **15**, 35-43.

Rosenberg, B A (1980) 'Mental-task instructions and optokinetic nystagmus to the left and right', *Journal of Experimental Psychology: Human Perception and Performance*, **6**, 459-72.

Rothen, W & Tennyson, R D (1978) 'Application of Baye's theory in designing computer-based adaptive instructional strategies', *Educational Psychologist*, **12**, 317-23.

Scandura, J M (1977) 'Structural learning approach to instructional problems', *American Psychologist*, **32**, 33-53.

Scarr, S (1981) 'Testing of children: Assessment and the many determinants of intellectual competence', *American Psychologist*, **10**, 1159-66.

Schroder, H M, Driver, M J & Streufert, S (1967) *Human Information Processing*, Holt, Rinehart & Winston, New York.

Schroder, H M, Karlins, M & Phares, J O (1973) *Education for Freedom*, Wiley, New York.

Skinner, B F (1958) 'Teaching machines', *Science*, **128**, 269-77.

Snow, R E (1980) 'Aptitude processes', in Snow, R E, Federico, P A & Montague, W E (eds), *Aptitude, Learning & Instruction, Volume 1: Cognitive Process Analyses of Aptitude*, Erlbaum, Hillsdale, NJ.

Streufert, S & Streufert, S C (1978) *Behavior in the Complex Environment*, Winston, Washington.

Tennyson, H H & Tennyson, R D (1982) 'Microcomputers as a tool in clinical assessment and treatment', *International Review of Applied Psychology*, **31**, 523-37.

Tennyson, R D (1982) 'Interactive effect of cognitive learning theory with computer attributes in the design of computer-assisted instruction', *Journal of Educational Technology Systems*, **10**, 175-86.

Tennyson, R D (1981a) 'Improvement in college teaching using historical objectives and contemporary instructional science', *International Journal of Instructional Media*, **10**, 339-47.

Tennyson, R D (1981b) 'Use of adaptive information for advisement in learning concepts and rules using computer-assisted instruction', *American Educational Research Journal*, **18**, 425-38.

Tennyson, R D (1978) 'Pictorial support and specific instructions as design variables for children's concept and rule learning', *Educational Communications Technology Journal*, **26**, 291-99.

Tennyson, R D (1974) 'Applications of computers in education', *Audiovisual Instruction*, **19**, 49-52.

Tennyson, R D (1972) 'A review of experimental methodology in instructional task sequencing', *A V Communications Review*, **20**, 147-59.

Tennyson, R D & Boutwell, R C (1974) 'An audio-tutorial instructional approach to individualizing college geology', *Improving Human Performance: A Research Quarterly, 3*, 15-21.

Tennyson, R D & Park, O (1980) 'The teaching of concepts: A review of instructional design research literature', *Review of Educational Research, 50*, 55-70.

Tennyson, R D & Park, S (in press a) 'Process learning time as an adaptive design variable in concept learning using computer-based instruction', *Journal of Educational Psychology.*

Tennyson, R D & Park, S (in press b) 'Review of the research and theory of the empirically-based Minnesota adaptive instructional system', *Journal of Computer-based Instruction.*

Tennyson, R D & Rothen, W (1977) 'Pre-task and on-task adaptive design strategies for selecting number of instances in concept acquisition', *Journal of Educational Psychology, 69*, 586-92.

Tennyson, R D & Rothen, W (1979) 'Management of computer-based instruction: Design of an adaptive control strategy', *Journal of Computer-based Instruction, 5*, 126-34.

Tobias, S (1976) 'Achievement treatment interactions', *Review of Educational Research, 46*, 61-74.

Tulving, E (1972) 'Episodic and semantic memory', in Tulving, E & Donaldson, W (eds), *Organization of Memory,* Academic Press, New York.

Tulodziecki, G & Breuer, K (in press) 'Zur Entwicklung von Unterrichtskonzepten', in Tulodziecki, G, Breuer, K & Hauff, A, *Konzepte fuer das berufliche Lehren und Lernen,* Klinkhardt, Bad Heilbrunn.

Wickelgren, W A (1977) *Learning and Memory,* Prentice-Hall, Englewood Cliffs, NJ.

APPENDIX
List of stages and steps in the instructional design guidelines
STAGE 1 Course specification profile analysis
    Step 1: Content analysis
        A. Original form
        B. Imagery capability
        C. Manipulative aspects
    Step 2: Student analysis
        A. Aptitude
        B. Prior knowledge
        C. Perception
    Step 3: Learning analysis
        A. Acquisition of content
        B. Formation of semantic networks
        C. Development of schemata
    Step 4: Instruction analysis
        A. Presentation of information
        B. Demonstration of information
        C. Practice of information
    Step 5: Interpretation of profile
        Step 1: Content analysis
        Step 2: Student analysis
        Step 3: Learning analysis
        Step 4: Instruction analysis
Example (following Steps 1 to 5)

STAGE 2 Media selection
    Video technology
    Computer technology
    Attributes of video and computer technology
    — Visual
    — Audio
    — Calculation
    — Sequence
    Matching profile analysis with video and computer attributes
    Step 1 (macro analysis)
    Step 2 (micro analysis)
Conclusion

3. Interactive Video in Higher Education

Diane M Gayeski and
David V Williams

SUMMARY

Interactive video presents many challenges and opportunities as a new instructional technology in higher education. But how can it be most effectively employed and how can colleges and universities begin implementing these systems? This chapter discusses the variety of hardware/software systems available, describes the utilization of interactive video in a number of college and university settings, and recommends procedures whereby institutions can go about selecting and developing interactive video teaching materials.

The uses of both video and computer-assisted instruction (CAI) technologies in colleges and universities have grown over the past two decades. However, educators have experienced the shortcomings of each medium as well. Video programs present information in a lock-step fashion regardless of student comprehension or attention, requiring no active participation and providing no measure of achievement to the instructor. CAI, on the other hand, requires activity in responding to questions, and presents information appropriate to those answers through branching, often recording student progress at the same time. However, it lacks the ability to present the vivid audio and visual information that video can recreate so well. In the late 1970s, advances in microprocessor technology brought about the integration of these two media, 'interactive video'. This new technology promises the best features of both individualized, participatory CAI and realistic, captivating video.

Many people conceive of interactive video in terms of its hardware (generally stereotyped as a microcomputer linked with a videodisc player). However, interactivity is a behavioural concept and an instructional style more appropriately defined by the *outcomes* of the technology for the student and instructor (Gayeski & Williams, 1980). We have developed a model of 'levels of interactivity' which interrelates hardware, program design, and the information provided to the learner and the managing instructor (see Figure 1). The first level is 'direct address'. Rather than specialized technology, the technologically simple but instructionally powerful technique of scripting that 'speaks' directly to the viewer, is employed. This can involve asking questions for the viewers to answer 'in their heads' or pointing out significant aspects of the scene. Direct address also requires a thorough understanding of

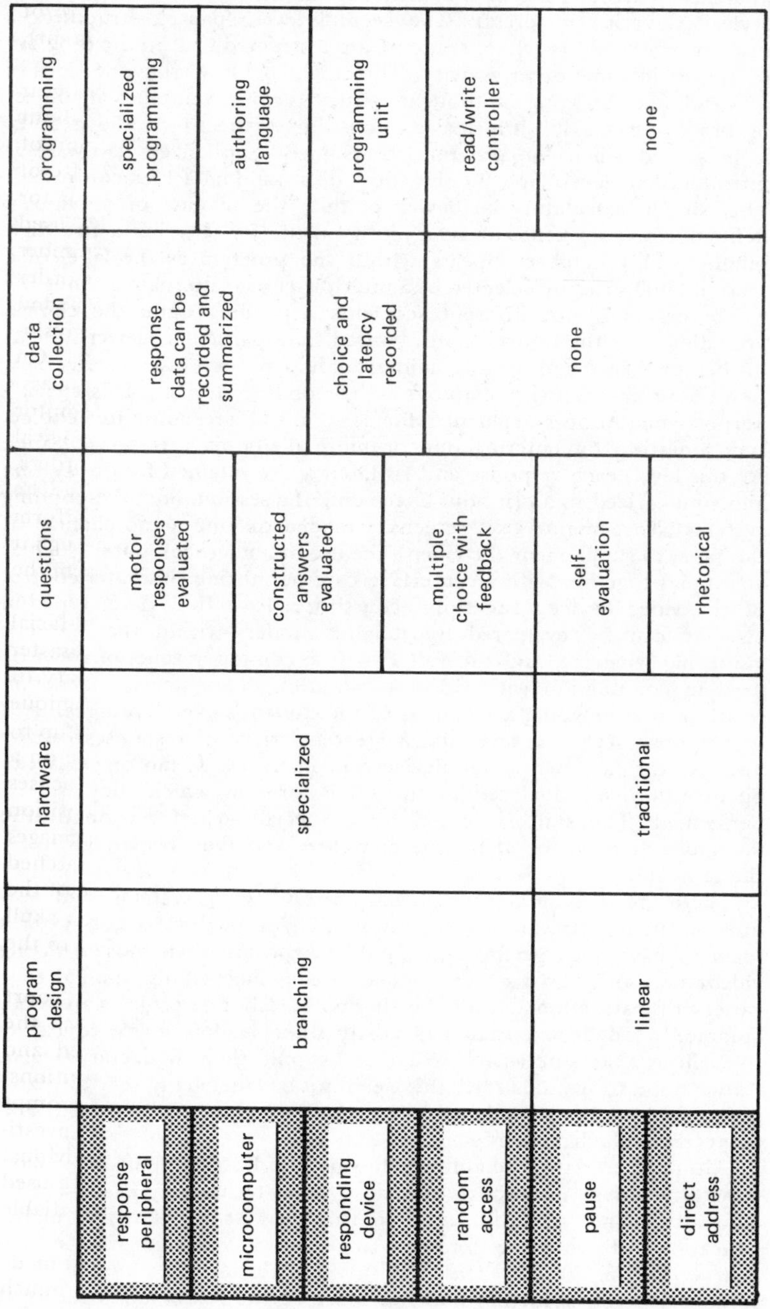

	program design	hardware	questions	data collection	programming
response peripheral	branching	specialized	motor responses evaluated	response data can be recorded and summarized	specialized programming
microcomputer	branching	specialized	constructed answers evaluated	response data can be recorded and summarized	authoring language
responding device	branching	specialized	multiple choice with feedback	choice and latency recorded	programming unit
random access	linear	specialized	self-evaluation	none	read/write controller
pause	linear	traditional	rhetorical	none	none
direct address	linear	traditional		none	none

Figure 1. *Levels of interactivity*

audience characteristics so that the program relates its content to their styles (Gayeski, in press). The second level, 'pause', structures a program with points where students are instructed to stop the program to engage in some other activity. This might be answering questions in a workbook, engaging in thought or discussion, examining an object or practising a skill. Information for self-assessment of the activity is presented when the program is resumed. Specialized hardware is introduced in level three in the form of a 'random-access controller'. This simple calculator-like device permits the playing of previously defined video segments in an arbitrary order by entering a two-digit number. This number appears within the program as the label of a section which can be selected or a multiple-choice alternative. Thus the video 'branches' to different segments depending upon the choice, providing only the information required by a particular viewer in light of his or her demonstrated understanding or expressed preference. Level four interactivity employs a 'responding device'. This special-purpose microprocessor enables the selection of a response to a choice-type question by entering one or more digits via a response panel. At this level, each response and its latency are retained by the system and summarized in a print-out at the end of a session. Some responding systems also generate text screens, encoded on one audio channel of the tape, to supplement the video. The use of a microcomputer (such as an Apple) together with an interface card permitting computer control of the video device's functions, constitutes level five. Here, typed-in answers can be evaluated by judging models within the system's authoring language, and the full range of computer functions can be used in conjunction with video. In addition, branching can occur in relation to an ongoing assessment of the student's overall progress and/ or response style. At level six, a greater variety of responses can be assessed through peripheral devices. In many cases, motor skills can be quantitatively analysed in the same form in which they will be performed. The skill is sensed by a specially-wired version of the manipulandum, analysed by the computer and then responded to by the program.

There are a number of such hardware/software systems, and new ones are being introduced almost monthly. Although videodisc systems seem to have been getting more public exposure than those utilizing videotape, both playback vehicles are being successfully applied to a variety of instructional needs. Furthermore, elaborate projects are more commonly publicized than less costly ones, leading many educators to believe that interactive video is beyond their budgetary reach. As we hope to demonstrate, this need not be true; many very effective programs have been produced using simple production equipment and inexpensive playback hardware.

Although to date, the military, business, industry and medicine have used interactive video most extensively, the technology has found its way into higher education as well. However, its impact upon higher education will be more complex since this technology affects both *instruction* and *research*, as well as constituting both *method* and *content* in each academic domain. Most of the initial applications of interactive techniques have been in its role as a method of instruction.

The Nebraska Videodisc Design/Production Group (of the Nebraska ETV Network at the University of Nebraska, Lincoln) was created in 1978 to explore the potential of videodisc technology and to become a service agency for videodisc production. Since that time, it has been involved in the making of over 40 videodiscs, mostly for industrial clients. They also sponsor videodisc symposia and workshops on disc mastering and production (Nugent & Christie, 1982). However, they have produced a college-level interactive videodisc, 'The Puzzle of the Tacoma Narrows Bridge Collapse' which teaches physics principles. Using historical footage of the disaster, the system allows students to perform nine experiments, each of which can be experienced at three levels of difficulty depending upon the mathematics required and the physical principles discussed (Kearsley, 1981).

The Architecture Machine Group at the Massachusetts Institute of Technology has been a pioneer in developing hardware/software systems. Some of them include 'vicarious travel' in which the viewer seems to turn left or right, pause to move closer to an object of interest or even converse with a passer-by. These choices are indicated by touching symbols or parts of the scene. In one version, the viewer's chair is wired to convey the desired changes in orientation. These systems usually involve two or more videodisc players, a mini-computer, a colour graphics processor, video special effects hardware, and a monitor with a touch-sensitive screen. A demonstration program was developed on the topic of bicycle repair. The two-disc paradigm allows visuals from one disc to be mixed with audio from another, and enables switching from segment to segment without breaking the visual continuity. Titles, text information, and control functions are generated by the computer and overlaid on the screen. The touch-sensitive screen allows the student to indicate responses directly in terms of words and objects presented (Backer, 1982). Informational systems of this type were featured in the US Pavilion at the Knoxville World's Fair.

The National Science Foundation has sponsored several college level interactive programs. WICAT Inc (a Utah-based computer and interactive video production company) produced a videodisc for introductory biology based on excerpts of existing films with enhancements of still frames and computer text. The disc consists of 10 lessons, reportedly about one-third of an introductory college biology course. A joint project by Utah State University and the University of Utah resulted in a program on quantum mechanics, electronics and gravitational fields. The original was developed on interactive videotape and then transferred to disc (Kearsley, 1981).

The power of interactive video to simulate conditions which are rare, dangerous, distant, or otherwise difficult for students or researchers to encounter is one of its most significant attractions. This is especially true in medical training situations. The Allied Health Institute of South Oklahoma City Junior College has produced a videodisc/microcomputer program to simulate medical conditions, complete with a visual and auditory data bank of video events, enacted scenes, shots from existing media, and graphic displays and sounds of medical equipment coupled with measures of patient symptoms generated by microcomputer. Students follow an assessment procedure, and in response to their requests, the system provides the appropriate data. For instance, if examination of the patient's eyes is selected as a diagnostic step, a video image of the pupil appears on the monitor. The system also reports errors, and lets students experience the consequences of their choices; for instance, if the student recommends an inappropriate treatment, the video patient may respond by having convulsions (DeChenne & Evans, 1982).

The National Technical Institute for the Deaf (Rochester, New York) developed an interactive videotape and microcomputer program which assists the deaf student in practising speech-reading and job interviewing skills. The student first fills out a typical job application displayed on the screen by typing on the microcomputer keyboard. Then, the videotaped interviewer appears on the screen and asks questions based upon the general information provided by the application. The student answers by typing in a response, and the interviewer responds accordingly (the microcomputer program having analysed the student input and branched the tape to an appropriate segment). If the student is unable to understand the interviewer's question, he or she can ask him to repeat, just as in real life. After three tries, the interviewer looks a little upset, and writes the question down on a piece of notepaper. This ability to simulate a stressful and challenging interpersonal situation before actually encountering it is a unique contribution of interactive video to the educational process.

At Ithaca College, we are using interactive video for individualized instruction in a variety of content areas. The first project was the production of an interactive videotape presenting the 'Levels of Interactivity' for use in our classes and workshop presentations. This early project employed an industrial Sony Betamax videorecorder and an inexpensive random-access controller. In this situation, the technology was at once the method and content of instruction. The same technology was used to produce an interactive videotape to teach television studio lighting through simulation. In this production, a student is presented with information about the basics of lighting, and is then given questions about the material in the form of choices of various lighting configurations; depending upon the answer, the tape branches to a segment showing what the studio scene would look like if the student's concept were carried out. As in many instructional situations, the optimal way to teach lighting is to allow each student to practise different schemes; however, this is not only impractical, but carries with it the possibility of injury. By simulating various lighting plans, students can vicariously place lights and see what the effect looks like when shot on video.

Ithaca College's Office of Career Planning has also produced two interactive videotape programs with the assistance of the School of Communications faculty and students. The small staff of the Career Planning Office has difficulty in scheduling all the students who desire assistance, especially just before graduation. To reduce the repetition of basic information and yet provide a personal and convenient service to students, the Office has produced an interactive tape on job interviewing. Turning the situation around, the student-viewer takes the role of the job interviewer, selecting which questions he or she would like to ask the 'candidate' by selecting from a 'menu' on the screen, to which the videotaped candidate replies. By taking the role of the interviewer, students experience the information-exchange from another perspective, imagine how they would reply if asked that question, and see how the candidate in the program handles the situation. (Andrade, 1982). Another interactive videotape was produced for use in peer counsellor training. Finally, the Office and a student in the Interactive Video class have collaborated in producing an 'interactive resumé' for the student, a 1982 graduate of the School of Communications. The videotape will be sent to prospective employers who will select certain questions which are answered on the tape, segments of the student's video portfolio, and even interviews with the student's references. Each of these programs was executed using moderate-cost video production equipment, and random-access half-inch videocassette players using an inexpensive controller (level three).

A problem faced by higher education today is assisting students in relating the content of general introductory-level courses to their own experiences. Especially in large classes with a diverse student population, incorporating examples or explanations tailored to all the groups represented is impossible. A good example is in teaching the development of behavioural objectives, a concept included in a variety of courses, including educational psychology and theories of communications media. To make the topic a bit more lively and immediately useful to our students, we have produced an interactive videotape which takes the humorous approach of having the student teach a 'poor, lost freshman' how to survive on campus. Of course, in the process of that 'instruction', the need for developing clear objectives becomes evident. After the concept has been developed, students may select examples of behavioural objectives as applied in various professional settings, from developing advertising campaigns to coaching sports.

Interactive technology is also becoming an important part of the content of all curricula concerned with human communication. Ithaca College's Corporate/Organizational Media Department has developed an entire course in the design and production of interactive video and includes interactive content in other related courses, such as instructional media theory, and media facilities design. In the Department of Psychology, the design and evaluation of interactive hardware and software systems through behaviour setting analysis has become a topic for an undergraduate research team, while in the course on tests and measurements, the role of interactive systems in assessment and psychological research is demonstrated. The sign language of the deaf is the topic of an interactive system which provides immediate visual feedback through alternate recording and playback. Each year, the College sponsors an Interactive Video Workshop open to the public, presenting the theory, application, and production of interactive tape and disc programs. In this way, faculty and students interface with professionals in the fields of industrial training, librarianship, biomedical communications, and marketing/advertising in terms of their common interests.

Interactive video, properly understood and implemented, could well become a highly effective adjunct to traditional classroom teaching and established mediated self-instruction, as well as an important research tool. Using this new family of technologies, programs can be produced which:

- [ ] simulate mechanical, organic, or interpersonal processes allowing students access to additional practice in situations which would be impractical for them to encounter in actuality
- [ ] provide drill-and-practice and tutorial instruction incorporating audio, still and moving visuals, and computer-generated text and graphics
- [ ] tailor themselves to a variety of levels of knowledge, skill, or interest, branching to remedial or more advanced material or different examples depending upon a student's input
- [ ] incorporate existing film, video, slide, graphic, computer, and/or text materials into one package which, by its design, mandates active student attention and participation
- [ ] provide feedback to both the student and the managing instructor in terms of individual answers and overall progress
- [ ] open new avenues for behavioural research and psychological assessment through the introduction of less obtrusive measures, more vivid non-verbal stimuli, and adaptive, individualized testing.

Despite these potentials, interactive video in higher education has a number of barriers to overcome before it can become widely accepted. The multitude of incompatible systems currently on the market, and the small chance of any one system emerging as the 'standard', make it difficult to develop materials for mass marketing. Other more traditional and standardized media formats, such as 16mm film and slide/tape have not enjoyed as wide an exposure in higher education as they might have because each institution and, in fact, each professor, believes his or her course to be 'just a bit different' from everyone else's. As yet, no major producer or distributor of materials has taken the creative and financial leap to produce materials uniquely suited to interactive technologies. They are reluctant to do so since they do not believe there is enough hardware in place; of course, consumers will not be likely to buy hardware until there is some software to use with it. This situation, nonetheless, is not unique to interactive video; in 1973, Anastasio and Morgan wrote of the 'vicious circle' of the problems of CAI marketing (see Figure 2).

Because of the absence of and reluctance to buy mass marketed interactive software, colleges and universities wishing to incorporate this new technology into their curricula must produce it themselves. While some are doing so, there are several areas of deficiency: funds, faculty interest, and in-house staff training. In a recent survey of media and learning centre directors in New York State colleges and universities, it was found that 84 per cent of the respondents reported a positive attitude toward interactive video. Only 25 per cent have already incorporated it into their media centre, although 58 per cent plan to do so in the future. Some respondents said that interactive video has 'excellent potential due to user involvement and flexibility' and 'the growing utilization of computers and individualized instruction is changing the face of education' (Simcoe, 1982).

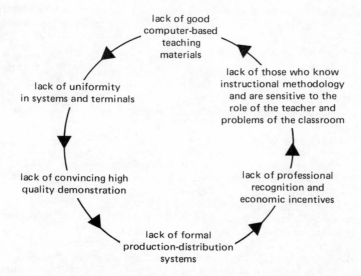

Figure 2. *'The Vicious Circle' of the problems of CAI marketing (Source: Anastasio and Morgan, 1978)*

Some of the reluctance of instructional designers and media producers in higher education to consider producing interactive video is due to the confounding of the controversies surrounding videodisc with the overall field of interactive video. Most have noted with disbelief the introduction of a list of incompatible systems and the collapse of one of the first major companies to produce disc hardware and press disc software, Discovision Associates. Videodisc production also involves the careful production and precise editing of a high-quality videotape master, and the expensive and time-consuming process of disc stamping at one of the few plants operating in the world. Once pressed, of course, the material cannot be altered. Although videodiscs offer very rapid and accurate assessing of segments and individual frames, variable motion control, and cheap replication in quantity, new videotape players can nearly match most of those characteristics without the necessity of introducing yet another new format and the expense and trouble involved in producing a master that probably won't be duplicated in quantity anyway. New half-inch and three-quarter inch VTRs also offer noise-free still frames, slow and fast motion, and rather rapid search times (it is unusual to branch between segments at extreme points in a program in any case), and many of the new interface cards can access tape frame accurately.

Interactive video can be more widely implemented in higher education by:

☐ seeking grants to underwrite acquisition of start-up hardware and production of a pilot program

Photo "A". *A student using the Sony random-access controller to answer questions posed on a videotape. This controller is itself a microprocessor which controls the branching of an interactive video program, eliminating the need for another computer such as an Apple.*

- [ ] beginning with interactive techniques which can utilize existing hardware, with the addition of a small amount of specialized equipment
- [ ] upgrading skills of instructional designers, video producers, and computer specialists to those necessary for the production of interactive materials by taking courses, attending workshops, or sponsoring seminars on the topic
- [ ] stimulating faculty support and interest by informing them of successful interactive projects, and making available means by which they can learn to help in the production of materials themselves
- [ ] co-operating with other institutions, sharing budgets, equipment and expertise for projects which will benefit each
- [ ] actively communicating with manufacturers of equipment and producers of software, letting them know what products would be desirable to your market
- [ ] seeking the help of consultants in producing the first few programs while developing skills and concepts needed to produce future projects independently.

As higher education budgets tighten and student demographics become more diverse, we will need to make use of the most powerful informational technologies available. These new media will surround our

Photo "B". *Students interacting with a computer-based instructional program. The picture shows our interactive carrel, housing a monitor, Apple II computer a Sony Betamax videotape recorder and, underneath, a printer. Controls in front of the printer are the Sony random-access unit, and 'paddle' controls for the Apple. Students at the college have produced and use interactive programs on the following topics: television lighting, operation of a portable mini-cam and VTR, writing behavioural objectives, and handling customer complaints in retail stores. Two of our graduate students have also produced interactive programs for their places of work: one is on inspecting printer assemblies for NCR, and another on chronic lung disease for patient education at the Robert Packer Hospital in Sayre, Pennsylvania.*

student-clients in every other realm of their lives: homes will be equipped with two-way shopping, entertainment, and informational services, and they and their parents will be trained for their jobs, select vacation spots, choose the model of car best suited to them, and learn about how to take care of their 'tennis elbow' using such interactive systems. One need only observe the local video games arcade to see the fascination which participatory, auditory and visual stimuli have for our future students.

REFERENCES

Anastasio, E J & Morgan, J (1978) in Branson, R & Foster, R *Educational Applications Research and Videodisc Technology*, Florida State University.

Andrade, S (1982) 'Interactive Video: Television with the Teaching Touch', *Journal of College Placement*, 15-16.

Backer, D (1982) 'One-of-a-Kind Video Programs', *Instructional Innovator*, 26-27.

DeChenne, J & Evans, R (1982) 'Simulating Medical Emergencies', *Instructional Innovator*, 23.

Gayeski, D (in press) *Corporate and Instructional Video*, Prentice Hall Inc, Englewood Cliffs, NJ.

Gayeski, D & Williams, D V (1980) 'Program Design for Interactive Video', *Educational and Industrial Television*, 31-34.

Kearsley, G (1981) 'Videodiscs in Education and Training: The Idea Becomes Reality', *Videodisc Videotex*, 208-20.

Nugent, R & Christie, K (1982) 'Using Videodisc Technology', *Video Systems*, 16-21.

Simcoe, D (1982) 'Survey of Media Center Administrators with regard to Interactive Video', unpublished report, Ithaca College, Ithaca, NY.

4. Video Production Technology in Australian Higher Education

Bob Haynes

SUMMARY

The paper describes the present state of the art of video program production in Australian tertiary education, discusses the identity of the decision-makers in the production sequence, and assesses the importance of video aesthetics. Against the background of some Australian media departments' production and hardware philosophy, the author describes four series of programs produced at the ACUE.[2]

Since the 1960s the technology of the television industry has developed significantly. The miniaturization of electronic equipment, particularly in the video field, has fostered the beginnings of both a domestic and an educational video boom. The present development of video technology was preceded by the highly successful portable monochrome video recorder which, with only a limited working knowledge, anyone could use in the classroom or in the field. The availability of instant replay was an important educational advantage of this equipment. The development of the video editing recorder enabled teachers to produce concise and interesting educational programs.

What has emerged from this development process is the electronic field gathering camera (EFG) and the portable videocassette recorder. Such equipment can be linked into an editing system to provide a basic facility for the production of video programs; this is often referred to as a 'post-production studio'.

While little of the above will be new to most readers, it should serve as a reminder of how technology has changed, and changed rapidly.

EDUCATORS AND VIDEO

Today's students are different to those of a decade ago; they have grown up with such modern technology as computers, video games and high quality communication receivers. Now that video technology has become a normal and accepted fact of life, educators will have to reconsider their attitudes to its use in teaching and learning.

Some administrators and educationists still believe that technology of any kind is a threat and that it will interfere with the educational process. However, the introduction of videotapes into teaching laboratories has *not* caused teacher redundancies. Rather, video has been widely used in conjunction with other aids, such as charts, models and handouts, to enrich and diversify teaching. In some cases where staff loss through financial constraints has been a problem, video technology has actually enabled teaching to continue at a satisfactory level.

One of the least thought-of parts of the video production is the control of program content. The people who make decisions on content in the production sequence may be called 'gatekeepers'. For example, the gatekeepers of television news service are the journalists presenting their views and the news editors who decide what is most newsworthy to go out on air. These people make the decisions on content.

In the educational system there are gatekeepers, too. There is the lecturer who wants a program to use in teaching in his department. He or she will usually have discussions with the director of an educational video unit and a video producer, and they will together plan program production. So there are at least three decision-makers who have an influence on program content. At the ACUE, a series of set questions is used as a basis for decisions on video program production (ACUE, 1975):

Educational questions

1. How is the subject taught at present?
2. Why is video to be substituted for the present method of teaching?
3. Is the video medium the most appropriate one to achieve the aims you have in mind?
4. How will the videotape be used in teaching?
5. What are students expected to learn by viewing the proposed videotape?
6. What knowledge, skills and attitudes would students be expected to have before viewing this tape?
7. Will students be expected to carry out any experiment or discussion after viewing this tape?
8. How will the effectiveness of the videotape be assessed?

Technical questions

1. Is video playback equipment available to the user? What are its technical characteristics?
2. In what format is the finished program required?
3. Are the university's facilities adequate to undertake the production? If not, what hiring of equipment will be necessary?
4. What materials (eg videotapes, audiotapes, graphics, slides, props) and special effects are required in the program?

Administrative questions

1. When is the finished program required?
2. Can the department provide staff to assist (and maybe train) in the production of the program?
3. What are the projected costs of the production?
4. When can the full production crew come together for the production?

5. Who will be responsible for: (a) supervising the production (the producer), (b) writing the script, and (c) preparing materials (graphics, slides, props, etc)?

EVALUATION OF VIDEO PRODUCTIONS

Among the more neglected gatekeepers are the students who view the video material. Evaluation is carried out at the University of Adelaide by the students filling in questionnaires on the videotape they have just viewed (Appendix I reproduces the form used by the ACUE). This feedback helps producers to make changes if necessary to the content or presentation of the program in subsequent revision.

In one science department, evaluation has shown that the advantages of the videotapes used in the teaching laboratory considerably outweigh the time, effort and expense of production for the following reasons:

1. Students obtain a more consistent and better presentation of the procedures they are about to carry out.
2. Students are able to start their practical work earlier in the session than previously, to work more effectively and with considerable time savings.
3. Students have better opportunities for preparation and revision than formerly.

SOME ASPECTS OF VIDEO AESTHETICS

The making of video programs for educational purposes creates a need for the understanding of 'video aesthetics'; Malik & Murphy (1972) consider video aesthetics to be the coincidence between logical, rational and emotional thinking in presenting information.

Academics who produce video programs have the opportunity to use video in a highly personal way. For example, when working with portable video equipment in the field, they can at any instant change the focus of view, and can communicate their own perceptions and values to make their own visual images. However, some educational programs are made with too little attention to picture *quality*; video technologists are certainly aware of any loss of definition, but there is more to picture quality than that — there are more serious effects to the view if the information structure is lost. The more emphasis there is on livelier pictures, composition, the information impact on the students, and visual relevance, the better. Such 'video aesthetic' factors are not necessarily related to technical quality.

There are, of course, limits to the technical quality that producers of educational video programs can achieve, depending on such factors as the availability of skilled production crews, good quality equipment, and money to support production costs. The technical quality limit, according to Charmer (1980), is functionally related to the educational value placed on the materials produced and the degree to which marginal reduction in picture resolution and colour quality are found to be acceptable.

In some Australian universities there are those who oppose this view of the acceptability of low quality video; they believe that video teaching material has to be of the highest quality. Indeed, some have large budgets to produce video in broadcast studios, and others have the staff and broadcast-quality equipment to produce high standard programs as a series of visits to tertiary institutions over the past few years has shown.

TERTIARY MEDIA UNITS

The standard of content of educational television programs is similar throughout Australian higher education, but there are big differences in technical quality. This is because of varying technical standards; some units use a simple three-quarter inch U-matic system, while others use expensive broadcast-standard equipment.

One major metropolitan university has four broadcast-standard colour TV cameras which can be interchanged between the studio and a mobile unit, and five C-format videotape recorders, four of which are suitable for editing and one for portable use. With a staff of 21, the director of the television unit believes that this university's service has three major roles: providing support to teaching and research; acting as a centre of expertise for other video centres in the university; and making high quality productions which can be circulated widely outside the university and even broadcast nationally.

Several other universities also have high quality broadcast equipment, and produce programs that are being shown around Australia as well as being used effectively by their own university departments.

At the ACUE we have passed through several stages of development. When the colour television studio was established, TV was not being broadcast in colour in Adelaide. There was not at that time the range of equipment that is available today, and for economic reasons we were forced to purchase equipment the technical quality of which left a lot to be desired. Nevertheless, it was educationally effective. Four years later, to improve the technical quality and reliability, we sold the studio equipment and invested the money in a basic post-production studio. The system now includes two professional colour cameras (Ikegami 2400 and 350), a professional editing suite, titler, professional sound mixer and various other pieces of ancillary equipment. As resources become available, we will add a new vision switcher and effects generator, time base corrector and a broadcast editor-recorder. Figure 1 illustrates the present facility, with dotted lines representing the planned expansion.

Judging by the demand for ACUE services, video in Australian universities has taken off in the last couple of years. There have been 16 video productions from the ACUE this year (January–March), and there are more productions in progress. Some highlights of recently completed programs are described below. I believe that the ever increasing demands made weekly for video productions fully justify further investment in equipment.

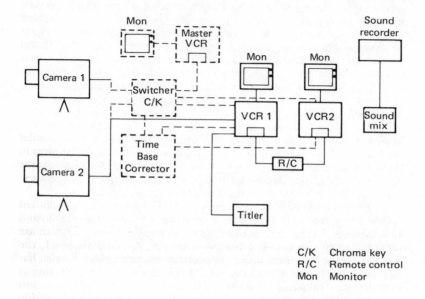

Figure 1. *The video system at ACUE (proposed expansion shown in dotted lines)*

VIDEO PROGRAMS PRODUCED BY THE ACUE

The first productions to be described are videotapes on applied neurology. This series was a multi-disciplinary effort by the departments of Anatomy and Neurosurgery and the ACUE. The purpose of the videotapes was to show students the relevance of what they were learning to clinical practice. The videotapes were centred on selected patients with neuro-anatomical problems. The reactions of the large number of students who have seen the tapes has been very favourable indeed; their interest in the subject-matter was aroused and they were able to see its relevance to their future clinical studies.

However, the evaluation questionnaires did reveal some criticisms. The first and most common criticism was that some of the programs were too long; they were up to 55 minutes in length. They would have preferred tapes to be about 30 minutes long. The second criticism was that some of the clinical terms introduced were ill-defined, so that the students were left guessing as to what some of the clinical content was about. They found some information hard to digest and to retain. At times they found the videotapes dealt with anatomical features that were rather complicated and too involved for them to appreciate at the present stage of their course. In the light of this feedback, the videotapes have been re-edited and modified, and they will be useful for years to come. It is encouraging that other (less official!) comment in the student-produced 'Counter Calendar of the University of Adelaide' expressed the view that the tapes produced by the ACUE were of greater value, in terms of clinical content (particularly local content), than those bought commercially by the teaching department.

The second type of program to be considered is used by second-year physiology students in practical sessions. These programs came about as a result of a donation of $3,000 by the Anti-Vivisection Union of South Australia to the Department of Physiology for the purchase of a BioVideograph machine, to reduce the need to use live animals for experiments and practicals at the university. Only one animal is used for experiments which before took up to 40, depending on the number of students. The BioVideograph is connected to a videocassette recorder in such a way that, as the operation on an animal is recorded in sound and vision onto videotape, technical data from some form of physiological sensing device are recorded on the second audio channel. On playback, the VCR is connected to several pen recorders in the classroom so that, as the students watch the technique on the monitor screen and listen to the commentary, the pre-recorded physiological data are fed through the BioVideograph to their own pen recorders, and they can collect and analyse their own experimental results. The BioVideograph improves the quality of teaching by providing a uniform set of data for student analysis and staff-student discussion, although it can never fully replace practical sessions in which students perform the experimental technique themselves.

The third type of program to be discussed is about cranio-facial superimposition, a time-saving method of identifying crime or disaster victims from their remains. A team of scientists led by University of Adelaide odontologist, Dr Kenneth Brown, developed this technique using video cameras. As Figure 2 shows, one video camera is set up to display an image of a photograph of the suspected victim's face on a television screen while another camera, on a mobile dolly, focuses on the skull, which is mounted on a ball-joint tripod so that its position can be adjusted. After previewing each camera, the two video images are fed through a special effects generator, superimposed and matched up with each other on a large screen. By adjusting the orientation of the skull, slowly and accurately, and by micro-adjustments of the skull camera, the relevant anatomical features of the skull are related to the corresponding features of the face as shown on the photograph.

The technique is videotaped and the programs can be used in court cases, as well as in teaching medical students, an area in which the ACUE plays an important role. These tapes have been edited and distributed to other universities and to forensic science institutions. In the Truro murders case, a much publicized affair in which prompt identification of the victims was an important factor in the investigation, videotapes of the seven skulls of the victims revealed individual victims' characteristics. Cranio-facial video-superimpositions were used to support the identification of some of the victims, not identifiable from dental records in the conventional way.

Recently, another videotape produced for Dr Brown was a test made on the behaviour of dingoes. This tape was presented to the much publicized inquest into the death of Azaria Chamberlain, and was also

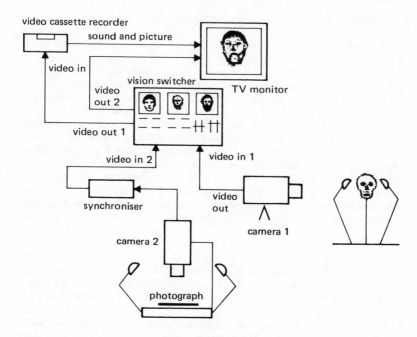

Figure 2. *The set-up for cranio-facial video-superimposition*

edited to produce a teaching tape emphasizing the importance of teeth marks in the collection of forensic evidence.

The final series of productions to be mentioned are three programs recorded in the field by a lecturer in the Department of Anthropology. In preparation for a study tour of Spain, the lecturer spent three months in the ACUE (including much of his free time) learning how to use portable video equipment. His experience inside cathedrals, recording artists and sculptors at work, illustrates well the benefits of portable video equipment. While he was at work, quietly and unobtrusively, a major television company was producing a program on the same event. The documentary team had a large crew, setting up lights and other equipment and generally disturbing the artists. Eventually, the production group was asked to leave, because of the obtrusiveness of their TV equipment and technology, while the lecturer was given free access and was able to record the artists, sculptors and craftsmen at work, building effigies and so on, without 'staging' or interference with their normal routine. The ensuing programs presented a realistic picture of the subject to students and have been applauded by professional anthropologists as a simple but effective representation of the Spanish people and their culture.

CONCLUSION

The last example illustrates an important difference between 'television' (complex, expensive and inflexible) and 'video' (simple, inexpensive and flexible) production technologies. Video production technology has become predominant in education for three rather different reasons. First, the availability of lightweight, easy to operate and relatively inexpensive equipment of acceptable technical quality has enabled educators to achieve reasonable video results for teaching purposes. The second reason is economic: at the time when many institutions were gearing up to move into colour 'television', they were confronted with severe economic restraints which made the move extremely difficult or impossible. Finally, many educators have realized the advantages of simple video production techniques which remove − or at least vastly reduce − the 'controlling' influence of the 'professional gatekeepers' on educational video production.

Notes
1. This chapter is a reprint of an article by T R Haynes (1982) under the same title in the *Journal of Educational Television*, **8**, 2, 119-26. The journal editors' kind permission of copyright is gratefully acknowledged.
2. Advisory Centre for University Education (ACUE), the University of Adelaide, Adelaide, SA, 5000 (Australia).

REFERENCES

Advisory Centre for University Education (1975) Paper 15, 'Teaching Materials', University of Adelaide.

Charmer, F (1980) *Media Service Unit: Report to the Professorial Board*, Perth, University of Western Australia.

Malik, M F & Murphy, D (1972) *Videophysiology − Video Psychology − Video Aesthetics*, Concordia University, Montreal, Canada.

APPENDIX I

The University of Adelaide Advisory Centre for University Education
Evaluation of Videotape

Introduction and instructions
Your evaluation of the videotape you have just watched is sought to
help in the design and production of future programs. The evaluation is
confidential. There is no need to write your name on this sheet.

Please indicate your present thoughts about each of the following items
by placing a tick (√) on the five point scale below. For example, if you
found the videotape fairly interesting, you should show this as follows:

a b c d e

interesting   boring

The videotape   a b c d e
1.   interesting   boring
2. content was well presented   content was poorly presented
3.   organized   content was poorly organized
4.   presentation too fast   presentation too slow
5.   pictures conveyed   pictures did not convey
       information clearly   information clearly
6.   important information   all information seemed the
            stressed   same
7.   quality of   quality of
       soundtrack good   soundtrack poor
8.   I have learnt a lot   I have learnt nothing
9. Please describe briefly what you recall as the main message of the
   videotape.
   . . . .
   . . . .
   . . . .
10. If you have any other comments about the videotape, please write
    them here.
   . . . .
   . . . .
   . . . .

Thank you for answering this questionnaire. Please return it now to
your lecturer or tutor.

5. Video and the Control of Knowledge

Ian Hart

SUMMARY

No one denies the potential of video for teaching at all levels, but in the 22 years since it was first used in a tertiary institution in Australia it has not succeeded in becoming a significant educational force. Its failure has been due less to technical factors than to a power struggle over the control of knowledge between academics (specialists), video producers (generalists) and educational researchers (theorists). As today's tertiary institutions come under pressure to cater for different types of students the struggle may be resolved by pressure from students and administrators.

At the 1982 Australian Society for Educational Technology Conference Richard Hooper of Prestel did his best to convince us that in the age of the silicon chip intelligent machines can take over the jobs of factory workers and teachers alike. Of course post-Toffler prophets have been announcing this from the backs of their band-wagons for some time. Frederick Williams, in his breathless celebration of geewizzery *The Communications Revolution* (1982) uses the word 'explosion' six times in as many pages. (Though maybe it is significant that, in placing education last in his catalogue of soon-to-be-radically-altered human pursuits, he recognizes that it, at least, has been something of a damp squib.) In the 1950s and 1960s it was television that was going to transform the classroom and make teachers redundant. It didn't happen.

Considering it has been with us now for 20 years, video has had remarkably little impact on education at all levels in Australia. In the 1980s, age of the cheap VTR, most recordings in the video libraries of colleges and universities are (illegally taped) evening entertainment shows: plays, documentaries, current affairs. They have become the new 'texts' in soft-option subjects like mass media studies, sociolinguistics and the unhappy remnants of English literature and history where academic rigour has been replaced by fashion and topicality.

It is a pity. Video has immense potential in tertiary education, as distance teaching institutions have demonstrated. It can create opportunities for people who, for many reasons, have previously been unable to attend colleges or universities. It can widen the horizons of even the highest institutions (by exchanging tapes). It can even have a positive influence on the standard of face-to-face teaching, for in the act of producing a videotape it is necessary to rethink the whole presentation of the course.

In this paper I make the conventional distinction between *television* (broadcast) and *video* (non-broadcast). It is a distinction which is becoming confused by cable, RSTV and other distribution systems. It is also a distinction which is hard to make in terms of quality, subject matter or treatment because of the influence that big, expensive, socializing television has had on small, cheap, narrow-band video. Television has created codes of communication which we all understand and accept; the video program which ignores these codes is not going to communicate effectively.

This is one of the reasons that video has not been used to its full potential in tertiary education. It has a bad name. It is infected with the disease of television: frivolity. Academics distrust it. There are other reasons, some of them technical, but most of them tied up with a pedagogical power struggle over the control of knowledge. Until the struggle is resolved it is unlikely that any of the new technologies will find comfortable places in the hallowed halls of learning.

Academics are *specialists* who feel very protective about what they know. They have spent their lives acquiring it, they guard it jealously and they let it out in small doses to students. It is the academic's duty to tame knowledge, define it, organize it; how often have you seen the philosopher compared to the gardener? The 'God-Professor' is not just an Oxbridge fable; we all know some university lecturers who aspire to deification!

Academics and other specialists find it difficult to come to terms with the video medium. They have problems tying it down, defining exactly what it is. On the one hand Sony, National and JVC tell them that any old tennis star can use the equipment to remake *Star Wars*; on the other hand it is obvious that to do a good job a large number of highly skilled people are needed. It is a technology which requires high priests in darkened rooms and acolytes in white coats to make it perform miracles. The academic who considers using television to present part of his course in, say, physics, is going to feel justifiably anxious about whose program it actually *is* in the end. During the production he will be demoted from God-Professor to mere performer (or, in the often ironical jargon of the trade, 'talent'). A person born and bred to words, he will be surrounded by people who talk a language he doesn't understand, a language of visual abstraction, with words like *pan, zoom, cut, focus-pull* and incomprehensible mumbo-jumbo: 'ped up and dolly in to a keyed title super . . .'

Unfortunately, some producers behave as though they own the medium and they have all the answers. 'The medium is the message' they chant, '*any* content can be made interesting by imaginative use of production techniques.' They cannot understand the academic who holds back from the opportunity to make his semester's lectures in mediaeval poetry into a 13-part series. These producers, I suspect, see academics as little more than sources of program material, rungs on their ladder to personal fulfilment.

A film producer once told me how to go about making a film on medical engineering. 'Words are everything,' he said. 'You pick up a bit of engineering jargon and use it on the doctors and then you get a few medical terms and use them on the engineers. Each side thinks you're an authority on the other and because academics respect authorities they'll accept you and let you film anything you like.' The unfortunate thing about this attitude is that it usually works.

Not all producers are like this of course. A good video producer is a true *generalist*, which does not mean that he knows a little bit about everything. His craft requires a wide range of skills from writing to computer editing as well as an appreciation of music, literature and design. His principal objective is to communicate knowledge rather than to acquire it for its own sake. He is a teacher.

Educational video production will fare better in the hands of producers who are willing to reject shortcuts, formulae and razzle-dazzle; to approach each new assignment with interest and enthusiasm. Such a producer can contribute a great deal to the education process.

Both academics and producers have some common ground in their distrust of educational researchers, whom they see as wanting to measure and quantify their skills; whom they suspect of attempting to replace them by a set of formulae. For many years now video has been a fertile field for empirical research which could give a doctoral student instant entry into the prestigious club of learning theorists.

In the 1960s researchers tried to isolate variables and define the elements of the 'successful' video program. Most of their conclusions showed 'no significant difference' between the results of students taught by television and those subjected to live instruction.

When you think about it, such experiments are ludicrous. What were they testing; knowledge of facts? Of course television can teach facts! (One is reminded of Jerry Mander's (1980) wonderful revelation that federally funded scientific tests have shown, at last, that mother's milk is better for babies than cow's milk.) Non-funded thinking reveals that broadcast television is very good at teaching other things too: the commercial television industry is founded on the principle that it can teach greed, envy, intolerance and the enjoyment of vicarious experience. Could it not also, just as effectively, teach enthusiasm for learning, tolerance, respect for the environment, methods of inquiry...? Deane Hutton, another contributor to this book, sets out this hidden agenda for his children's TV program *The Curiosity Show* in the Proceedings of the Third International Conference on Experimental Research and Televised Instruction (1980).

In the end it seems the medium proved to be more complex than the experiments which sought to measure it. The approaches of recent researchers such as Salomon (1979), Baggaley (1980) and Olsen and Bruner (1974) which draw upon the theoretical schools of semiology, sociology and psychiatry are heading in more productive directions.

The most valuable research to the educational production team is applied research which is of direct relevance to their program. The results feed back into the process and become a formative factor in the development of the next script. I have discussed this at length elsewhere (1982) so I won't elaborate on my complaints about navel-gazing research.

To summarize so far: There is a fundamental culture gap between *producers*, who are naturally generalists, manipulators of a complex technology, who see content as only one part of the program;

academics, who are specialists and see the content as all-important, who are jealous of their reputations and who fear being misrepresented; and *researchers*, who are theorists, seeing the program (both content and technique) as a means to the abstraction of a theory of universals.

The first thing we must do is get them talking to one another in the same language.

OBSTACLES

Writing and producing a video production, or any other complex audio-visual program, takes considerable time and effort, more than can usually be fitted in between teaching and research commitments. Writing for video, as most readers will probably know, is a frustrating business indeed: the script needs to go through so many revisions that the writer sometimes loses track of what he was trying to do in the first place (the word processor, another new technology, can overcome much of this frustration).

At our college there is a current proposal that members of staff who want to develop new teaching strategies should be given periods of student-free time, ranging from a few weeks to a semester, to work with the Media Centre or Computer Centre. The pay-off for the other staff members who have carried the teaching is to be improved resources and less lecturing in the long term.

A second obstacle is a general lack of comprehension of the medium. Most people have a fixed view of video, equating it with what they see on television. But video can be both 'heavy' broadcast-type television and a 'light', flexible tool. As Robert Lefranc puts it in an article for the ICEM, (1978, 24):

> One of the characteristics of television is that it is, by itself, a multi medium. What I mean is that it comprises a great many media at the production stage: photographs, films, graphs, sounds and recorded music, etc. Television is, by its very nature, a medium of synthesis.

Nevertheless, video is not a magic bullet. In fact, to be fully effective a video program usually needs considerable support from the tutor as well as some form of accompanying documentation.

Users of video, academics and producers alike, need to be aware of the potential of video in *all* its aspects and the best way of doing this is through experience. It is a chicken and egg situation.

A third and very important obstacle has been the fear that the video program will replace the teacher in the classroom, an assumption nurtured by those 1960s research reports showing 'no significant difference'. Like the Chinese who feared losing a part of their spirit when photographed, untenured staff have good reasons to anticipate that, having recorded their lectures on videocassette, the institution will fire them but retain their electronic shadows. There is little incentive here to spend precious time on instructional design.

INCENTIVES

One incentive to making lectures available on videocassette is that students seem to like it. Surveys in this and many other colleges have produced strongly positive results. Video lectures are convenient and flexible for students who can't attend for one reason or another; the direct (above line) cost is low; they reduce ego threat to older students or people with language problems; they allow citizens who are housebound to have the benefit of tertiary education; and

> live lecturing is ephemeral whereas a video recording of a lecture can be examined, modified, corrected and used as a basis from which to produce a better video recording. It has also been observed that increasing competition results in continuous attempts to improve quality. This improvement by evolution is cheaper, quicker and often better than attempts at improvement by design (Stephen, 1982, 4).

The operative word is 'competition'. In Australian, and most other free enterprise societies, tertiary education is a buyer's market. Education is joining tourism and golf in the big league of leisure industries. In Canberra, with a population of less than 200,000 we have a university, a college of advanced education, schools of music and art, and three technical and further education colleges. In addition, four other tertiary institutions are currently advertising degree courses by correspondence: 'Let Your Home Be Your Classroom'. If the move to utilize the new media does not arise from the academic staff the pressure will eventually come from the administration which sees its territory invaded and its students seduced by the prospect of painless learning in the comfort of their living rooms. My institution is planning for an enrolment of significant numbers of 'home study students' over the next triennium.

THE USES OF VIDEO

I have referred to video above as a 'new technology' even though it has been around since the early 1960s. I saw my first rat dissected on video in 1962 on one black and white monitor in a theatre seating 600 students. Things have improved a little since then and it's hard to believe that it is only since the general availability of the U-matic cassette that accurate editing has become a possibility in low budget educational video. About eight years.

The flexibility of editing, combined with increased portability and reliability, released video from the control of technicians and allowed people to use it creatively. Documentary film makers understand about editing. They like to take the camera to the scene, to be unobtrusive, to use the expressive possibilities of the medium. The marriage of educators and film makers has been one of the most interesting television events of the last 10 years. It started with great educators like Sir Kenneth Clark, Jakob Bronowski, Richard Attenborough and Alistair Cooke. They demonstrated that knowledge in large dollops could be interesting. It even spilled over into radio with Robin Williams' *Science*

Show giving opportunities for programs like Peter Mason's magnificient history of science documentary series *Couchu the Weeping Wood* (ABC, 1980). These have become the models which adventurous academics, using video, are attempting to emulate.

Thankfully at this college the requests to 'videotape my lectures this semester for when I'm on study leave' have begun to diminish. At the other extreme, to produce programs approaching the complexity of these BBC/Time-Life documentary series requires both a producer/ director with great skill and a writer/presenter with vision and acting ability (not to mention time). The conjunction of these talents and events is not common on small tertiary campuses in Australia.

Video can be used less ambitiously, however, to great effect. Video can be a purely practical tool, like a notebook or camera, for recording events, and those recordings can be edited and used in lectures or as a student reference. This type of use has applications in almost any subject one can think of. The professional journals are full of reports of innovative uses of video in teaching. A quick search of one or two volumes of recent publications shows, for example, language teaching: Lonergan (1982) and MacKnight (1982); tertiary teaching: Stephen (1982); opinion surveys: Baggaley (1982b); collaborative learning: Bruffee (1982); and system-wide integration with teletext: Lefranc (1981).

SIGNAL/NOISE

One thing that a producer can do for an educational video is to lower the communications 'signal:noise ratio'. *Signal* is what we want to communicate; *noise* is what gets in the way. At its simplest, *noise* can be literally ambient noise on the sound track. It can also be poor focus or composition, bad exposure or flare. At a more sophisticated level, *noise* concerns cinematic codes.

Video, like television and film, is a storytelling medium which relies on movement for its impact. Stories are told using the conventions of cinema which have grown up since the beginning of the century: close-ups, subjective camera, inserts, off-camera narration, music . . . combinations of icon, index and symbol which are meaningful to any practised viewer. Like any language the codes evolve with time, and yesterday's cinema is recognizable by its use of these conventions as well as by the models of the cars and the lengths of the skirts. A video which makes poor use of codes (like an essay with bad grammar and spelling) will distract attention and interfere with communication.

The video vaults are stuffed with programs in which a window behind the subject caused the aperture to stop down, where the angle was too high in the speech demonstration and you couldn't see the lips moving, where the camera operator suffered from telephoto St Vitus' Dance or imagined he was playing *76 Trombones* on the zoom lens, or where the program was in an entirely inappropriate medium (I have seen a film made to show, step-by-step, how to thread a 16mm film projector). The equipment may be light, portable, reliable and of remarkable quality for the price, but it needs someone with a good eye and a knowledge of production to operate it effectively.

One very common problem arises in the videotaping of events such as an experiment or a demonstration. The subject specialist will tend to see the event itself as the thing of prime importance and the video camera as an intruding spectator. The video producer will recognize that unless the camera has the best position, the light and sound conditions are adequate, and the process can be stopped or repeated for close-ups, the result will not be of much use to anyone. It is necessary to establish right from the start which is more important, the event or the production? If the event is more important it would be preferable to restage it for the camera.

More difficult processes may require more production technique; for instance, phonetics tutors have a need to illustrate the relationship between the position of the vocal cords and the wave forms of the emitted sounds. To do this they swallow a thin tube tipped with a photo-receptor and when it is positioned correctly they shine a bright light onto the throat at the larynx. The photo-receptor records the fluctuations caused by the opening and closing of the glottis and displays it on an oscilloscope. As you can imagine, it is a very uncomfortable procedure, especially if they need to explain to the class what is happening at the same time and if they have four or five tutorial groups to demonstrate it to in a week. In a videotape demonstration one can take time to get the best results (swallowing and reswallowing the receptor if necessary) and, by using split screen, juxtapose cause and effect. One can edit in order to repeat events, stop frame, superimpose or add inter-titles and we can record a voice-over on the soundtrack to be used when the lecturer is not present. The entire production takes about half a day; the tape can be used to replace a hundred painful demonstrations.

RESEARCH

Today's research into educational video has come a long way from the kindergarten-level, single-variable studies of 20 years ago. Researchers are looking at *how* people learn from video and the *type* of learning which the medium promotes. It is obvious that some areas are absolutely inappropriate for video, such as learning vocabulary and pronunciation of foreign languages, literature, librarianship . . . or are they? Video can make unexpected contributions in many areas. I have seen it used very effectively in explaining concepts in mathematics, computing, accountancy and secretarial studies. The John Cleese/Video Arts films on business management show what a little humour and imagination can do.

Much research seeks to be prescriptive. Starting out with the intention of helping the academic and the producer to cultivate the desired response in their audience, the research ends by providing rules, algorithms and questionnaires which have the effect of restricting choices. It denies the possibility of an elegant solution from a creative mind.

I would assert that the best way to find out what type of program to produce is to make one first and then test it, then to modify the next program in the light of that test. One good 'crash' often teaches more than 50 experiments! Development and modification is easy with today's video equipment where it was not a workable strategy with film or studio television.

It is unfortunate that experimental research often seems based on out-moded styles of production. Experimenters test factors that no longer exist. Perhaps this is because researchers don't watch television, but it is more likely that it is due to lack of communication with experienced working producers. The research carried out by the Children's Television Workshop provides a model for the analysis of educational television. It is practical living research, based on an understanding of the audience and the production process. It is a team approach.

CONCLUSION

Video is one of the most powerful tools available to the educator, but it has not been effectively used on a large scale in Australian tertiary institutions. Video is a medium which needs a team approach involving, among others, the subject specialist who provides the content, the producer who puts it into the language of the medium, and researchers who provide information on the program's success in achieving its aims.

If the academic insists on controlling the production, he runs the risk of failing to communicate what he set out to achieve. The program is ineffective because it is, in the words of Tennyson and Breuer (Chapter 2 in this book), a 'transmediation' rather than a video communication in its own right. If the producer takes control we run the risk of ending up with a program which entertains but does not inform, or in the worst instance, misinforms. There must be a close and trusting relationship between teacher and producer, and if the researcher is not also involved in the team he runs the risk of chasing shadows and testing variables which do not exist.

How is such a trusting relationship to be achieved in a normal tertiary institution? Remote teaching centres, like the British Open University, have had many years of experience at developing procedures with considerable successes and some spectacular failures. Perhaps we should be looking to institutions like these for our models rather than to Oxford and Harvard. Tertiary institutions are changing, teaching new types of courses, attracting new types of students: housewives, retired people, unemployed, retrainees. We hear words like Polyversity, Unicoll and Metropolitan Institutes of Higher Education (MIHE).

The power structures in tertiary institutions are shifting too. Once it was the duty of academics to do research, to publish and to teach (in that order). Today's tertiary teacher often needs to spend regular periods of time working in the 'real world'. His relationship to his students is no longer that of 'shepherd/gardener', it is more like mentor/ co-worker. Many teachers recognize that we can do a bit better than follow the mediaeval lecture/tutorial system of instruction: twentieth-century educational technology is both effective and available.

This is not to imply that there has been much of an improvement in the last 20 years. Video producers, where they are employed at all, are still either equated with the technician who operates the equipment or regarded as some kind of creative arts fellow. They are rarely seen as an integral part of the institution's overall education policy.

In western societies the social, economic and technological structures are changing very rapidly and education is coming under the influence of free-market forces. At present we are still trying to adapt video and the other new technologies to the nineteenth-century educational practices of the tertiary education system. It would probably be just as bad if, by over-reacting, we ended up adapting the system to the needs of the technology.

Let's hope that we can find a more sensible middle ground.

REFERENCES

Baggaley, J (1982a) 'TV Production, Research and Media Development', *Media in Education and Development*, 15, 46-48.

Baggaley, J (1982b) 'Electronic Analysis of Communication', *Media in Education and Development*, 15, 70-73.

Bruffee, K A (1982) 'CLTV: Collaborative Learning Television', *Educational Communication and Technology Journal*, 30, 26-40.

Cassidy, M F (1982) 'Toward Integration: education, instructional technology, and semiotics', *Educational Communication and Technology Journal*, 30, 75-89.

Hart, I (1982) 'Educational Television: The Gulf Between Researchers and Producers', *Journal of Educational Television*, 8, 91-99.

Hooper, R (1982) Keynote address to the Second National Conference of the Australian Society for Educational Technology, Kuring-gai CAE, (published on microfiche).

Hutton, D (1980) 'Tacit and explicit processes in television design, production and presentation' published in Proceedings of 3rd International Conference on Experimental Research in Televised Instruction, Memorial University, Newfoundland. (Edited by Dr J Baggaley).

Lefranc, R (1978) 'The obstacles to effective school television', *Educational Media International*, 1978/2, 22-25.

Lefranc, R *et al* (1981) 'The EPEOS experiment', *Educational Media International*, 1981/3, 8-12.

Lonergan, J (1982) 'Video recordings in language teaching', *Media in Education and Development*, 15, 49-52.

MacKnight, F (1982) 'The video camera in EFL teaching', *Media in Education and Development*, 15, 99-101.

Mander, J (1980) *Four Arguments for the Elimination of Television*, Harvester, New York.

Mason, P (1980) *Couchu, the Weeping Wood* (audio-cassettes), Australian Broadcasting Commission, Sydney.

Olson, D R & Bruner, J S (1974) 'Learning through experience and learning through media' in Olson, D R (ed.), *Media and Symbols: The Forms of Expression, Communication and Education* (Part 1), National Society for the Study of Education, Chicago.

Salomon, G (1979) *Interaction of Media, Cognition and Learning*, Jossey-Bass, San Francisco.

Stephen, K D (1982) 'New trends at the tertiary level', *Media in Education and Development*, 15, 3-6.

Williams, F (1982) *The Communications Revolution*, Sage, Beverly Hills.

6. Influencing Human Interaction: Interpersonal Process Recall (IPR) Stimulated by Videotape

Norman Kagan

SUMMARY

IPR is a model of developing an awareness of processes of interpersonal and group dynamics. It can be applied in professional, para-professional and teacher training as well as in general undergraduate sessions on communication skills. The core of the model consists of three phases: A trainee's performance being videorecorded, immediately played back, and studied in an unusual review process in which a trained facilitator or 'inquirer' encourages the trainee to recall and verbalize underlying thoughts, feelings and motives. No advice, critique or interpretations are offered by the inquirer. After the initial training, supported by a package of materials 'Influencing Human Interaction' (including films and vignettes on videotape) students can use the model on their own practising with their peers as 'inquirers'.

ORIGIN

In 1962 my colleagues and I observed a phenomenon which seemed useful in understanding and improving human interaction (Kagan, Krathwohl & Miller, 1963). We named the technique evolving from our observations IPR (interpersonal process recall). Five years of controlled studies (Kagan & Krathwohl, 1967) elucidated and defined the method's utility; but it took an additional 10 years to develop a film package which would enable instructors in medicine and a variety of mental health programs to offer an IPR course to their students (Kagan, 1976).

We observed in 1962 that if someone is videorecorded relating to another and shown the recording immediately afterwards, the person can recall detailed thoughts and feelings in depth. Self-evaluation usually accompanied an intricate account of how the participant felt affected by the other. If participants were given a remote-control switch and encouraged to stop and start the playback freely, they could usually verbalize a multitude of underlying thoughts, feelings and motives. We also found, during these initial experiences, that the method worked more reliably when a trained facilitator encouraged the viewer to verbalize perceptions and elaborate upon them.

The person who facilitated the recall was most effective when soliciting a description of underlying thoughts and feelings rather than emphasizing critique or self-confrontation. The successful facilitator asked such questions as: 'Can you recall more of the details of your feelings, where did you feel these things, what parts of your body responded?' and 'What do you think (the other) thought about you at that point?' The catalyst's role is that of an interested, inquiring colleague. We chose the word 'inquirer' to describe the facilitative person in an IPR session. The basic discovery, then, was not just of the value of video playback, but of this unique combination of human role and technology.

IPR proved in time to be a method by which mental health workers and a myriad of other professional and para-professional groups could learn to improve their ability to interview, communicate with, and help other people. It also proved to be a useful vehicle for developing affective sensitivity scales (Campbell, Kagan & Krathwohl, 1971; Danish & Kagan, 1971) for formulating theory about human interaction (Kagan, 1975), and for the study of medical inquiry (Elstein *et al*, 1972).

Analysis of our early failures led us to develop some interpersonal developmental tasks for influencing human interaction. We sequenced these tasks from the least threatening to the most threatening phases.

ELEMENTS OF FACILITATING COMMUNICATION — EXPANDING A REPERTOIRE OF RESPONSE MODES

The first phase grew out of our attempts to develop a behavioural counselling rating scale. In developing this scale, we analysed videotapes of counsellors whose skills usually led to positive client comments on recall, and compared these with videotapes of counsellors who seemed ineffective to their clients as well as to experts who reviewed the tapes. In addition we consulted the literature. We concluded that successful counsellors:

☐ focus much attention on client affect
☐ listen carefully to the client's communication while conveying that they are trying to understand
☐ can be honest (but gentle) rather than manipulating the client or responding evasively
☐ encourage the client to explore and assume an active part in the counselling process.

In the first stage of the training system, a narrator on video or film discusses these four concepts, offering examples and simulation exercises for student practice.

COUNSELLOR RECALL — STUDYING ONESELF IN ACTION

The next phase was designed to help counsellors overcome two behaviours that often interfere with understanding the client and communicating that understanding. We had repeatedly observed in IPR sessions that people perceive and comprehend much more than one would suspect in observing an interaction. It appears that people read subtle communications well, but as socialized beings often acknowledge only the surface phenomena, the official message. Beginning counsellors acted unaware of meaning behind many client statements, but during recall indicated that they had understood but had been unable to act on their perceptions. In recall sessions focusing on the counsellor alone, the 'feigning of clinical naiveté' becomes clear. 'I knew she (the client) was very unhappy underneath that put-on smile, but — and I know this sounds stupid — I was afraid she might cry if I told her I knew she was hurting, and then I would feel that I had made her cry', or 'I knew (the client) was lying, but I didn't call him on it . . . I was afraid he wouldn't come back for a next session if I was honest with him . . . he might even get up and walk out of the room . . . I guess I would feel hurt if he did these things, and yet I know he probably wouldn't, but I couldn't risk it.' The second issue we confront, in this phase, is the problem of 'tuning out', of failing to see or hear the other person for periods of time during the session. This usually occurred when the students were especially concerned about the impression they were making on the client. For instance, medical students often heard their patient say things of importance during recall which they had completely failed to hear during the interview! The most frequent explanation was: 'I kept worrying about how to say things in such a way that I would appear to be older and more experienced than I am. I kept thinking about how I should look and how I should phrase my statements at those times. Even though I look as though I'm listening I really haven't heard a thing the patient said.' Teachers often missed important clues about their students. The young teachers, not really comfortable with their subject matter, were so often rehearsing the material to themselves that they were closed to external stimuli.

After recall sessions students were less prone to tuning out and feigning clinical naiveté. The second phase, then, was to set up a counselling session and do no recall with the client, but rather to conduct a recall session of the student. Typically, students learn how they fail to hear and deal with client messages, and they usually become more sensitive to their own feelings in interaction.

INQUIRER TRAINING — PEER SUPERVISION

The next phase is learning the inquirer role. In doing so, most students also learn that assertive behaviour is not necessarily hostile behaviour. While remaining fairly non-judgemental, the inquirer is confronting and assertive. One asks such questions as, 'How did you want that other person to perceive you?'; 'Were there any other thoughts going through your mind?'; 'Were those feelings located physically in some part of your body?' Students feel more secure reviewing a videotaped interaction than in a face-to-face interview where they are uncertain of the upcoming material. There is additional safety in the clearly structured cues to be used in the inquirer role. This non-threatening framework usually enables the student to try assertive behaviours without being hostile or defensive. Students practise the inquirer role in a series of exercises, learning to conduct recall sessions without reliance on the instructor. They also develop important new and useful skills in interaction. From the instructor's point of view, of course, an extremely time-consuming process can now be assumed by students. For the administrator, an expensive supervisory process is replaced by one of modest cost.

CLIENT RECALL — FEEDBACK FROM THE CONSUMER

Students seemed better able to help their clients or patients when sensitive to their own feelings and frequently inappropriate behaviours, but awareness of self was often not enough. Typically the students needed additional help in becoming more involved with their clients. By the time the second phase was completed, the student was also ready to receive feedback about client dynamics. We fashioned an IPR tool to provide client feedback and to afford the student additional experience using exploratory probes, the primary mode used in recall. In this phase, the students themselves are required to perform the function of inquirer with another student's client. Thus, the counsellors have an opportunity to try new behaviour with the realization that they are working with their peer's client, not their own. Two counsellors exchange clients for a recall session. They may agree to exchange notes later, to listen to audio-recordings of their partner's recall, or even to observe the session through a one-way mirror, to understand their client's reactions. Thus both students learn, one in the counsellor role, and one in the inquirer role. By this phase the students are ready for such feedback and are not overwhelmed by it (especially since it is a peer, not the supervisor, who is the client's inquirer). The instructor or a staff member is available to assist with any technical problems and to discuss with students their reactions to the role of inquirer and the feedback they got from their clients. Students usually learn, often to their amazement, that they can be both confrontive and supportive, that questions raised by the interviewer which might be embarrassing in most social settings are appropriate and productive in a counselling or medical interview when accompanied by communication of concern. Students learn, too, which behaviours clients found helpful and which they did not. Most often students are also amazed to learn the extent to which clients are concerned about the counsellors' feelings about them. The discussion during the recall session is likely to be very different from the recorded interaction, when the client's attention is focused on the client-counsellor relationship. The knowledge gleaned from client recall creates in students a readiness for the next phase of the system.

MUTUAL RECALL — THE RELATIONSHIP AS CONTENT

It is one thing for students to learn experientially that an important part of clients' concerns involve the counsellor, but it is quite another thing for students *to learn to use the relationship itself* as a case in point to help clients understand their usual interpersonal behaviour and to learn to relate in new ways. Again, with the developmental task defined and awareness of the probable readiness of the student for new learning, an IPR experience was fashioned to help achieve the goal.

Counsellor and client are videotaped as before. During the recall *both* counsellor and client remain in the same room and are joined by an inquirer. During the recall session both counsellor and client are encouraged to recall their thoughts, feelings and especially how they perceived each other and what meanings they ascribed to each other's behaviours. A situation is thus created in which two people, a client and a student, are helped to talk about each other to each other. Such mutual recall sessions typically enable students to become better able to communicate with clients on the level of the here-and-now. Students usually become more involved, more concerned, more assertive, and more honest with their clients and use the ongoing counsellor-client relationship as a case-in-point to help clients understand their relationships with other people.

AFFECT SIMULATION – COPING WITH INTERPERSONAL NIGHTMARES

After the studies cited above validated the revised system, affect simulation or 'stimulus' vignettes were added to the model (Kagan & Schauble, 1969; Danish & Brodsky, 1970). The idea for such trigger vignettes on film or videotape came from the experience of conducting hundreds of recall sessions. In numerous IPR sessions we observed that people feared behaviours which in all likelihood they would never be subjected to. Clients often feared, for instance, that if they told their counsellor or psychotherapist 'the truth' about themselves that the counsellor would walk out of the room in disgust. Teachers often fantasized that if they gave up 'too much' control in the classroom chaos would follow. Medical students often feared being discredited or even mocked by patients because of their age and fallibility. In general, the fears could be categorized under four general rubrics:

☐ fear of the other's hostility towards the student
☐ the students' fear of loss of control of their own aggressive impulses
☐ fear that the other would become too intimate or seductive
☐ the students' fear of their own potential seductiveness.

These 'interpersonal nightmares' were often examined during recall session if the student was introspective enough and if the encounter in the videotaped interview stimulated the nightmare sufficiently, but it seemed to us that it might be possible to create a more reliable way of helping people face their interpersonal fears. It occurred to us that if we filmed actors looking directly at the camera lens (so the resultant image looks directly at the viewer) and portraying one of the more universal nightmares, it might help students discuss and understand their interpersonal behaviours. A series of filmed vignettes were made. These were to be used for a wide range of subjects, so actors were instructed to portray the various types of affect with varying degrees of intensity, but to avoid words which would give them a role or too specific a story. For instance, in one vignette an actor looks at the viewer for a few seconds, tears appear in his eyes and between sobs he asks, 'Why did you do that? I did nothing to you.' In another vignette a woman slowly licks her lips and tells the viewer, 'If you don't come over here and touch me I'm going to go out of my mind.' Students are told to imagine that the actor is talking privately to them. Students are then asked such questions as: 'Did the vignette have any impact on you? What did you feel? What did you think? Has anything close to that kind of situation ever actually happened to you? How do you usually respond? How do you wish you could bring yourself to respond? What did the person on the screen really want of you?' Most students are easily involved in the process.

After our initial experiences with the filmed simulation of inter-personal threat, we turned to creating vignettes of the kind of threat which might influence performance in a specific occupation. A series of films were made especially for teachers and instructors based on some of the fears teachers typically have. Similarly, vignettes were made for physicians, medical students, and other health care groups, for instance, 'We've been to so many doctors who were just awful! But we're sure *you'll* be able to help us!' The vignettes are used with students in small groups. Other formats have also been used. In one, students and the image on the screen are videotaped using two cameras and a split-screen technique as the student watches the film. At the conclusion of the simulated experience students are engaged in a recall of the videotape. In another format, each student's heart rate, skin conductance, respiration, and other physiological processes are also recorded and included in the videotape so that during the recall students not only see how they looked during the playing of each vignette but also how their physiological processes responded.

EVALUATION

Did the newer model (expanded to include affect-simulation) work? Controlled studies (Spivack & Kagan, 1972) indicate that the model reliably enables students to make significantly greater gains than control treatments. We also found the model effective in other cultures (Kagan & Byers, 1973, 1975). Especially exciting for mental health workers was the finding that the IPR model could be used to help para-professionals learn basic counselling skills. Robert Dendy (1971) provided a 50-hour program for undergraduates. Among his findings were significant improvement in interviewing skills, significant growth on an affective sensitivity scale, and no loss of skills during a three-month no-training period. Before the program was undertaken, independent judges rated the undergraduates' interviewing skills and also rated tapes of PhD-level supervising counsellors employed at the university's counselling centre. Both groups interviewed clients from the same client pool. Before the 50-hour program, there were large differences favouring the PhDs, but, after training, independent judges found no significant differences between the groups on scales of empathy and other basic communication skills.

James Archer (1973) then found that these same undergraduates could, in turn, train other undergraduates so that the peer-instructed students scored significantly higher than other students who experienced an encounter group of similar duration. They also scored higher than a comparable no-treatment group, not only on measures of affective sensitivity and self-actualization, but also on scales given to room-mates and other peers not in the study. When given lists of all participants, dormitory residents selected the IPR-trained students as the ones they would be willing to talk to about a personal problem much more frequently than they rated either the encounter-trained students or the control group members. Apparently, then, dormitory residents were able to identify the increased therapeutic skills of those peer-instructed students in the IPR group.

It must be pointed out, however, that the undergraduates used in both the Dendy and the Archer studies were carefully selected and were highly motivated. Mary Heiserman (1971) applied a 16-hour variation of the model to a group of court caseworkers who did not perceive their role as requiring or including counselling skills. No significant gains were found. The learning potential of IPR is not irresistible! Nor have we yet achieved measurable success in rehabilitating alcoholics (Munoz, 1971) with IPR.

The majority of IPR evaluation studies have been pre-post evaluations of the impact of all or major segments of the model. There have been relatively few intra-model studies to examine the impact of *each* of the major elements. We obtained some evidence by making recordings of people's physiological reactions while they watched stimulus vignettes (Archer *et al*, 1972). We then showed the participants videotapes of themselves watching the vignettes and again recorded their physiological reactions. Major shifts in recorded pattern during the initial viewing of the films were too often repeated during the videotape review for such repetition of pattern to have been a chance occurrence. This strictly clinical observation has not been quantified but certainly is convincing evidence that the recall process is a re-experiencing rather than a fabricated story to explain one's previous behaviour. David Katz and Arthur Resnikoff (1977) found a more systematic, controlled way to test the validity of the basic recall process. They trained people to provide an ongoing account of the intensity of their experimental groups. In another intro-model study, evidence to support the basic premise that the affect simulation vignettes do indeed have an impact on people was found by Robert Grossman (1975). He produced vignettes of an actor presenting five antagonistic messages to the viewer. The same actor was also filmed presenting non-inflammatory information to the viewer. The antagonistic vignettes were then presented to two groups of 10 men and women and the informational scenes were shown to two other groups, each of 10 people. Limb tremors were measured with an accelerometer which the viewers were asked to hold in their arms. There was significantly greater change in magnitude of limb tremor for the groups receiving antagonistic messages than for the groups receiving the informational messages. If we are to believe the data obtained in studies using IPR to examine covert processes (that is, to demystify medical inquiry) then more such studies of the validity of basic IPR processes need to be encouraged.

ADDING A FRAME OF REFERENCE — AN INTERPERSONAL THEORY FOR EVERYDAY COMMUNICATORS

Karen Rowe (1972) found that when in addition to the experiential processes of the model, students were also exposed to relevant theoretical constructs, their skill development was significantly augmented. Based on her findings, theoretical constructs about interpersonal communication were added to the IPR model.

Students are cautioned that acceptance or rejection of the theory is not crucial to learning from the IPR model. Instructors are encouraged to modify or substitute their own theoretical constructs. For the purpose of this book, it is not necessary to describe the elements and manifestations of the theoretical concepts (as in Kagan, 1978), but to point out that the ideas are *offered* to the student as a set of constructs or cognitive roadmaps. Students and instructors are encouraged to use these concepts as stimuli for their own theory building. As a point of departure for discussion, students may reject all or any part which does not make sense to them, and substitute other constructs which are more compatible with their beliefs or experiences.

PACKAGING

Since our first publication reliable replication of the model by others has been a primary concern to us. The inquirer role, so basic to the process is very difficult to communicate in writing. Even the filmed stimulus vignettes could easily be used in ways which would not encourage productive learning by students. This concern has led us to experiment with 'packaging' the entire model so as greatly to simplify the task of the instructor and to make the model reliably replicable without the need for 'outside' consultants. Our first attempt was limited to a black and white film and videotape series containing illustrations, instructions, demonstrations, and didactic presentations. It was aimed primarily at mental health workers. The package was used by more than 40 universities, schools and social agencies, most of which reported satisfactory experiences. A controlled evaluation by one of them (New York University) has indicated that counselling students taught by instructors using the package made significantly greater gains than a control group receiving an equivalent amount of other curriculum offerings (Boltuch, 1975). The package, entitled 'Influencing Human Interaction' was revised and expanded so that it now consists of colour films or colour videotapes (see Appendix) and contains illustrations from a wide variety of disciplines including medicine, teaching and family therapy. The new series also contains scenes which can be used by instructors to stimulate discussions of sexism and racism. An extensive instructor's manual and student handouts were also prepared.[2] The new package is currently in use in medical, pharmacy and law schools, hospitals, secondary schools agencies and prison personnel programs in the US, Canada, Australia, Sweden, Denmark, Norway, Germany, Puerto Rico, Israel and elsewhere.

NEW APPLICATIONS AND THE 'SELF-CONTAINED' FORMAT

The most recent modifications in the model grew out of an interest my colleagues[3] and I have had for some time in the possibilities of influencing the productivity and happiness of entire communities of people by offering IPR training to large numbers of people who would then be expected to use the skills and knowledge, not so much as counsellors for others, but as a way of relating more directly and being capable themselves of more intense involvement with those they live and work with. For instance, prison inmates who received IPR training at the prison reception centre prior to assignment to the prison they would serve their 'time' in, were later rated by guards as more approachable than a control group of inmates (Singleton, 1976). Teachers were rated by junior high school students as being more human and more likeable after the teachers received training (Burke & Kagan, 1976). In all of the IPR formats discussed thus far the instructor or a trained cadre of instructor-aides had to conduct the first recall sessions for the students (prior to the students learning the inquirer role and conducting recall sessions for each other). The number of students enrolled in such a course then would have to be limited to the number of inquirers the instructor could recruit or the number of recall sessions the instructor could reasonably conduct. Would it be possible to teach the inquirer role to students *prior* to the first IPR session so that their first interview is then followed by a recall session conducted not by the instructor or instructor-surrogate, but by one of the student's peers? In other words, is it possible to teach students to supervise each other in this model right from the start? A controlled comparison (Bedell, 1976) of the model using 'outside' inquirers and a 'self-contained' version indicated that very little was actually sacrificed for the increased efficiency.

It is therefore now possible for one or two people to have a positive influence on an entire school community (Burke & Kagan, 1976). Based on class groups of 25, it has been possible, for instance, for each IPR instructor at Michigan State University to offer 100 students every academic quarter the kind of individualized experiential learning which had previously been reserved for medical students or for graduate students pursuing mental health careers. A typical 10-week course is presented in Figure 1.

Such courses are now also offered on a regular basis at MSU and elsewhere to nutritionists, nurses, prison personnel, a wide range of students majoring in chemistry and business administration, and to persons who want to improve their ability to relate with others in professional or personal interactions.

WHY DOES IT WORK?

Why is IPR an effective learning program? Undoubtedly there are several vocabularies which could be applied and more than one learning theory. I prefer to explain it in the following ways:

Sessions	(3 hrs each)
1 and 2	Presentation: Explain background of IPR, development, uses, and course objectives Presentation: Elements of Effective Communication
	Lab Sessions: Individual Recalls with Experienced Inquirer
3 and 4	Discuss lab experience with students Affect Simulation, The Process, Film 1 and 2, and Vignettes Individual Recall Film example; eg, a film from the 'A' series
5 and 6	Inquirer Training: Inquirer Role and Function — film 8 Relate students' experience of inquiring in their labs to a discussion of learning the role for themselves Individual Recall Film Example; eg, a film from the 'A' series
	Lab Sessions: Inquirer Training in team of five to six
7	Individual Recall Discuss lab experience in small groups Filmed examples; eg, a film from the 'B' series
	Lab Sessions: Client recall, teams of three Students acting as inquirers for each other
8	Discussion Film (small group interactions) Followed by lab session in teams of three
9 and 10	Mutual Recall Discussion Discuss lab experience in small groups Filmed examples; eg, films from the 'C' series Followed by lab sessions

Figure 1. *Basic course outline*

1. *Intimate interpersonal encounter is not a dominant theme of life in our society.* Most people simply have never had opportunities to develop adequate skills that enable and facilitate such involvement. The program confronts this problem by beginning with exercises in skill definition and skill practice. Also such activities probably offer the least threatening type of interpersonal activity and are the least likely to raise excess student anxiety.

2. *Skills are not enough.* If people are frightened of each other, then simply teaching them ways to get closer may be of limited use. People need to be helped to come face-to-face with their most feared interpersonal nightmares. If these can be experienced from a position of maximum safety and security, it is possible for people to learn to deal with and overcome such fears. Film simulation seems

to offer this security by permitting people to talk about and gradually come both to experience and *label* the kinds of stress that ordinarily would evoke too much anxiety to permit acknowledgement, awareness and understanding. Simulation enables people to enter what would otherwise be overwhelming experiences without being overwhelmed. A great deal of control and mastery can come through such experience followed by labelling and cognitive analysis. Finding words for what had been vague feelings is often described by students as 'freeing'. It is as if the ferocious wolf, on close examination, is found to be old and toothless. Videotape feedback of one's reactivity to experienced simulated threat seems to give people an opportunity to look at some of the most frightening of interpersonal potentials, but from a secure position, so that the 'nightmare' can be experienced and also examined and understood. Whenever physiological feedback has been included, the potential for learning has been increased. As anxiety is reduced, new behaviours can be considered, learned, and used.

3. *Meeting in small groups with others to describe reactions to simulated situations affords people an opportunity to learn about other people's covert life.* This not only helps students expand their repertoire of descriptive words and phrases for covert behaviours, but offers them an experience of intimacy and sharing with others. They also learn that others may share some of their nightmares, thus reducing feelings of aloneness and shame.

4. In the IPR interviewer recall format, one is encouraged to make explicit one's perceptions and aspirations, thoughts and feelings about an actual recorded dyadic session. This leads to increased awareness of the way in which people frequently 'put their right hand in their left pocket' or frustrate the achievement of their own goals. The examination of an actual behavioural sample gives one an opportunity to recognize the daily expression of one's own ways of interpersonal distancing. Also of benefit, the recall process is in itself a *practice* of new behaviour. One says the things one perceived or was tempted to say during the recall process and hears the not unpleasant sounds of these statements. For instance: 'What I was really trying to ask throughout this entire session was, "there are times when your behaviour completely confuses me", but I couldn't find a good way to ask it . . . I guess I could have said it the way I just said it now . . .'

   Again, the careful management of anxiety level is a basic consideration. Student and inquirer are to be alone together during the initial recall sessions. If the inquirer is supportive and respectfully inquires about the student's experience, then the person is likely to be free to acknowledge and 'own up to' much of the covert experience. If the inquirer functions well, students have little to defend against except their own self-perceptions. If the inquirer is supportive, the student is encouraged to participate in an exciting learning-by-discovery experience rather than in analysis of whether 'appropriate' goals were achieved.

   Given this support, and the abundant feedback available from the

videorecorder, it is intriguing to hear neophytes describe complex
dynamics of which even astute supervisors were unaware. People
are truly the best authority on their own dynamics and the best
interpreter of their own experiences. Don Ronchi's (1973)
formulations further clarify why the inquirer role works. In a
sense, the inquirer is an active agent in fostering perceptions of
personal intention and personal control. Ronchi (1973, pp 7-8)
maintains:

> Peripheral awareness of the procedure as an attempt by an
> outside agent to modify behaviour may preclude an
> interpretation of personal intention. Recent work has provided
> insight into the way that external attempts to control behaviour
> serve to undermine what might be called 'intrinsic' motivation
> to perform the behaviour in general.

5. Assisting human beings to explore and struggle through complexities
   in their lives requires skills most people do not 'naturally' possess.
   Learning and practising the inquirer role does more than make the
   model more efficient, it provides people with skill at assisting others
   to learn-by-discovery.

6. *People ordinarily associate assertive behaviour with hostile
   behaviour.* Practising the inquirer role helps people learn assertive
   but non-punitive, non-hostile relationship skills. It is here as well as
   elsewhere in the program that 'interpersonal courage' is nutured.

7. I have already described the phenomenon of 'feigning of clinical
   naiveté'. *If one does not have to teach people to develop a 'third
   ear', but rather one has primarily to free people of their fears so that
   they are willing to risk labelling messages that they already perceive,
   then the simulation films and the interviewer recall should have
   helped students recognize and understand and be less controlled by
   their fears of others.* The response-skill training and inquirer-training
   phases should have given students specific skills with which to
   implement their new readineess for involvement.
   In the client recall phase of IPR, students learn about
   interpersonal communication and the nature of helping directly
   from the client. The student's previously unverbalized hunches are
   confirmed or denied. The student learns to recognize how the
   client's life style is enacted in the here-and-now of the client's
   relationships. Students learn that as clients talk with counsellors,
   teachers and others about concerns outside the immediate dyadic
   relationship, much of their energy is focused on the ways they
   want the other to feel about them.

8. *It is one thing for students to recognize and understand the
   importance of the here-and-now of an interaction, but it is another
   thing for them actually to incorporate this understanding into their
   behaviour,* to learn to respond to others in new ways, and especially
   to risk being more direct with others in the immediacy of the
   interaction. The mutual recall IPR format helps people reduce their
   fears and shorten the interpersonal distancing that blocks this kind

of interaction. In the presence of the third person and with the *here-and-then* of the videotape playback two people are usually able to risk describing what their perceptions had been of each other, the aspirations they had had for themselves and those they had had of the other. This here-and-then situation enables two people to practise relating in a new way with each other. Typically, in the early minutes of the mutual recall, each participant addresses the inquirer and talks about the other on the videotape as 'him' or 'her'. As the session progresses, the inquirer is usually bypassed as each participant finds the courage to address the other directly and to talk about 'you' and 'me', our fears about each other, our impressions, hopes and strategies.

9. Typically students go through these training sessions being clients for each other. At the end of the series, whenever possible, students then engage in interviewer, client and mutual recall sessions with people from the actual populations they are to influence. For instance, teachers are videotaped in their classrooms and conduct a teacher recall session with a colleague as inquirer. At another time, the colleague conducts a recall session of the students in the classroom without the original teacher's presence. Finally, a teacher is videotaped in the classroom and another teacher conducts a mutual recall in which both teacher and students are encouraged to describe their reactions and covert behaviours. This facilitates a transfer of learning beyond the IPR seminar and lab rooms. Trainees are also encouraged to use the methods in their daily work rather than to think of the experience as a 'one-shot' learning sequence or course. For instance, medical students are encouraged to use the methods during their clinical experiences and to focus on both affect and cognitive inquiry processes during recall.

It is difficult to identify all of the factors responsible for the apparent success of the learning program. The above constructs are my best approximation at this time. As we continue to use and test the model these ideas may well change.

WHAT NEXT?

The ongoing developmental process of IPR is opening up new ways to assist people who wish to improve their interpersonal understanding and skills. Offering the IPR program to any interested person on campus with absolutely no course prerequisites has proved a huge success at MSU. There are currently seven sections with 30 students in each section and these are fully enrolled well in advance of each term. In addition to the students who take IPR as a requirement in the medical schools, more than 800 people a year now go through the IPR program — a series of experiences once considered too expensive to offer to other than medical students or graduate students in counselling. The impact this might have on the lives of these people and on the quality of life at the university is probably researchable.

The model itself could be intensified. I am particularly optimistic about the possibilities of including self-study of one's own physiological reactions to interpersonal messages. The methods for this exist, we have only to find a practical, economical procedure to allow large-scale implementation.

What we have developed[4] thus far involves the following. A medical student sits in a comfortable chair facing a projection screen. As the student watches each affect simulation vignette a videorecording is made of (1) the student, (2) the vignette and (3) the student's heart rate, respiration and left and right hand skin conductance. An on-line computer also records the physiological events. After a dozen vignettes are viewed, and the student's physical and physiological reactions have been videorecorded, an inquirer reviews the video with the student. The recall session is conducted in the usual way except that the student can now see physical behaviour (grimaces, bodily shift, and so on), the vignette being reacted to, and a video playback of the student's physiological behaviour as it was being recorded on a polygraph. A second video monitor displays, at the student's direction, an *intra*-personal statistical analysis of the record. If the student wishes to know how his/her heart rate during the second vignette compared with his/her heart rate on all of the other vignettes, he/she presses a single key and the information is immediately displayed. Similarly, frequencies, amplitudes, slopes, and area under the curve are displayed for the vignette being viewed. We have found statistically significant improvement for those students who experience the new unit over students who receive the regular course with an additional lab session of a more traditional sort. The improvement is indicated by higher 'accurate empathy' scores from independent raters and by the use of a greater number of affective statements by medical students in a patient interview at the end of the course.

Ultimately the film series itself will be expanded. Vignettes and illustrations have been added which inevitably stimulate discussion of sexism and racism. Additional material on loss and grieving, on ageing and on problems associated with being a single parent could be included.

In 1979 the US Army experimented with teaching counselling skills to selected military personnel apparently in the belief that leadership in the future would be more dependent on interpersonal relations than it had been in the past. IPR is the model they settled on. Modifications in the film series were made, primarily the addition of military examples to the existing series. The IPR course has been a required part of the training of new drill sergeants in the US Army for the past three years. These sergeants have subsequently been an influence in the lives of literally hundreds of thousands of soldiers. All training sessions are conducted by military trainers, themselves drill sergeants.

The success the IPR model has seen in the past 20 years has given us a great deal of satisfaction and has encouraged us to continue research and development efforts.

Notes

1. This chapter is a revised and up-dated version of a paper prepared for a workshop at the Fourth International Conference on Improving University Teaching, 23-25 July 1978 in Aachen, West Germany. I wish to acknowledge the collaboration of the conference organizer, Dr Dietrich Brandt, in editing this paper. The original conference paper has also been edited for different purposes and published as Chapter 19: 'Influencing Human Interaction — Eighteen Years with IPR' in Hess, Allen K (1980) *Psychotherapy Supervision: Theory, Research and Practice*, John Wiley, New York. I wish to thank John Wiley & Sons Inc for giving me their kind permission to reprint parts of this chapter here.
2. The materials are available on videotape or film and are sold by Mason Media Inc, 1265 Lakeside Drive, East Lansing, Michigan 48823, USA (phone 517-3327880).
3. During the past ten years J Bruce Burke has directed or co-directed many of the IPR research and development projects.
4. A project supported by the National Institute for Mental Health Grant #ST-24-MH15473-02.

REFERENCES

Archer, J, Jr, Feister, T, Kagan, N, Rate, R, Spierling, T & Van Noord, R (1972) 'A new methodology for education, treatment and research in human interaction', *Journal of Counselling Psychology, 19*, 275-81.

Archer, J, Jr & Kagan, N (1973) 'Teaching interpersonal relationship skills on campus: a pyramid approach', *Journal of Counselling Psychology, 20*, 535-41.

Bedell, W P (1976) 'A comparison of two approaches to peer supervision in the training of communication skills using a videotape recall model', unpublished PhD dissertation, Michigan State University.

Boltuch, B S (1965) 'The effects of a pre-practicum skill training program, *Influencing Human Interaction*, on developing counsellor effectiveness in a master's level practicum', unpublished PhD dissertation, New York University.

Burke, J B & Kagan, N (1976) 'Influencing human interaction in urban school', NIMH Grant #1+21MH13526-02, final report.

Campbell, R J, Kagan, N & Krathwohl, D R (1971) 'The development and validation of a scale to measure affective sensitivity (empathy)', *Journal of Counselling Psychology, 18*, 407-12.

Danish, S J & Brodsky, S L (1970) 'Training of policemen in emotional control and awareness', *Psychology in Action, 25*, 368-69.

Danish, S J & Kagan, N (1971) 'Measurement of affective sensitivity: toward a more valid measure of interpersonal perception', *Journal of Counselling Psychology, 18*, 51-54.

Dendy, R F (1971) 'A model for the training of undergraduate residence hall assistants as paraprofessional counsellors using videotape techniques and interpersonal process recall (IPR)', unpublished PhD dissertation, Michigan State University.

Elstein, A S, Kagan, N, Shulman, L, Jason, H & Loupe, M J (1972) 'Methods and theory in the study of medical inquiry', *Journal of Medical Education, 47*, 85-92.

Grossman, R W (1975) 'Limb tremor responses to antagonistic and informational communication', unpublished abstract, Michigan State University.

Heiserman, M (1971) 'The effect of experiential-videotape training procedures compared to cognitive-classroom teaching methods on the interpersonal communication skills of juvenile court caseworkers', unpublished PhD dissertation, Michigan State University.

Jason, H, Kagan, N, Werner, A, Elstein, A & Thomas, J B (1971) 'New approaches to teaching basic interview skills to medical students', *American Journal of Psychiatry,* 127, 1404-07.

Kagan, N (1976) 'Influencing human interaction', distributed by Mason Media, Inc, Box C, Mason, Michigan 48854. Also available through Media Division, American Personnel and Guidance Association, Washington, DC.

Kagan, N (1975) 'Influencing human interaction — eleven years with IPR', *The Canadian Counsellor,* 9, 74-97.

Kagan, N & Byers, J (1973 & 1975) 'Assignment reports', IPR workshops conducted for the United Nations World Health Organization in New Guinea and Australia. WHO, Manila, Phillipines.

Kagan, N & Krathwohl, D R (1967) *Studies in Human Interaction: Interpersonal Process Recall Stimulated by Videotape,* ERIC Document Reproduction Service, ED 017 946.

Kagan, N, Krathwohl, D R & Miller, R (1963) 'Stimulated recall in therapy using videotape — a case study', *Journal of Counselling Psychology,* 10, 237-43.

Kagan, N & Schauble, P G (1969) 'Affect simulation in interpersonal process recall', *Journal of Counselling Psychology,* 16, 309-13.

Katz, D & Kesnikoff, A (1977) 'Televised self-confrontation and recalled affect: a new look at videotape recall', *Journal of Counselling Psychology,* 24, 150-52.

Munoz, Daniel G (1971) 'The effects of simulated affect films and videotape feedback in group psychotherapy with alcoholics', unpublished PhD dissertation, Michigan State University.

Resnikoff, A (1968) 'The relationship of counsellor behaviour to client response and an analysis of a medical interview training procedure involving simulated patients', unpublished PhD dissertation, Michigan State University.

Ronchi, D (1973) 'Attribution theory and video playback: a social psychological view', paper presented at the American Educational Research Association Annual Convention, New Orleans.

Singleton, N (1976) 'Training incarcerated felons in communication skills using an integrated IPR (interpersonal process recall) videotape feedback/affect simulation training model', unpublished PhD dissertation, Michigan State University.

Spivack, J S & Kagan, N (1972) 'Laboratory to classroom — the practical application of IPR in a masters level pre-practicum counsellor education program', *Counsellor Education and Supervision,* September, 3-15.

Werner, A & Schneider, J M (1974) 'Teaching medical students interactional skills', *New England Journal of Medicine,* 290, 1232-37.

APPENDIX
INTERPERSONAL PROCESS RECALL:
DESCRIPTION OF FILMS AND VIGNETTES

THE FILM SERIES

The films entitled, 'Elements of Facilitating Communication' (film 1),
'Affect Simulation' (films 2 and 3), 'Inquirer Role and Function' (film
8) and 'Discussion' (film 11) are devoted to skill development, consideration of conceptual frameworks, exploration of interpersonal stress and
contain descriptions of the lab assignments.

The 'A' series, 'B' series and 'C' series demonstrate to students some
of the ways in which IPR can be used to study and influence important
human interactions. The content of the films also serves to stimulate
student learning about interpersonal relations and to encourage students
to engage in analyses and discussions of their own IPR lab sessions.

The 'A', 'B' and 'C' series are films of actual interactions of physicians, patients, teachers, psychotherapists, students, counsellors,
administrators, dormitory workers, families and couples. Age, sex and
race are varied. The 'A' series contains excerpts from the recall of the
helping person — the therapist, administrator, physician, counsellor, etc.
The 'B' series contains excerpts from the recall of the client, patient or
students. The 'C' series contains excerpts from the recall of both or all
persons in the recorded session — physican *and* patient, family *and*
family therapists, etc.

Film 1 — 'Elements of Facilitating Communication'
This film is designed to help students expand their repertoire of ways of
responding to requests for help or understanding by another. The
following four skills are defined and illustrated:

☐ Exploratory responses — those which encourage a person to stay
  deeply involved in communicating and at the same time give the
  person freedom in what her/his next response will be.
☐ Listening responses — those which actively and deliberately
  communicate to the person that you are listening and trying to
  understand.
☐ Affective responses — those which identify the feeling tone of what
  the other person is saying and which focus on underlying attitudes,
  values and bodily reactions.
☐ Honest labelling responses — those which communicate to the other
  person that you are willing to deal directly and frankly, but not
  brutally, with what you have seen and heard.

The student is shown vignettes in which a person makes a statement
and an interviewer responds one way (non-exploratory) to her statement. In the next vignette the person repeats her statement to the
interviewer who responds differently (exploratory) to her statement.
Several occupational types are presented for each of the four sets of
concepts. The instructor points out that the non-exploratory, non-
listening, cognitive and avoidance response modes are those usually

associated with superficial social conversation, while the other response modes are those which are frequently contained in therapeutic communication. Students practise the new response modes with a series of actors on film who look directly at them and make statements varying in complexity and intensity. Students are reminded that the response modes being taught are helpful but are not used by effective interviewers in responding to every client statement and that indeed it is frequently inappropriate to use them.

52 minutes. Available on colour film or colour videotape.

Film 2 — 'Affect Simulation. The Process'

This film is on two reels. The first introduces the idea of affect simulation and explains to students the purposes of the unit, which are to help students increase their sensitivity to themselves and to recognize some of their 'interpersonal allergies'. Various formats for using the simulation vignettes are illustrated. Specific questions are posed for students to ask themselves and each other after viewing each vignette, such as: 'What did you feel? What were your bodily reactions? When else in your life do you feel that way? What did you think? What did you really want to do? What did you think the person was feeling about you?'

The second reel is intended for viewing after some or all of the affect simulation vignettes (film 3) have been reacted to by the students. The vignettes were created from those interpersonal situations which we are all concerned about. Specific discussion themes are introduced by the film; eg, how does creating a language for one's experiences help one overcome fears? The concept of interpersonal distance is also explored.

16 minutes. Available on colour film or colour videotape.

Film 3 — 'Affect Simulation, Vignettes'

This film is a series of brief scenes in which an actor looks directly at the viewer and makes statements which are likely to have an emotional impact. For example:

> *An older woman says, 'I want you to settle down and do the kind of job we both know you're capable of.'*
> *An older man says, 'I'd be proud to be your father. Any man would be. I'd be proud to be your father.'*
> *Man behind a desk, laughing, says, 'You are so funny. Well, just look at yourself sitting there. I mean, you don't take yourself seriously, do you?*

Film 8 — Inquirer Role and Function

This film is designed to enable students to understand the conceptual bases of the inquirer role and to permit students safely to practise the role, for the first time, through supervisory simulated situations on film. Knowing the inquirer role enables students to conduct IPR sessions for each other, and also further expands students' repertoire of ways of relating with or helping another.

In the first part of the film, episodes are presented which contrast traditional supervision with IPR inquiry. The inquirer functions so as to assist another person to learn through their own efforts. In addition to dealing with conceptual issues, there are a series of practice vignettes where the viewer assumes the role of inquirer. The film also contains a demonstration of how students may next practise the inquirer role with each other in small groups. The specific cues one uses in the inquirer role and the learning-by-discovery philosophy of the recall process are useful to students with or without videotape. In addition, from the instructor's point of view, an extremely time consuming process can now be assumed by students for one other.

51 minutes. Available on colour film or colour videotape.

THE 'A' SERIES — SELF STUDY

The purpose of the experiences illustrated in the 'A' series is to help students learn to study themselves in action.

The process is based on the observation that *all* students perceive infinitely more information about the nature of other people's concerns and communication than they acknowledge. The developmental task is to help the student learn to identify, organize and put to use the information she/he possesses.

In these individual videotaped playback sessions the inquirer encourages the student to relive her/his helping experience in as much depth and detail as possible. The inquirer assists the student to remember what she/he was thinking and feeling, what she/he wanted the other to think and feel, making explicit concerns which interfered with achieving her/his goals for the session. The IPR format helps the trainee take interpersonal risks, using data about the other which had previously been ignored or avoided.

An example from the 'A' series: Film A-2, 'Psychotherapist, On-going Therapy'
This is a film of a young woman client and a male social worker with whom she had been in therapy for several weeks. During the session she describes the previous week's events. She cries as she recounts that a collection was taken up at school to buy winter boots for her children. The recall session is of the therapist who articulates his compassion and concern as well as his strategies.

Recall of session
Therapist: I do have a tendency to lead a little too much in therapy . . .
I want to steer clear from that, especially with somebody that really
needs to own their accomplishments in therapy.

23 minutes. Available on colour film or colour videotape.

THE 'B' SERIES — STUDY OF OTHERS

The purpose of the experiences illustrated in the 'B' series is to help students to learn more about helping processes. What do people want when they present a concern of theirs to us? What are some of their more subtle messages? The purpose of this unit is to expand student knowledge of patient or client wants, perceptions, aspirations, and of how people avoid, deny and suppress, or learn to grow and change.

Students seem to learn more about patient or client dynamics through discovery than through demonstration or lecture and so this unit is an experience through which the patient or client her/himself becomes the student's instructor. A student interviews a person. At the end of the interview she/he asks the person to review the videotape recording with one of the student's colleagues. The person is told that in order for the experience to be of value, the person should recall her/his thoughts, feelings and moment-by-moment reactions as completely and as honestly as possible. The student introduces the inquirer to the client and then leaves the room. The colleague assumes the role of inquirer and then learns from the client the moment-by-moment impact, the aspirations, the kinds of interventions which started new thought processes and those which were perceived as meaningless. Most clients are able to provide considerable feedback. Students conduct two or three such recall sessions for each other. In this way students learn about human dynamics not from a supervisor's wise counsel or interpretations, but from an almost unimpeachable source, the consumer.

Typically students learn many things about human dynamics. One is the awareness of the importance of the here-and-now interaction between participants; students learn that, almost no matter what the content of the session, a large proportion of the patient's or client's energy is devoted to concerns about how the person was being perceived and how the person wanted to be perceived by the student.

An example from the 'B' series: Film B-1, 'Client, On-going Therapy'
This film is of the same client and therapist who are in film 'A-2'. They have had four non-videotaped sessions since the 'A-2' session was conducted. This time the client's recall was elicited and recorded.

During the session the client described a painful quandary — if she has nothing to do, she feels miserable and yet in ways which are unclear to her: 'nothing ever lasts . . . it seems like things come to an end . . . when I come across something happening good I don't ever want it to stop, but it does.'

During her recall session she reflects on how her own childhood influenced her perception of herself. She also talks about the meaning her relationship with the therapist has for her and she reflects further on her own responsibilities for her plight.

Recall of session
Client: When I mentioned something about how things come to an end

*. . . um . . . it's like I go so far and then I don't want to be used . . .
so I stop it before I find out what the results are.*

18 minutes. Available on colour film or colour videotape.

THE 'C' SERIES — STUDY OF INTERACTIONS

The purpose of the experiences illustrated in the 'C' series is to help
students learn to use the here-and-now, to bring them to act overtly on
patient or client behaviour as it occurs. An interview between the
student and a patient or a client is videorecorded. During the recall,
both participants are present with the inquirer.

The inquirer encourages *each* participant equally to talk about their
unexpressed intentions, feelings, thoughts, strategies and their expectations of one another. The inquirer helps the participants to talk with
each other and to listen to each other in new ways and at deeper levels,
as well as to confirm or refute perceptions they had had of each other.

Mutual recall allows the student an opportunity to learn how to use
the on-going interview as a vehicle for understanding the life style of
the other, and of helping the other toward better self-understanding
and change.

**An example from the 'C' series: Film C-2 Supplement, 'Physician and
Patient'**
This film is of a first contact between a young mother and a male
physician. The film is not of the same picture quality as the rest of the
series but the content of this physician-patient interview and recall is
fascinating and instructive. During recall the physician becomes critical
of some of his own behaviour.

Recall of session
Physician: . . . *it's a necessary evil for the system that we use for
interviewing — I have to write a certain number of notes . . . I don't
know. As an individual I have a little trouble dealing with silence . . .
and I'm thinking that maybe if I was watching her a little more
carefully through that questionnaire process, and then would jot a
note or two . . . that maybe I could have picked up on some of that
. . .*

11 minutes. Available on black and white film only.

7. When Professors Confront Themselves: The Use of Video Self-Confrontation (VSC) in Improving Teaching in Higher Education

Arye Perlberg

SUMMARY

The use of VSC as a technique to improve teaching in higher education[1] has been growing in recent years. This paper discusses the process of externally mediated self-confrontation which is not limited to media in general, or to video in particular, but which is viewed as a preliminary step to internal self-confrontation leading towards self-actualization and self-fulfilment. The paper reacts to some recent criticism which over-emphasizes the magnitude of arousal, stress and anxiety in VSC. It is based on the dissonance theory and the belief that, since dissatisfaction is a precondition to any viable behavioural change, users of VSC in higher education should take advantage of its potential to improve instruction. They should however also be aware that if not properly used, the process can be harmful or the effort wasted.[2]

INTRODUCTION

The limitations of this chapter do not enable a comprehensive discussion on the phenomenon of self-confrontation (SC) in general, and VSC[3] in particular. Therefore, we have chosen to touch upon selected issues, which are related to higher education and which to our best knowledge have received not enough attention or none at all in the literature.

Even though there is a growing use of VSC in higher education and it is strongly recommended as a technique for the improvement of teaching, (Perlberg, 1970, 1976; Koffman, 1973; Bergquist & Phillips, 1975; McLeod, 1976) there is not yet enough quantitative and qualitative data reporting the unique problems of VSC in higher education. The following discussion will therefore be based on research evidence and testimonials obtained from various fields in the behavioural sciences, from the writer's personal experience, and from the experience of other researchers and practitioners throughout the world, who have communicated with the writer during the last decade.

TERMINOLOGY AND DEFINITIONS

There is a measure of latitude shown by writers and practitioners in the use of terms related to the topic of this paper. In the title of our paper we use the term 'confront', and only in the subtitle do we explicitly

114

mention 'video self-confrontation'. Geerstma and Mackie (1969) and Fuller and Manning (1974) did likewise. This is no accident. In recent years, video playback has been the medium most widely used in SC, and therefore these terms are used almost synonymously. We should be aware of the fact that this prevailing habit narrows the scope of SC.

When using the term VSC, we assume a definition of confrontation as 'the reflection of information about the self from outside sources' (Kaswen & Love, 1969). However, if we refer to external channels of feedback to mediate SC, we must remember that in addition to video there are other devices, such as mirrors, photographs, audiotape recordings and motion picture.

Moreover 'external mediators' in SC should not be synonymous with media. Any oral or written, verbal or non-verbal communication to a person on his behaviour and his interaction with his environment may trigger a process of SC. In the specific case of higher education it is of special importance to recognize that the whole range of techniques and procedures of evaluation of instruction which have been highly recommended in recent years (Perlberg, 1979) is basically a trigger of SC processes. As such, they embody the advantages and disadvantages, the benefits and dangers of this process.

A BASIC CONCEPTUALIZATION OF SELF-CONFRONTATION

We mentioned above the role of 'external mediators', but a person can and should be able to reflect on his [4] behaviour without external mediators. Researchers and practitioners recommend that even when one uses external mediators to provide feedback, the person involved in the SC processes should try and recall his experiences in relation to his own goals and intentions, even before viewing himself or receiving another kind of feedback (Fuller & Manning, 1974). Our basic conceptualization is that external mediators in general, and in particular videorecordings which are considered the most potent mediators in the process, are only instruments used to trigger behaviour which will eventually lead to *internal self-confrontation*.

This conceptualization of SC stems from a basic psychological and philosophical humanistic concept, which views the psychologically healthy person as one who strives constantly for self-actualization and self-fulfilment which is a never-ending process (Maslow, 1954). Such a person is psychologically secure to be able to face reality without distorting it by defence mechanisms, and has the courage to accept this reality. He has a high degree of self-awareness and sensitivity and is able to perceive the fine and sometimes hidden aspects of his behaviour and interaction with his environment. He has the tools and techniques to analyse and diagnose the gaps between reality and his goals and intentions. We believe that the above-stated philosophy and description of the self-actualizing growing person has important implications to faculty development in higher education.

In their attempt to conceptualize VSC for teacher education, Fuller and Manning speak about 'three different views of behaviour change: the self-theory or experiential view, the learning theory or a behaviour modification view, and the attribution theory'. They suggest that these three views are not antithetical but rather complementary, 'each with a different contribution to make to current cyclopean conceptualizations about video playback'.

Some researchers have suggested that greater attention should be given to cognitive processes and information processing models in SC (Bierschenk, 1974; Finlayson, 1975; McLeod, 1976). The call for greater attention to cognitive theories does not negate the basic construct advanced by Fuller and Manning, and we concur with them that all these theories are complementary. Our discussion, however, will focus on the role of self-theory and the experiential view and their potential for conceptualizing VSC.

VIDEO SELF-CONFRONTATION AND DISSONANCE THEORY

In their conceptualization, Fuller and Manning depend mainly on the dissonance theory (Festinger, 1957) which postulates that the discovery of discrepancies between experienced performance and observed performance or between experienced and observed behaviour and intentions or goals, is both an activating and motivating force, leading to its own reduction, that is, change in self-perception or behaviour or both. This description of the dissonance process seems rather simplistic and harmless. However, based on their review of voluminous research reports and testimonials, Fuller and Manning (1974) conclude that this process is much more complicated. 'Self-confrontation is a stressful, arousing, partly covert experience with potential for harm as well as help. Its most frequently observed effects are intense focusing on the self, general activation of the system, and increased realism about the self.' McLeod (1976) objects to this extreme view of discrepancy theory. He suggests that we should look at the 'self-viewer in teacher education as a rational and internally consistent processor of information'.

Finlayson (1975) and McAleese (1977), also cast some doubts on the validity of Fuller and Manning's conclusions in regard to the magnitude of arousal, stress, anxiety and other highly emotional manifestations caused by SC. McAleese admits that research evidence points to the fact that psychological stress is present, but he suggests that the magnitude of this stress should be put in perspective. He would prefer to view it simply as 'arousal stress'. Based on his work with 260 trainees over a period of five years, McAleese states that 'in general, trainees respond very favourably to VSC'. Could we generalize from the above that VSC is a pleasant experience?

During a decade of intensive work with VSC in different settings and countries, we have worked with over 1,000 trainees: children, children tutors, student-teachers, experienced teachers, supervisors and helpers in teacher education, higher education faculty, consultants to higher education faculty, and various functionaries in other settings. We experienced reactions from trainees which ranged from extreme expressions of self-satisfaction and enthusiasm through moderately favourable reactions, various degrees of pain and stress during the discovery of discrepancies, deeper arousal, stress, anxiety, expressions of agony up to outbursts of tears and expressions of despair. These experiences and similar ones, reported by colleagues, induce us to concur with Fuller and Manning that VSC is inherently a stressful situation. The magnitude of the stress and the degree of anxiety differs from person to person and from situation to situation.

There remains the question of how it is possible that some trainees, even in our case, expressed satisfaction, favourable reaction and feelings of enjoyment after VSC which by its nature is a stressful experience. There are various answers to this question. Firstly, it is important to remember that people often have ambivalent feelings of distress and satisfaction simultaneously. Secondly, there is the narcissistic phenomenon (Nielson, 1964): people are curious about themselves and enjoy seeing themselves, notwithstanding the fact that they know beforehand that the experience may be stressful. Thirdly, there is the novelty and status of seeing yourself on television. In an era when television dominates such a large portion of our lives, many people are ready to overcome the fears and arousal involved in being videotaped, in order to resemble celebrities on TV. They are curious to see themselves on television and this overcomes their fears. Fourthly, some of those who have confronted themselves voluntarily may cover their stress and anxieties by rationalizing that 'after all it was not so bad'. They had expected it to be worse and anyhow they will not experience this ordeal again. This happens in many training situations where trainees have only one or two opportunities to confront themselves and where during the rest of the time, they watch their peers going through the same procedure. Frequently the overall satisfaction after SC in a group is derived from the person's feeling that he was not the only one to experience stress — other group members were also 'beaten' and often more than himself. Finally, the expressed satisfaction of student-teachers, or trainees in other settings, after VSC may stem from their comparison of the effectiveness of this training technique with other training techniques they have gone through.

A theoretically orientated training program which tells what is desirable but does not show how to do it, may also cause stress and frustration. As one trainee put it: 'At last I know exactly what is wanted. Even though I realize now that I have to change a lot, I am relieved. This is much better than the many painful hours of floundering around, of feeling and knowing that you are not good but not being able to put a finger on it.' VSC coupled with other laboratory techniques was found to be more effective than traditional training programs and was received favourably and sometimes even enthusiastically. These are but a few explanations to the puzzle of how a person can react favourably to an experience which is inherently stressful and may trigger anxiety.

THE IMPORTANCE OF AROUSAL, STRESS AND DISSATISFACTION

As was stated above, some writers object to the over-emphasis on stress and anxiety and would prefer to view VSC as 'simply arousal stress'. When VSC ends without any expression, overt or covert, of arousal and stress, it should be considered a failure of the helper, the person involved and his peers. If this occurs too often to the same person, there is a danger that he will become immune to VSC.

In our attempts to reduce arousal, stress and anxiety we may forget that they are necessary elements in any change process and that behaviour cannot be changed without experiencing them in some degree. Thus, the aim is not to eliminate these phenomena, but to control them and use them in a way which will disrupt or unfreeze the present situation and enable change, rather than freeze and fixate the situation as a result of overstress and anxiety. The optimal degree of stress depends on the individual and the situation.

From the above discussion it may appear that arousal, stress and even some degree of anxiety, must be seen as negative experiences — as necessary evils. We would like to posit that they could also be seen as positive elements necessary for human growth as, for example, in Berlyne's (1960) concept of curiosity as depending on conflict and arousal, or in Maslow's (1954) concept of the growth needs in contrast to the deficiency needs. While satisfied deficiency needs relax and satiate a person, growth needs are never satisfied. In satisfying his need for self-actualization and self-fulfilment a person is constantly aroused and activated. He may experience stress and even some anxiety. In satisfying his cognitive needs, such as learning and curiosity, the person discovers how little he knows, and is aroused to learn more. Scientists and artists alike are aroused, develop strong drives and go through stages of stress and conflict.

Those involved in VSC should view the process as one leading towards self-actualization. It is the consultant's duty, therefore, to establish an accepting atmosphere and an adequate climate for growth and self-actualization.

ATTITUDES TOWARDS TEACHING AND CHARACTERISTICS OF TEACHERS IN HIGHER EDUCATION

Any attempt to apply VSC as a technique for improving teaching in higher education must take into consideration the general attitude towards teaching in higher education and the characteristics of the various populations from which clients for VSC are drawn.

It must be stressed that higher education systems do not reward teaching and that faculty members are not motivated to engage in activities designed to improve teaching (Perlberg, 1970, 1976). Any attempts to improve teaching which *are* made as a result of public or student pressure tend to be only token, half-hearted measures.

It can be said, therefore, that faculty members and their consultants, involved in this type of activity, are working in a non-rewarding, non-appreciative and at times even a sceptical and cynical environment. The number of candidates for such work may thus not be large.

Another important fact is that most faculty staff in higher education are not selected for their teaching ability and have received no formal training in teaching and education. Moreover, many of them, like many teacher educators, are sceptical about the effectiveness of traditional teacher programs and are often also disappointed with the traditional programs in 'teaching improvement centres'.

Most faculty staff are torn between the demands which teaching and research make on their time. However, even the large number in junior colleges, polytechnics and so on, whose main task is teaching, often find that their reward system depends only partly on teaching. They are usually encouraged to advance in their professional discipline but not in professional education. They have developed similar attitudes towards teaching as their colleagues in universities.

VSC, experienced in a teaching laboratory, has great potential to solve some of these problems. The novelty of seeing oneself on television, or seeing oneself as others see one will motivate or lure some candidates in the first place. Once videotaped, the person discovers discrepancies which disrupt his equilibrium. If he participates initially because of external pressure, he may soon discover that the video feedback systems and the teaching laboratory can be more effective than other techniques for the improvement of teaching. Many participants see immediate changes in their mastery of certain teaching skills. They are reinforced both externally and internally by such improvement and are motivated to continue. Others find that the experience sharpens their perception and improves their ability to communicate with students, colleagues and everyone else. They appreciate that the benefits of participation go beyond the improvement of teaching.

However, when the novelty of television wears off, they find themselves torn between a feeling that they ought to do something about their teaching, and a conviction that nobody would appreciate it if they did. Here the consultant and the peer group must come into the picture and with proper techniques sustain the person's motivation to continue and work towards his self-actualization and self-fulfilment. The consultant should help him to focus on his discrepancies and realize that for his own mental health and sanity he must do his best and invest time and effort in order to reduce these discrepancies. All this in spite of a non-appreciative and non-supportive system.

THE ROLE OF THE CONSULTANT IN VIDEO SELF-CONFRONTATION IN HIGHER EDUCATION

The role of the consultant is very important and, at times, crucial. Fuller and Manning (1974) stressed the importance of 'focus' in VSC, of different strategies of 'focusing' and of the characteristics of the 'focuser' who, in the literature, is variously referred to as 'helper', 'supervisor', 'clinician' or 'consultant'. The semantic aspects of the terminology may seem of little significance, but we have found that in higher education it is important since the terms used can arouse antagonistic feelings. The terms 'clinician', 'clinic to improve university teaching' and 'clinical supervision' have a pathological connotation. 'Helper' is associated with the 'helping professions' and connotes weakness. 'Supervisor' suggests an administrative line position. The term 'consultant' refers to a member of the teaching staff at a faculty development centre. Among other functions and techniques, he utilizes VSC as a trigger for analysis, discussion and development of teaching behaviours and in connection with various aspects beyond teaching such as course development and evaluation procedures.

VSC is used extensively in various therapeutical situations where the people involved are seeking help and put themselves voluntarily in the helpers' hands. In most educational situations the participants are 'captive', the supervisors having chosen VSC as a training method. In higher education the consultant deals with a very sensitive population. At times, every participant behaves like a *prima donna*. The consultant may have general problems in higher education which affect the VSC situation among others. For example, his academic rank or professional status: he requires enough professional know-how and confidence to enable him to work with colleagues who may be above him in rank and stature. Many teaching experts in schools of education perform very well with students or school teachers, but are hesitant and insecure in advising university professors.

The difficulties in any consultancy situation in higher education are more acute with VSC, because after discovering discrepancies, the person confronting himself, highly-charged with emotion, may direct his frustration and hostility against the consultant as a defence mechanism. This can happen particularly if the consultant focuses on various behaviours which the person tries to ignore. Conflicts have to be controlled and resolved by the consultant. On the other hand, in cases where the person involved is not activated and aroused, the consultant's role is to activate and to arouse, to create the feeling of dissatisfaction which is a prerequisite to learning and adapting new perceptions and new behaviour.

The consultant needs to be highly skilful to manoeuvre this delicate and complicated process. There is very little evidence that consultants using VSC techniques are prepared for this role. Various writers referred to in this paper who have recommended the use of these techniques, or who have reported their own experiences, have neglected the crucial role of the consultant and the importance of his special training.

THE MORAL AND ETHICAL DILEMMA OF THE CONSULTANT IN HIGHER EDUCATION

In an American Educational Research Association (AERA) symposium in 1974, the late Frances Fuller argued that VSC is a stressful situation, at times dangerous and harmful. Since the subjects who might benefit most from VSC are the 'YAVIS' (young, attractive, verbal, intelligent and successful) (Garfield, 1971) and since many professors don't fall into these categories, it is morally wrong to involve them in VSC, especially without adequate trained personnel. As a member of the academic community, Fuller described very realistically all the forces working against the improvement of teaching in the university. She argued that helping to discover discrepancies and creating stressful situations without being able to help the person overcome the system, and eliminate these discrepancies is not ethical. Our response in that symposium was based on experience with VSC in higher education, which Fuller did not have. We argued that helping people to help themselves, to do a better job, to actualize themselves and to derive satisfaction from teaching, which is an important facet of their professional life, is moral, ethical and a very humane task. Our experience is that VSC can be used successfully even with older people in senior positions, whose behaviours are deep-rooted. In order to achieve this goal, we have to employ powerful techniques which arouse, activate and create dissatisfaction with the present situation. We are aware of the dangers as well as the great positive potential.

We hope that, as the number of people confronting themselves increases, and their need to improve teaching is intensified, this will in the long run help to change prevalent attitudes and behaviour towards the role of teaching in higher education. Pressure for change will be greater if it comes from people of high status. We concur with Fuller that there is a moral dilemma which places a great responsibility on the consultant to use the techniques of VSC correctly. Training is vitally important.

CONCLUSION

The growing use of VSC techniques in many walks of life should please all those who have predicted this development. However, our pleasure should not override our concerns. Too many people are using VSC techniques without really appreciating its potential benefits or harm. Too many people are subjected to VSC and to the arousal and stress which may come with it without really achieving the goals of bridging discrepancies. For too many, it is a wasted investment of pain and agony, without any benefits.

On the other hand, too many people just see themselves on TV, enjoy the novelty, enjoy a group discussion, paying attention to cosmetic effects, and enjoy the reinforcement techniques and 'pats on the back' from their peers and helpers without really getting down to the matter of analysing their behaviour.

In both cases a powerful tool and technique is wasted. It has become commercialized. Some are using it as a gimmick or a fad, and as the novelty of its use wears off, it will not attract anymore. A person who goes through VSC without achieving anything might become resistant to any real confrontation in the future.

Technology advances very rapidly. Recent developments in video technology make it possible to predict that many higher education faculty members, who are now our target population, will soon be owners of portable video equipment for home use. Video will be as popular as audio-tape recorders or 8mm movie cameras. However, very few people use audio-tape recorders for feedback and self-confrontation on their own initiative. How many will use the videorecorder? The present users of VSC have to realize that they are taking a great responsibility. They should be fully aware of the great potential of this powerful tool, if used properly, of its potential dangers and on the great loss of its advantages if used improperly.

Notes

1. Even though we refer in the title to 'professors', our discussion relates to higher education faculty as a whole.
2. This chapter is based on a paper presented at the Fourth International Conference on Improving University Teaching, July 26-29, 1978, Aachen, West Germany.
3. Throughout the paper we shall use the abbreviation 'SC' for self-confrontation and 'VSC' for video self-confrontation.
4. The male pronouns are used throughout for simplicity without any intention of sexism.

REFERENCES

Bergquist, W H & Phillips, S R (1975) 'Components of an effective faculty development program', *Journal of Higher Education*, **XLVI**, 2, 177-210.

Berlyne, D E (1960) *Conflict, Arousal and Curiosity*, McGraw Hill, New York.

Bierschenk, B (1974) 'Perceptual evaluative and behavioural changes through externally mediated self-confrontation, *Didakometry*, **41**, Malmo, Sweden, 1-58.

Festinger, L (1957) *A Theory of Cognitive Dissonance*, Stanford University Press, Stanford, California.

Finlayson, D (1975) 'Self-confrontation: a broader conceptual base?' *British Journal of Teacher Education*, **1**, 97-103.

Fuller, F F & Manning, B A (1974) 'Self-confrontation reviewed: a conceptualization for video playback in teacher education', *Review of Educational Research*, **43**, 4, 469-528.

Garfield, S L (1971) 'Research on client variables in psychotherapy', in Bergin, A E & Garfield, S L (eds), *Handbook of Psychotherapy and Behaviour Change: An Empirical Analysis*, John Wiley, New York.

Geerstma, R & Mackie, J B (eds) (1969) *Studies in Self-Cognition: Techniques of Videotape Self-Observation in the Behavioural Sciences*, The Willaims & Wilkins Co, Baltimore.

Kaswan, J & Love, L (1969) 'Confrontation as a method of psychological intervention', *Journal of Nervous and Mental Disease*, **148**, 3, 224-37.

Koffman, M L (1973) 'A study of the effects of videotape feedback and analysis of the classroom behaviour and student achievement of university teaching assistants', EdD dissertation, University of Massachusetts.

Maslow, A H (1954) *Motivation and Personality*, Harper and Brothers, New York.

McAleese, R (1977) *An Archetype of Self-Confrontation in Teacher Training*, University of Aberdeen, Aberdeen.

McLeod, G (1976) 'Self-confrontation revisited', *British Journal of Teacher Education*, **2**, 3, 219-26.

Nielson, G (1964) *Studies in Self-Confrontation*, Howard Allen, Inc, Cleaveland.

Perlberg, A & O'Bryant, D C (1970) 'Videotaping and microteaching techniques to improve engineering instruction', *Journal of Engineering Education*, **60**, 741-44.

Perlberg, A (1976) 'The use of laboratory systems in improving university teaching, *Higher Education*, **5**, 2, 135-51.

Perlberg, A (1979) 'Evaluation of instruction in higher education — some critical issues', *Higher Education*, **8**, 2, 141-57.

8. Video Self-Confrontation as Microteaching in Staff Development and Teacher Training

Ray McAleese

SUMMARY

This chapter analyses the use of close circuit television (CCTV) and videotape recording in the training of teachers in one institution in the United Kingdom. The model that underpins the operational description is discussed. The roles of the trainer/consultant who uses the video self-confrontation, the trainee and other participating trainees (peers) are examined. The chapter concludes with an examination of a model or archetype of self-confrontation in the university context.[1]

INTRODUCTION

This chapter is an attempt to conceptualize the process of video self-confrontation in the context of staff development and teacher training. It is a detailed case study in one institution of some of the ideas that Perlberg has detailed in the previous chapter.

The emphasis is on the system developed in the University of Aberdeen in the 1970s. The starting point for the discussion is self-confrontation and micro-teaching.

SELF-CONFRONTATION

Self-confrontation (viewing oneself carrying out activities) has been used to change performance in a wide variety of social areas: teaching, management, counselling, and so on (Fuller & Manning, 1974). Its origins can be traced back to the early days of film (Gesell, 1935; Nystrom & Lea, 1939). By the time the videorecorder was in common use (about 1950), recording and playback of performance had limited use in social skills training. It was not until the marriage of the portable videorecorder and teaching skills training at the University of Stanford in about 1962 that self-confrontation in teacher training 'took off'. The portable videorecorder made possible accurate and immediate replays of teaching performance. Allied to the technology was skills analysis and the concept of feedback to change performance. The growth of self-confrontation in teacher training was more rapid in the USA than elsewhere: by 1969, Ward reported 125 colleges involved with micro-teaching using CCTV and videotape recording (Ward, 1969).

Isolated examples of self-confrontation existed in Britain in the 1960s; for example, audio-tape recordings were used in university staff training in Aberdeen in 1966 (Nisbet, 1967).[2] By about 1969 simple CCTV equipment, developed in Robert Gordon's Institute of Technology, Aberdeen, was also used. It was not until about 1968, when the University of Stirling and the New University of Ulster embarked on large-scale programs of micro-teaching using CCTV and videotape recording, that self-confrontation was used extensively (McAleese & Unwin, 1971b).

However, micro-teaching is not self-confrontation. Although self-confrontation is an essential element of micro-teaching or skills training (Brown, 1973) it is only a part of the process. The 'narrow' definition of micro-teaching means short practice of specific skills, followed by self-confrontation (usually) followed by further practice (see McAleese, 1973b, for this definition).

As self-confrontation is only an element or component of micro-teaching, no discussion will be undertaken here of the more general aspects of skills training, such as the relationship between teacher performance and student achievement (see for instance Heath & Nielson, 1973), the extent to which micro-teaching is a simulation of real teaching (McAleese & Unwin, 1971a) or the criticisms made of the behaviouristic connotations in micro-teaching. Micro-teaching has been used in a 'broad' sense in Aberdeen. This discussion will focus only on self-confrontation. Perlberg is one of the few trainers who have reported on the use of specific skills training for teachers, although McKevitt (1967) and more recently Brown (1976a, 1976b) have used a 'skills approach'. No evidence exists that would suggest a 'performance-based' training program.

Self-confrontation takes place in a variety of settings. The instance used in Aberdeen is where the trainer (or supervisor or consultant), a trainee, and one or more peer trainees work in lecture recording sessions. The trainer organizes the session and acts as a teaching supervisor. The trainee is concerned with finding out more about his teaching competence. The trainee's peers form a micro-class for the purpose of discussion. Several questions arise about the recording sessions:

1. What is the context?
2. What is the role of the trainer/consultant?
3. What role do peer trainees perform?
4. What is the goal structure for the sessions?
5. What is the nature of self-confrontation?
6. How does the trainee respond?
7. What type of self-confrontation should be used?

The context

Trainees give 10-minute lectures to their peers. The lectures are recorded on videotape and played back to the group as a whole. Equipment comprises a fixed vidicon camera, a one-inch reel-to-reel videorecorder and a cheap omnidirectional microphone. Playback is through a 19-inch monitor. The trainer starts, stops and times the videorecorder and supervises technical arrangements. Trainer, trainee and peers are grouped around a table in front of a blackboard. No additional lighting or other technical support is provided. The recordings are made in a normal classroom that is set aside for such recordings (see Figure 1).

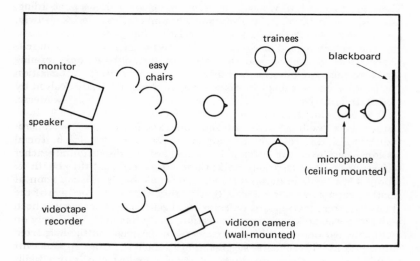

Figure 1. *Classroom setting and video equipment used at the University of Aberdeen in teacher training*

The role of the trainer/consultant

Trainers or supervisors are central to orthodox micro-teaching practice (Olivero, 1970; Stewig, 1970; Parry & Gibbs, 1974). However, doubt has been cast as to their efficacy in achieving change in teaching practice and performance (McAleese, 1973c). Very little consideration has been given to the role of the supervisor, *vis-à-vis* the process of self-confrontation, in the research literature. Supervision itself is well documented and researched. In general the teaching aspect of supervision (as opposed to the judgemental aspect) has received less attention in the training literature. What has appeared has been based mostly on clinical or military experiences. The model for such supervisory conferences is the five-stage model suggested by Goldhammer (1969): that is, pre-observation conference; observation of trainee; analysis of the trainee's performance; supervisory conference and analysis of supervisor's performance. The role of the trainer (as a supervisor) fits this model adequately. In Aberdeen, the recording sessions provide four of the five elements; the trainer does not formally evaluate his performance after the sessions — even though he should! According to the Goldhammer model presented by Fraser (1977), the process of supervision is:

> Basically analytical, the mode of analysis is a detailed examination
> of the learner's behaviour, [the] precepts and methods are rational
> and open . . . the learner participates . . . the supervision should
> produce real measurable accomplishments . . .

Therefore the supervisor has been seen among other things as an agent
of change in relation to performance. Blumberg and Cusick (1970)
present some interesting data on the relationship between supervisors
and trainee teachers. They question the degree of change that supervisors effect in trainees and the nature of their interactions: 'one is
forced to raise the question whether . . . what currently . . . transpires
. . . in the name of supervision is not largely ritualistic [and] deals with
a great deal of trivia.'

It is doubtful if the trainer/supervisor directly effects change in a
trainee as a result of self-confrontation experiences. How does the
trainer fulfil this role? In a study of the nature of 'talk' in these
sessions[3] just over two-fifths (43 per cent) of the discussion after the
self-confrontation was trainer talk; these utterances tended to be short
(about 11 seconds in duration); their tone could be classified as neutral
(neither supportive nor critical; they were mostly concerned with the
trainee's lecture (as opposed to lecturing in general or other comments))
and there was an equal use of questions and statements. Differences
were detected between different trainers, in particular in the length of
contributions. These data suggest that trainers are (as opposed to
should be) mostly concerned with a trainee's performance rather than
their socio-emotional support for the trainee. It is interesting to
compare the performance of the trainees in the same study. Trainees
contributed just over one-fifth of talk (24 per cent). These utterances
were short (about 11 seconds in duration); their tone was mostly
critical; they were predominantly concerned with their own performance. Trainees seldom asked questions, preferring to make statements
(in nine cases out of 10). (Blumberg and Cusick, 1970, have similar
evidence with regard to trainee teachers.) In contrast to the trainer the
trainee is much more critical. Over and above the numerical data, it
was observed that trainees could be very self-critical in their introductory comments. One could guess that this was a social strategy that
permitted them to retreat to a safer neutral position when the trainer
and the peers joined in the discussion. The trainer's role was a facilitative
one, mediating the critical trainee comments and incorporating the
peer comments (see below).

The facilitative role is well exemplified in Kagan's work (see Kagan
in this book and 1978, for a survey of his most important findings).
Kagan, along with others, has developed a system of 'interpersonal
process recall' (IPR) and calls this role the 'inquirer role'. In IPR, after
watching their teaching performance, or performance in a counselling
situation, trainees are able to recall the details of interpersonal trans-
actions (or thoughts) with the help of an 'inquirer'. Kagan chose
the word 'inquirer' to describe the facilitative person in an IPR session.

The role described is not that of a critic but of a support person.
It might be argued that trainers should be more critical and incisive in

their 'supervision'. For example, evidence suggests that trainees prefer the supervisor to play a more directive supervisory role during self-confrontation experiences (Copeland & Atkinson, 1978). The intention in Aberdeen was to help the trainee put his performance in context, helping him draw out salient points and helping with the analysis.

The role of the peers

As was suggested, peers are not essential for the success of self-confrontation experiences. Their presence, however, acts as a brake to the trainee's (self) critical comments. A study of the Aberdeen sessions[3] showed that peers contributed two-fifths of the talk; their utterances were longer than those of either trainees or the trainer (about 14 seconds in duration); their tone was neutral; they were largely concerned with lecturing in general; and they mostly used statement. The main difference was in the focus of their statements, which was external and general as opposed to specific and trainee-centred. They did, however, act as a brake on the trainee's critical comments and in a number of cases took a strong supportive role, suggesting that the trainee was too critical.

Apart from the logistical benefits of using peers for training (dispensing with the need to organize real students), they make a contribution to the self-confrontation sessions in at least two other ways. First, they shift the focus of the discussion from a teacher-taught dyad (trainer-trainee) to a group discussion. The trainee is not put in a dependent relationship with the trainer. In the absence of peers it is difficult for the trainer to be facilitative (although not impossible). Second, peers widen the discussion focus into more general topics, concerned with making points about lecturing (sometimes their own) and giving emotional support to the trainee. Evidence on the stressful nature of self-confrontation (see below) suggests that if peers can create a warm socio-emotional climate it can counter the critical trainee climate. Further, there is some evidence from an analysis of peer statements followed by trainee utterances that this in fact happens.

Goal structure

A further question that might be asked about these sessions relates to their goal structure (see, for example, Johnson & Johnson, 1974). In one important sense the sessions represent 'multi-goal situations'. Goals for sessions can be either competitive, co-operative or individualistic, depending on the expectations individuals have for the session. The supervisor's goal in these sessions could be described as co-operative (that is, changing the perceptions of the group to teaching), whereas the analysis of utterances (above) suggests that participants may have had more individualistic goals (that is, self-directed). Their goals might even have been competitive, that is, trying to do one better (in terms of the comments made and received) than their colleagues. Success or failure of the sessions is therefore not easy to judge. A session could be successful if the supervisor's goals were achieved yet the participants may have had different goals (Johnson & Knapp, 1970). Not only can the specific nature of the goals be different, but the general typification can be as different as individualistic and competitive versus co-operative.

The nature of self-confrontation

In the major reviews on self-confrontation that have appeared in recent years (Fuller & Manning, 1974; Biershenk, 1974), there has not been any critical attempt to conceptualize self-confrontation. By far the most wide-ranging review is that by Fuller and Manning who consider the evidence on self-confrontation both inside and outside education. Macleod (1975) has taken them to task for an over-inclusive approach and quite rightly concludes that 'the self-viewer in teacher education [is] a rational and internally consistent processor of information'.

In contrast, the Fuller and Manning view is that the trainee may seem anxious and narcissistic (see also Nielson, 1962). The role of rational processor of information is the one which is consistent with experiences in Aberdeen.

What is the nature of self-confrontation? What processes go on 'inside' the trainee? Two differing conceptualizations can be brought together. First, there is the self-concept view. When the trainee views himself teaching, he is experiencing a process of self-discovery: he is seeing an external representation of his self; his self as a teacher. In conjunction with his external self-perception there is an internal schema of the self as a teacher. This concept of self as a teacher is a part of the total self-concept built up over time. For the novitiate this internalized self-perception is weak and ill-formed, but for the experienced teacher it may be very highly structured, based on many years' experience at the job of lecturing (McAleese, 1973a). The formation of self-concept is not very clearly understood (see Shavelson et al, 1976) but it is sufficient to suggest here that it is based on feedback of information or results from performance of tasks and experiences — that is, perception of self while lecturing (see, for example, Gagné, 1976, on the formation of attitudes).

As Stanton (1978) quite correctly points out, 'self-concept is not, of course, a physical entity'. It is nevertheless useful to use it as a construct to explain the process of self-confrontation.

The process of 'teaching self-confrontation' is a meeting of internalized perception of self as a teacher and an externalized realization of the same concept. If there is congruity between the two perceptions, then the encounter should be non-anxiety (or non-stress) creating. If on the other hand there is a manifest difference between the two realizations of the concept, then there will be a state of anxiety in the subject. The relevance of stress in self-confrontation is that, for skills training to be effective, it is posited that playback experiences should be as stress-free as possible (McAleese, 1973b). Some authors have expressed a view that conflict (cognitive dissonance due to two 'conflicting' drives) is potentially useful in learning (see Festinger, 1957; Berlyne, 1965). There is conflict in self-confrontation with the drive to see oneself (narcissism) being opposed by self-consciousness. No evidence exists in staff development to suggest that conflict is beneficial in the videotaping sessions. However, research evidence points to the fact that psychological stress is present (Gilmore, 1975; MacLeod, 1975; McAleese, 1973b). The stress may be simply arousal stress; its magnitude is put in perspective when it is considered that stress in lecturing may be considerably higher.[4] Whether the reported stress is as strong as Fuller and Manning suggest is doubtful as the trainees are not usually in a totally stressful context where 'failure' means disaster. It is stress *in relation to a non-anxious resting state.*

The second view of self-confrontation is derived from learning theory. Viewing oneself teach is a special case of experiential learning. One view of learning theory is to cast it in terms of an information-processing model (Lindsay & Norman, 1968; Gagné, 1974; Gagné, 1976). Sensory receptors detect an input and unless it can be assimilated and cross-referenced it is not built into any schema in the long-term memory. Attitudes (conscious) and established long-term concepts have to permit the incorporation of external input before new schema are built up. Stress is a manifest dissonance between input stimuli and either recalled schema or unconscious schema. The process of self-confrontation then is a process of assimilation and cross-referencing of the externalized self into the established schema of 'self-as-a-teacher'. It is however recognized that 'self-as-a-teacher' is only part of the view that is changed. The observed 'cosmetic effect' (McAleese, 1973b) in micro-teaching students shows that a more total self is perceived. This concept of self as a teacher then is experienced by trainees when they view videorecordings of their teaching. The process is one of changing perceptions, firstly of the self as a teacher, and secondly (in a more general sense) of teaching in relation to self and teaching in general. Without further evidence it is only possible to hypothesize that there may be a hierarchy of perceived or experienced states: self-as-a-teacher; followed by teaching in relation to self; lastly teaching in general (see for possible corroboration, Shavelson *et al*, 1976). A further hypothesis would be that trainees must range along this continuum in respect to their subconscious preferences. However, it is sufficient in the meantime to accept the general proposition that the trainee is perceiving 'self-as-a-teacher' at some stage in the viewing. Braucht (1970) corroborates this view in his findings that self-concept accuracy is increased by self-confrontation but that self-esteem is unaltered. Further evidence is found in the 'free-wheeling effect' (McAleese, 1973c),[5] where it was possible to detect a 'free-wheeling' of students' self-perceptions in micro-teaching when there was no trainer present.

Trainees' responses
As has been suggested above, trainees respond to self-confrontation with statements that can be classified as critical as opposed to supportive and a focus on self-as-a-teacher as opposed to teaching in general. Further responses can be used in analysing the trainee's experiences, namely physiological stress and kinesic (movement) behaviour. An increase in heart rate by up to 45 per cent (McAleese, 1973a; McAleese, 1973b) indicates physiological arousal. Kinesic responses of trainees show a performance of viewing self, as opposed to the class, in a split screen experimental situation.[6]

This narcissism is in line with the findings of Nielson (1962) and with the hypothesis regarding what is perceived by the trainee (see above).

In general, trainees respond very favourably to self-confrontation. Based on 260 trainees' responses over a period of five years, self-confrontation sessions were rated as having a mean of 2.2 on a four-point scale (1 : highly favourable, 4 : low) — see McAleese (1978) for details. Trainees' attitudes to self-confrontation sessions must be seen in terms of their expectations and their experiences. The self-confrontation sessions were almost entirely the first occasion on which the trainee had experienced 'self-meeting'. As the sessions are novel to the participants, one might expect a favourable 'experimental' effect ('it's new, therefore it must be good'). This is supported by the evidence in Aberdeen, which shows a favourable climate of opinion. It is interesting, however, that the trainees showed no preference for type of self-confrontation or type of trainer intervention. The plausible explanation is that unless trainees had experienced different forms of supervision, they would be unable to make distinctions. As the majority of the trainees had not encountered such supervision before, they would have no way of making comparisons.

Type of self-confrontation
Self-confrontation can be achieved by either audio-tape or videotape. Film, to all practical purposes, is of no value: the immediacy of the self-confrontation is an essential component. However, the training protocols developed suggest that self-confrontation of teaching shortly after its occurrence (that is, up to one hour, allowing time for change-over arrangements) is ideal. Social factors and trainees' expectations make a short delay essential. As there seems to be no benefit from delay, immediate feedback (self-confrontation) is standard.

The argument is really over videotape versus audio-tape. There are other considerations, apart from the pedagogical one — for example, cost. On a direct comparison videotape equipment is at least five times more expensive to install, maintain and operate than audio-tape equipment. Logistics and technical complexity also favour audio-tape. It is, however, the overall balance of technological (cost, logistical, technical) against pedagogical that determines the chosen medium. Pedagogically, the type of self-confrontation used can be examined from two sides: firstly, the information processing model of learning, and secondly, the attitudes of the trainees. Broadbent (1958), Lindsay and Norman (1968) and Gagné (1974) suggest that channel blockage occurs when too much information is picked up by the sensory receptors. There is a sifting or selecting process in the short-term memory (the 'cocktail-party' effect). (See also Shiffrin and Schneider, 1977, on the limiting capacities of the 'short-term store'.) Subjects will selectively choose those inputs that have highest priority. That is, signals are not selected randomly, but on the basis of some set of priorities that the subject has already set up (internalized). If one considers the trainee, the relative merits of videotape and audio-tape become apparent. Videotape is a two-channel medium, audio-tape mono-channel.[7] The visual component of television is very strong. In line with the eyes' ability to process considerably more information than the ears, the picture on a videotape replay of a lecture contains a large amount of information.[8] McAleese (1973b) suggests that there are 16 identifiable events in one minute of video (picture only). Against this flow of information, one must consider the importance of the visual element to the lecture. Although it has a contribution to play (gestures for emphasis, facial cues, and so on), the verbal content of lectures is by far the most important pedagogically. It is for this reason and the additional evidence from the flow of information, that one must hypothesize that, other things being equal (see below) the trainee will prefer the audio channel. In selecting his channel he gives highest priority to the audio cues, which are more important and arrive less frequently. Why then is there such overwhelming support for CCTV and videotape playback?

No simple answer exists to this question. Considerations outside the pedagogical context may influence the choice of the medium. Institutional preferences for CCTV or videotape recording may override any educational or even commonsense considerations. Video or CCTV has the capacity to confer status, and because it is available, it is used. This view is supported by evidence from the number of colleges that use CCTV and/or video micro-teaching. There is evidence in Aberdeen that trainees like videotape self-confrontation even though they may not know how actually to use the visual component of the television signal. When trainees are asked immediately after a replay, 'What did you think of that?', they invariably refer first to something that they said or didn't say as the case may be. Videotape and CCTV have a powerful influence on the trainee's perceptions. It may be that (again, other things being equal) trainees like the visual component because it allows them to 'see themselves as others see them' − a 'cosmetic' or narcissistic experience, not a pedagogical one. There is equivocal evidence between what trainees prefer and what they use or are capable of using.

One has to conclude that while there are sound pedagogical reasons based on the information processing model why audio-tape should be preferred, in fact videotape is the most useful medium. This has, of course, far-reaching implications for training. (See McAleese, 1982 for an analysis of self-confrontation in different settings.)

AN ARCHETYPE OF SELF-CONFRONTATION

Self-confrontation in teacher training is a situation where the trainee's perceptions of himself as a teacher are changed. Stanton (1978) argues that it is the general *self*-concept that changes in a micro-teaching self-confrontation situation. The trainer is a facilitator of such an outcome, but he is not an agent of change, in that change in performance is not an expected outcome. Peer trainees act by modifying perceptions and in social and emotional support for the trainee. Perceptions are modified in a process that can be explained in terms of a special case of general learning theory. Video or CCTV is the preferred medium for self-confrontation although there is conflicting evidence (see, for example, Coates & Thoresen, 1976, for a review of teacher anxiety and feedback). As self-confrontation is concerned with changing perceptions, not performance (Brown, 1975), what are the strategies that the trainer should adopt to maximize gain? Focused activity would seem to be essential in order to control the internalization of perceived stimuli. Focused or 'purposeful' is 'meant to denote the act of behaviour which may be interpreted as directed to the attainment of a goal' (Rosenblueth *et al*, 1968).

Due to the process of selection, and the more detailed consideration given by the information processing model, where perception can be defined as 'the selection, structuring, evaluation and accentuation of information' (Biershenk, 1974), information seeking is necessary for an individual to develop an organized conceptualization. Focused activity is achieved through the trainer structuring the confrontation and by purposeful trainee observation of the replay.

An example of this purposeful focusing would be any form of systematic observation used during replay (McAleese, 1975). This archetype of self-confrontation is not intended to be explicative — or predictive — but to represent a 'systematic repertoire of ideas' (Black, 1962) that permits discussion. Figure 2 indicates the general relationships between the participants and the videorecording.

Experience suggests that peers and videorecordings have considerably more interactive effect on the trainee than the trainer. Again, whether this should be the case is problematic, and a lot more empirical evidence is necessary before a model might be built. One would have to suggest

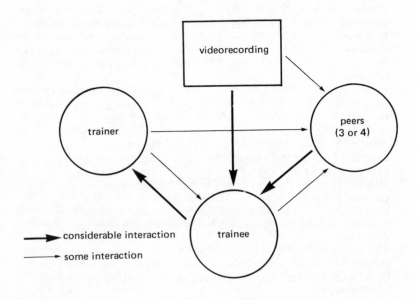

Figure 2. *The relationships between the participants in micro-teaching and videorecording*

that the reason for the conflicting views on self-confrontation from practitioners and researchers is a reflection of an inability to build such a satisfactory model. For example, Fuller and Manning (1974) believe: 'Practitioners have good reason for their optimism about self-confrontation . . . researchers have good grounds for scepticism . . .'

Notes

1. This chapter is a revised version of part of a paper presented at the Fourth International Conference on Improving University Teaching, 26-29 July 1978, Aachen, West Germany.

2. The use of audio-recordings was part of the first formal course in Aberdeen, March 1965. Nine students took part. The reactions were mixed, three considering the recordings 'very useful', three 'moderately useful', one 'occasionally useful' and two 'of little use'. Earlier, in 1962, some departments had tried this training technique with little success.

3. Ten supervisory sessions were recorded on audio-tape without the trainer, trainee or peers being aware. The recordings were coded using systematic observation techniques. Utterances (defined as meaningful units of speech) were coded for Tone (critical; supportive; neutral); Form (question; statement); Topic (lecture-centred; general; irrelevant; organizational); Emitter and Target (trainer; trainee; peer trainee). The frequency and duration of each utterance was computed.

4. Evidence from studies in Aberdeen suggests that heart rate can reach 170 beats/minute in a stressful lecture situation. For example, when a lecturer is asked a particularly difficult or unexpected question.

5. In this study, student teachers, who were unsupervised in micro-teaching practice, thought they improved their performance more than independent raters considered they did. It was suggested that trainee teachers 'used' supervision to 'control' their self-evaluation.

6. In the experiments referred to, subjects looked at a horizontal split screen presentation with themselves on the top half and the class on the bottom. Using a rather crude estimate of eye gaze, the part of the screen being perceived was recorded. Eye gaze position was detected by estimating, using a half-silvered mirror and a camera at an angle of $45°$ to the subject's line of viewing, where the subject's eyes were 'pointing'.

7. Mono-channel here means using only one sensory channel, that is, the ears. The signal might be stereo- or even quadrophonic. This is a simplification, but in teacher education it is most unlikely that trainees will have to cope with left and right audio channel differences.

8. The human eye can process about 10^7 bits/second of information; the ear, 8^3 bits/second, but the central nervous system not more than 50 bits/second. A television picture may contain up to 5^7 bits of information.

REFERENCES

Berlyne, D E (1965) 'Curiosity and education', in Krumboltz, J D (ed) *Learning and the Educational Process*, Rand McNally, Chicago.

Bierschenk, B (1974) 'Perceptual evaluative and behavioural changes through externally mediated self-confrontation', *Didakometry*, 41, Malmo, Sweden.

Black, M (1962) *Models and Metaphors*, Cornell University Press, Cornell.

Blumberg, A & Cusick, E (1970) 'Supervisor-teacher interaction: an analysis of verbal behaviour', *Education*, November, 126-34.

Braucht, G N (1970) 'Immediate effects of self-confrontation on self-concept', *Journal of Consulting and Clinical Psychology*, 35, 1, 95-101.

Broadbent, D (1958) *Perception and Communication*, Pergamon, London.

Brown, G A (1973) 'Some case studies in micro-teaching', New University of Ulster, Coleraine (DPhil thesis).

Brown, G A (1975) 'Some case studies of teacher preparation', *British Journal of Teacher Education*, 1, 1, 71-86.

Brown, G A (1976a) 'Micro-teaching', *Impetus*, 4, 2-11.

Brown, G A (1976b) 'Teaching and learning in universities', a course held in the University of Nottingham (Mimeo).

Coates, T J & Thorensen, C E (1976) 'Teacher anxiety: a review with recommendations', *Review of Educational Research*, 46, 2, 159-84.

Copeland, W D & Atkinson, D R (1978) 'Student teachers' perceptions of directive and non-directive supervisory behaviour', *Journal of Educational Research*, 71, 3, 123-26.

Festinger, L (1957) *A Theory of Cognitive Dissonance*, Stanford University Press, Stanford, California.

Fraser, G W (1977) 'Approaches to supervision in training', *RAF Education Bulletin*, 14, 52-65.

Fuller, F F & Manning, B A (1974) 'Self-confrontation reviewed: a conceptualisation for video playback in teacher education', *Review of Educational Research*, 43, 4, 469-528.

Gagné, R M (1974) *Essentials of Learning for Instruction*, Dryden Press, Hinsdale, Illinois.

Gagné, R M (1976) *The Conditions of Learning* (3rd edn.), Holt, Rinehart & Winston, New York.

Gesell, A (1935) 'Cinemanalysis: a method of behaviour study', *Journal of Genetic Psychology*, 47, 3-15.

Gilmore, S (1975) 'Student reactions to self-viewing on videotape', University of Stirling (Mimeo).

Goldhammer, R (1969) *Clinical Supervision*, Holt Rinehart & Winston, New York.

Heath, R W & Nielson, M A (1973) 'The myth of performance based teacher education', Far West Laboratory for Educational Research and Development, A73-10, California (Mimeo).

Johnson, D W & Johnson, R T (1974) 'Instructional goal structure; co-operative, competitive or individualistic', *Review of Educational Research*, 42, 2, 213-40.

Johnson, D W & Knapp, J E (1970) 'Trainee role expectations of the micro-teaching supervisor', *Journal of Teacher Education*, 21, 3, 296-401.

Kagan, N (1978) 'Influencing human interaction: fifteen years with IPR', paper presented at the XIXth International Conference of the International Association of Applied Psychology, Munich, 30 July to 4 August (personal communication and pre-publication mimeo).

Lindsay, P H & Norman, D A (1968) *Human Information Processing: An Introduction to Psychology*, Academic Press, New York.

McAleese, R (1973a) 'Micro-teaching and the training of university teachers', paper read at the VIII International Conference on Educational Technology, Brighton, ERIC IR 005 365.

McAleese, R (1973b) 'Micro-teaching: a new tool in the training of teachers', *Educational Review,* **25**, 2, 131-42.

McAleese, R (1973c) 'The application of micro-teaching techniques to the training of university teachers', paper read at the Education Section of the British Psychological Society's Annual Conference, London, ERIC IR 005.

McAleese, R (1975) 'A meta language of training in higher education', *British Journal of Teacher Education,* **3**, 1, 83-87.

McAleese, R (1982) 'Skills training and self-confrontation in different settings' in Trott, A (ed) *Aspects of Educational Technology XVI,* Kogan Page, London.

McAleese, R & Unwin, D (1971a) 'A simulated teaching environment as part of a teacher training programme', in Packham, D *et al* (eds) *Aspects of Educational Technology,* **V**, Pitman, London.

McAleese, R & Unwin, D (1971b) 'Skill in the classroom: art or science', *Times Educational Supplement,* 21 January.

McKevitt, O (1967) 'The use of television recordings in university staff training', *Australian Journal of Higher Education,* **3**, 1, 83-87.

Macleod, G (1975) 'Self-confrontation revisited', *Research Intelligence,* **2**, 46-48.

Nielson, G (1962) *Studies in Self-Confrontation,* Munksgaard, Copenhagen.

Nisbet, J (1967) 'Courses on university teaching methods', *Universities Quarterly,* March, 186-98.

Nystrom, C L & Lea, R (1939) 'The recording machine as a teaching device', *Quarterly Journal of Speech,* **25**, 433-38.

Olivero, J L (1970) *Micro-Teaching: Medium for Improving Teaching,* Merril, Ohio.

Parry, G & Gibbs, I (1974) 'A bibliography of supervision', *Programmed Learning and Educational Technology,* **11**, 3, 97-111.

Rosenblueth, A, Wiener, N & Bigelow, J (1968) 'Behaviour, purposes and teleology', *Philosophy of Science,* **10**, 18-24.

Shavelson, R J, Hubner, J J & Stanton, B C (1976) 'Self-concept: validation of construct interpretations', *Review of Educational Research,* **46**, 3, 407-41.

Shiffrin, R M & Schneider, W (1977) 'Perceptual learning and automatic attending', *Psychological Review,* **84**, 2, 155-90.

Spelman, B & St John Brooks, C (1973) 'Micro-teaching', *Trends in Education,* **31**, 14-19.

Stanton, H E (1978) 'Self-concept change through a micro-teaching experience', *British Journal of Teacher Education,* **4**, 2, 119-23.

Stewig, J W (1970) 'What should college supervisors do?' *Journal of Teacher Education,* **21**, 2, 251-57.

Ward, B E (1969) 'A survey of micro-teaching in secondary education programs of all NCATE accredited colleges and universities', University of Nebraska.

9. The Use of Video for Developing Symmetrical Communication

Stephen Kemmis

SUMMARY

In this paper, the notion of symmetrical communication is discussed. Symmetry in communication is evident in groups characterized by mutual recognition by members of one another as persons accepted and appreciated in their common striving for mutual understanding and consensus. The paper describes how a group of Deakin University staff members went about developing the arts of symmetrical communication in their own working group, and some of the things they learned in the process. The technique used by the group is based on informal videotape analysis and group discussion of blockages to communication. The development of such skills seems especially useful for improving the work of course teams which depend upon mutual understanding and consensus if the courses they develop and teach are to make the best use of the joint resources of the team.[1]

INTRODUCTION

At the May 1979 Annual Conference of the Higher Education Research and Development Society of Australasia (HERDSA), Dietrich Brandt of the University of Aachen offered a workshop on 'symmetrical communications'. According to Brandt and his co-workers Bruno Werner and Irene Drexler, symmetry in communications is evident in groups characterized by mutual recognition by members of one another as persons appreciated and accepted in their common striving for mutual understanding and consensus.

The thesis of the Aachen group is this: a working group tends to become communicatively incompetent, less satisfying for participants and less effective as a group capable of producing joint commitment to agreed action when communications in the group are distorted by considerations of status, internal power-politics or members' failure to respect one anothers' points of view. Suspension of status-considerations is necessary to achieve a climate where reason prevails and where group decisions are the most defensible ones, given the group's combined resources. Internecine politicking must be suspended to promote the community self-interest of the group and the attainment of consensus and joint commitment, and to avoid the group's coming to serve the self-interests of only a small part of its membership. Recognition and acceptance of members is necessary to achieve representation of all members' perspectives within the group forum and so to engage the disparate interests and perspectives of members and build these into a framework of common understandings and shared perspectives which promotes the community self-interest.

Brandt's workshop at the 1979 Annual Conference introduced participants to a technique for promoting symmetrical communication in groups in higher education. Groups are videotaped in the course of their discussions, the tape is replayed and the 'moderator' invites members to participate in the identification and analysis of blockages to symmetrical communication, and the formulation of strategies to achieve greater symmetry in communication.

At Deakin University, much of our course development work takes place in course teams. Like groups in higher education institutions everywhere, these teams have communications problems which are the product of asymmetrical communications. Since so much of our work depends on achieving joint commitment to courses developed as wholes — as curricula, not just aggregates of individual perspectives — it seemed to us to be useful to invite Dietrich Brandt to spend a few days with us helping us to learn techniques for developing symmetrical communications. This he did, using essentially the same approach as in the HERDSA workshop.

In this brief paper, the progress of the group in using the strategies suggested by Brandt is reported. A videotape is also available which depicts the use of the technique by the Deakin group.[2]

A number of interested staff at Deakin attended the Brandt workshop on Friday, 1 June 1979. The group consisted of 'course assistants' who work on course teams in a variety of roles (from clerical assistance through research assistance and editing to academic development roles), members of the university's production unit, and academic staff involved in course development and teaching (from a number of different course teams). One role for the 'Symmetrical Communications Working Group' (as it came to be called) was to explore the possibility of giving course assistants a role in the development of symmetrical communications in course teams.

For a variety of reasons, the focus of the group changed. These reasons included the availability of participants' time, the apparent intransigence of some course teams to the development of more symmetrical communications, the level of commitment required to develop the techniques over time, and the emerging interests of the participant group which settled down at about ten members of whom only three or four were course assistants. The focus remained largely on the development of symmetrical communications in course teams, though it was increasingly perceived as a matter for all course team members, not just course assistants. Course team chairpersons may have a special role in bringing about greater symmetry of communications, as might course assistants, but any member could intervene in the group process to reveal blockages to communication and help to achieve greater symmetry. Some participants in the Working Group also saw the wider applicability of the concept and the techniques for developing it; for this reason, the Working Group began to consider the variety of groups and committees throughout the university where symmetrical communications might fruitfully be developed. Members also considered the development of symmetrical communications in teaching/learning relationships.

We have some hopes of longer-term developments in symmetrical communications in our approach to teaching and learning at Deakin. A final possibility was that the Working Group might seek some kind of consultancy role with respect to course teams in the university more generally and use the techniques we had explored in this wider context. This last possibility was rejected on the grounds that seeking this 'service' or 'technical' role was contradictory to the basic principle of symmetrical communication. We recognized that we could accept such a role if invited to do so, but that we would then be obliged to adopt the strategy of the 'hidden compromise' developed by the Aachen team in their relations with higher education teachers: pretending to be 'expert' in order to gain access to and credibility with our colleagues, but only serving as 'moderators' of the process who helped members of groups to articulate their reactions to communications blockages they already experienced; developing group sensitivity about the signs, symptoms and consequences of communications blockages; helping the group to formulate strategies for overcoming asymmetry and the blockages to group process caused by asymmetry; and ultimately helping the group to become self-sustaining in the development of symmetrical communication (one sign of which would be dispensing with the services of the outside 'moderator').

It was not, and is not, the view of the Working Group that course teams can operate entirely without conflict or misunderstanding. On the contrary, the occurrence of conflict and misunderstanding is natural as groups work towards consensus and mutual understanding.

But conflict and misunderstanding may generate disaffection within a group which alienates members and reduces their commitment to the group project. Should this state of affairs become endemic to the group's process, then the prospect of joint commitment in a common task recedes, and the group project may disintegrate along the lines of self-interest (or sub-group interests) within the group. More commonly groups reach a dynamic equilibrium at some level of entrenched disaffection and internecine rivalry, sometimes remaining more productive, sometimes less. Hierarchy, compulsion and status may provide the 'glue' which holds such groups together, but its consequences may be experienced by group members in degeneration of group commitment, fragmentation of the framework of common understanding, and feelings of dissatisfaction, alienation or exploitedness among members whose interests are not being served in the working relationship.

'Symmetrical communications' as a concept is a description of an ideal process in which these dysfunctional tendencies are consciously recognized and deliberately countered. It is our project as a Working Group to discover strategies by which we might foster individually-satisfying and mutually-productive group relations.

Our method in our regular meetings was this:

1. The group met and discussed a topic decided in advance. The topic was usually one of particular concern to one or a few members but relevant (as far as possible) to all our interests. For example, in one

session we discussed a proposed evaluation of Deakin University Study Centres. In another, we discussed the possibility of producing a video program on the operation of course teams at Deakin.

2. These discussions were videotaped by a member of the group. The role of videotaping was shared among members in different sessions and was relatively inexpert: we all shared in the learning process [1] and developed some sense of more useful material for subsequent discussion of group processes and individual responses. We also chose to use the least sophisticated technology: black and white portapack equipment which could be readily replayed in the small seminar rooms where we met, no special lighting, no special microphones outside the one in the camera, and so on. We wanted equipment we could use rather than high-quality production equipment for public performances. (The 'production' videotape of our work is unrepresentative in this respect, since we were obliged to meet in a Deakin studio to produce higher-quality material, and we felt the discussion was slightly stilted under the bright lights and in the presence of studio technicians with their sophisticated equipment.)

3. After the videotaping session, which usually lasted about 25 minutes, we replayed the videotape. Whenever some member of the group noticed some blockage to communication, some individual reaction of discomfort, some especially constructive contribution or some other pattern of interaction which deserved comment, the videotape would be stopped. A relevant section might be replayed. Individuals involved in the incident of interest would be invited to enlarge on their actions or reactions, explain their points of view, speak to the significance of the incident in the group process, or otherwise help to make the group process transparent. Then wider group discussion would begin, with the group attempting to confirm the apparent pattern, find reasons for the blockage, or interpret the group effects of the incident. Where possible and appropriate, strategies for preventing the blockage or overcoming its immediate effects were suggested. Of course it was important to develop and maintain an attitude of trust, good humour, empathy and constructiveness. We were not a therapy group attempting to analyse each other as individuals; we were attempting, as far as possible, to understand the processes in which we played parts and the events we influenced and were influenced by. It should be remembered that we were an 'artificial' group meeting solely for this purpose, so we did not have to overcome the habitual forms and asymmetries which more permanent groups may need to confront. But it should not be thought that the fact of our transience made us so different: the group contained members who have constant working relationships, and we quickly recognized that we were developing stable roles and interests within our group, as well as importing some habitual patterns from other groups of which we are members into the Working Group.

4. Main points emerging from these discussions were recorded as 'minutes' on overhead transparencies when this was possible — in this way, all participants could see how our learnings (and the minutes) were shaping up. These transparencies were later

photocopied and distributed to participants as a record of the meeting.

This process was repeated in five meetings after the original workshop and before we began preparations for 'going public' — making the videotape which we hoped might serve as a discussion-starter for other interested groups in Deakin or beyond.

Some of the things that attracted our attention in the regular discussion sessions included:

☐ the development and the effects of 'rules' for 'turn-taking' in some discussions
☐ the effect of conversational gambits like 'that's a good question' or 'that's interesting' which could be used by one speaker to patronize or dismiss another while apparently supporting him
☐ the use of the 'filibuster' by a speaker to cloud the moment-by-moment interplay of a discussion and gain initiative or dominance
☐ the use of desks by participants as 'platforms' to gesture against or retreat behind
☐ the pervasive phenomenon that participants in group discussions simply don't listen to one another or hear one anothers' point of view as 'real' — and often systematically ignore one another while planning privately and waiting for an opportunity to make the next point
☐ the general relation of gesturing to speaking (sometimes small agitated movements indicated that a participant was about to speak or wanted to come into the discussion)
☐ the general phenomenon that small muscle movements often indicated tension or anxiety (our videotapes contained a great deal of footage of fingers, hands and feet moving restlessly)

Our analyses helped us to find patterns in our interaction which may or may not be typical of other groups, but which suggested more global group effects and strategies for overcoming some kinds of problems. For example:

☐ members becoming 'scapegoats' in moments of group crisis in discussion
☐ the politics of establishing a base for a point of view by appealing to likely supporters and isolating likely opponents
☐ the 'neutral chairmanship' role of sorting out problems in communication
☐ the strategy of documenting approaches to agreement in discussion by using an overhead projector, butcher's paper or a blackboard to keep 'visible minutes'
☐ the value of defusing contentious issues by seeking agreement on prior points, reflecting on claims made by speakers after conceding their potential merits or intervening in a debate to ask 'what's going on here?'
☐ possible roles for course team members in monitoring group interaction and interfering with group processes explicitly to establish mutual comprehension, to encourage members to contribute, to clarify issues or to support chairpersons in a non-threatening way.

In general, the group enjoyed the opportunity to meet for two or three hours about once a month to reflect on the processes in which we are constantly engaged: the processes of discussion and decision in groups. Even this little self-reflection seemed educative: too often we are involved in these processes as unconscious or intuitive actors, carrying habitual modes of response into new groups, reflecting relatively little, or learning not enough from our experience.

At its last meeting for 1979, the group began by doubting whether we had a sufficient commonality of interests or sufficient motivation to continue working together. Before too long, however, we had reached consensus that we should at least continue into 1980 to make a video-tape about the processes we had used, as a stimulus to others. More importantly, perhaps, we have begun to apply what we have learned in other groups of which we are members — as strategies for promoting symmetrical communication. It is, in a sense, an ideological commitment based on distaste for hierarchy, distrust of compulsion, and dissatisfaction with the cynicism and self-interest of small-time group politics. But there are positive reasons for employing the arts of symmetrical communication which transcend what is negative about group or committee work which has become a tedious and habitual experience of compromise and which preserves the shreds of self-interest in a climate of contention. At the risk of sounding too much the Pollyanna, these positive reasons are that groups can work together to serve common interests, achieve recognition and acceptance of their members as persons, and establish joint commitment to common projects when they do so on the basis of reasoned discussion and free commitment. For perhaps more tasks than we care to admit, such aspirations are achievable.

Videorecording, leading to group video self-confrontation and video analysis of group behaviour, is an effective tool and facilitating technique in the whole process of developing symmetrical communication and group consensus.

Notes

1. This chapter is based on a paper presented at the sixth annual conference of the Higher Education Research and Development Society of Australasia (HERDSA), in Canberra, 1980.
2. A copy of this recording is available on loan from the author.

REFERENCES

Brandt, D (1979) 'European approaches to staff development', in Unwin, D (ed), *Research and Development in Higher Education,* 2, Higher Education Research and Development Society of Australasia, Sydney, 29-38.

Werner, B & Drexler, I (1978) 'Structures of communication and interaction in courses for junior staff members of the Faculties of Engineering, TH Aachen', in Brandt, D (ed) The *HDZ Aachen — Activities and Context,* HDZ, Aachen.

10. Effects of Videotape Feedback and Modelling on the Behaviours of Task Group Members

Gordon Walter

SUMMARY

This study tests the relative and combined merits of two behaviour modification inputs for effecting predictable and productive task group behaviour change. Two hundred and seventy-seven subjects, mostly between 20 and 27 years of age, acted in problem-solving groups of five to seven members. Analysis of variance results indicates that videotape presentation of model groups and videotape feedback yield significant behavioural change. It is concluded that videotape feedback and modelling can be utilized in a constructively oriented behaviour modification effort in a task group context.

INTRODUCTION

Initial studies of the impact of videotape feedback in task groups and therapy groups indicate that the technique has tremendous potential to affect human behaviour (Kagan, 1963; Weber, 1971; Walter & Miles, 1972). Similarly, recent research on imitative behaviours in social learning has contributed greatly to understanding the role of models in the learning process (Bandura & Walters, 1963; Bandura, 1969; Allen & Liebert, 1969). The present study involves the combining of videotape feedback with models of desired task group behaviour in an effort to yield predictable and constructive task group behaviour modification. The development and testing of a combined videotape feedback and social learning paradigm for behavioural learning in a task group context is one goal of this research. The second goal is to gather data on the relative merits of the two independent behaviour modification inputs.

Schein and Bennis (1965) argued for the basic Lewinian premise that lasting behavioural and attitudinal change occurs via a three stage process: unfreezing, changing and refreezing. Discrepant feedback, feedback which shows the individual that his self-perceptions are not precisely shared by others, has the effect of unfreezing people in the T-group context. Weber (1971) argued that videotape feedback can play a role in task groups similar to that of interpersonal feedback in T-groups. The individual can thus develop an awareness of discrepancies between intended or perceived behaviour and actual behaviour as revealed during playbacks of a prior session. Once unfrozen, the individual will search within himself and his environment for clues and goals and will change. New behaviours which are positively reinforced or which are congruent with the individual's self-perception will be frozen into the individual's repertoire according to this reasoning. The effects of modelling for behaviours and attitudes do not emphasize the unfreezing aspect of the process. Instead, for example, Bandura and Walters (1963) emphasized the importance of the acquisition of imitative responses (changing) and performances of the imitatively learned responses (refreezing). A willingness and readiness to change seems to be assumed in the social learning paradigm. It is primarily the goals for change which depend upon identification with the model. Once the new behaviour or attitude has been performed, subsequent reinforcement contingencies determine whether the change will be lasting.

Both the videotape feedback and the modelling paradigms have inadequacies when viewed in the Lewinian perspective. Feedback emphasizes unfreezing while assuming that constructive change in refreezing is highly probable. Harrison (1965b) argued that in discrepant learning a heavy reliance on unfreezing via interpersonal feedback results in limitations in the 'change' process when there is a lack of adequate alternative models which provide desired behaviour patterns.

The individual may be ready for growth but fail to find in the behaviour of other members patterns which provide alternatives which are meaningful at the cognitive level at which he can respond. For example, a dependent person may be able to comprehend the opposite, counter-dependency, as a meaningful alternative. True collaboration in which authority is irrelevant, neither sought out nor defied, may be beyond his current range of understanding. (p 412)

Thus, Harrison emphasized that the individual needs to know where he is going as well as from where he came. He needs more than to be dissatisfied with his present behaviour. This criticism seems as applicable to videotape feedback learning experiences as it is to interpersonal feedback learning experiences. In short, videotape feedback appears to be weak on change and refreezing while modelling is weak on unfreezing, and it is quite likely that when combined they should yield greater behavioural change.

In addition, the generalizability of current video research findings is limited because most studies have occurred in either education or psychotherapy context (Danet, 1968; Kagan et al, 1963; Stoller, 1967). Another limitation comes from heavy emphasis on children as subjects and the primary focus on aggression and sexual behaviour rather than on less emotionally confounded issues in social learning studies. An exception to these criticisms is a study by Baron (1970) in which 48 undergraduate college students served as subjects. Further, models are generally presented to subjects in isolation rather than in groups and thus an oversimplified exposure to the model is inherent in these designs. Other features had led some to conclude that the experimental arrangements often lack social realism (Flanders, 1968). Finally, subjects' efforts to match behaviours with models are typically in terms of self-perceptions and these perceptions could be inconsistent with reality. This likelihood of inconsistency constitutes a basic premise in the video feedback paradigm.

The arguments above indicate the possibility that each of the techniques could benefit by combination with the other. In a combined learning paradigm the videotape feedback could be important for unfreezing, and social learning models could be used to facilitate changing and refreezing. Research evidence obtained in a task group context seemingly would provide improved generalizability to the behaviour modification evidence obtained to date. Also, a comparison of the relative impact of the two inputs can provide perspective, as to which aspect of the change process is most significant for the chosen subject population. A schematic paradigm for learning using feedback and models is shown in Figure 1.

The complex and contradictory results to be found in the small group literature offer special challenges to scholars interested in performance oriented behaviour modification in a group context. First, critical behaviour modification sub-processes, such as identification with the model, may be compromised in this setting due to alternative sources of social influence. Second, normative statements regarding group member behaviours which result in improved group performance are difficult to justify. In spite of these limitations, two goals of behaviour modification which are generally supported by small group research results have been chosen for use in this study. These goals are (1) non-evaluative idea generation and (2) exploiting ideational conflict.

Osborn (1953) noted that group members tend to evaluate ideas in a group as they appear, a tendency which inhibits or interferes with the generation of ideas. Groups can improve performance by incorporating a freewheeling period of idea generation where criticism of ideas does not occur. Dunnette *et al*, (1963) found evidence to support the notion that idea generation is best performed in isolation. None the less, brainstorming instructions have been clearly shown to improve group performance (Parnes & Meadow, 1959). Thus 'non-evaluative idea generation' type behaviour qualified as a goal for performance oriented behaviour modification.

Guetzkow and Gyr (1954) noted that successful management conferences were marked by substantial ideational conflict. Hoffman (1962) demonstrated the effect of conflict by encouraging low status members of a group to resist their superiors. The result was an increase in creative solutions. Thus, for certain problems, ideational conflict can also constitute a goal for performance oriented behaviour modification with the warning that ideational conflict which degenerates into interpersonal conflict can have negative performance consequences.

The direction of intended behaviour modifications in the non-evaluative idea generation mode of part one of the experiment, then, is for more neutral acts and fewer affective acts on the part of subjects. The direction of intended behaviour modification in the exploiting ideational conflict mode of part two of the experiment, then, is of fewer neutral acts and more affective acts on the part of the subjects. With both the directions of the behavioural change effort and the methods of attempted change articulated, it is now possible to describe the method employed in this study.

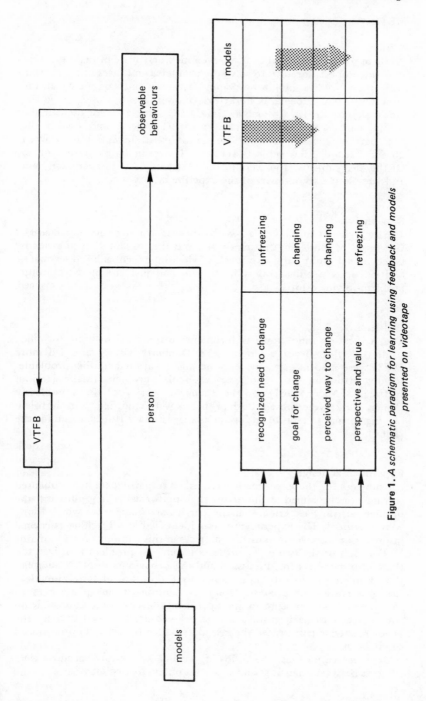

Figure 1. *A schematic paradigm for learning using feedback and models presented on videotape*

145

METHOD

Subjects
Problem-solving groups of four to seven members were brought together in a videotape laboratory to solve the problems and cases in connection with their studies in business administration and commerce at the University of California at Berkeley, Hayward State College, and the University of British Columbia. Only UBC subjects were used in the second part of the experiment and no UBC subjects were used in the first part of the experiment. The age of most subjects was between 20 and 27, but a few subjects as old as 50 were included in the sample. Of the 277 subjects, 133 were in the first part of the experiment, and 144 were in the second part of the experiment.

Data analysis
The experiment employed a two by two factorial design based upon two levels of modelling (no modelling and the presentation of a video-taped model group) and two levels of videotape feedback (no feedback and videotape feedback of subjects who had just completed a group problem-solving effort).

Problems
The 'education' and 'tourists' problems often used in brainstorming studies (Taylor, Berry & Block, 1958; Dunnette, Campbell & Justaad, 1963) were used in part one. For the high ideational conflict problem-solving effort in part two, the 'assembly' problem (Maier, 1952; Hoffman & Maier, 1967) and the 'change of work procedures problem' (Maier, 1952) were chosen. Both problems were modified from the role-playing format to a problem format as suggested by Hoffman and Maier (1964).

Experimental design
All subjects for the experiment were asked to participate in a problem-solving exercise aimed at improving their performance in groups as part of their learning experience in the particular course from which they were recruited. The experimenter was identified as a teaching assistant or professor who would assist the subjects in this learning effort.

For each of the two parts of the experiment, a problem was given to the group members for discussion and the behaviours displayed during the problem-solving attempt constituted the raw material for the first observation or pre-test. Upon completion of this phase of the experiment and exposure to an experimental event, a second problem was assigned to each group and the behaviours displayed during the problem solving constituted the raw material for the second observation of post-test.

In these conditions, the following events were experienced by the subjects between their first and second problem-solving efforts.

Condition 1, Control:[1]	No input, time allowed for discussion
Condition 2, Nominal:[1]	Brief verbal instruction and time allowed for discussion
Condition 3, Videotape feedback:	Presentation of subjects' first problem-solving efforts via videotape and the same brief verbal instructions of condition 2
Condition 4, Social learning:[2]	Presentation of a videotaped model group solving the first problem while demonstrating appropriate behaviour and the same brief verbal instructions of condition 2
Condition 5, Videotape feedback plus social learning:	The inputs of both conditions 3 and 4

The independent variables are the presentation of videotape feedback and videotaped social learning model groups but it was deemed necessary to give minimal verbal instructions. Weber (1969) showed that orienting comments are important for focusing subjects' perceptions during videotape feedback change attempts. Thus, to ensure adequate control, a condition entitled 'nominal' with only verbal instructions was provided.

The verbal instructions given experimental and nominal conditions were as follows: 'I was watching your group meeting while the recording went on and noticed that for this problem you might have done better in your attempt to solve the problem if you had tried to: (1) be more non-evaluative and just try to generate many ideas in the early part of your meeting or (2) be more evaluative of the major points which were most likely to yield good solutions,'[3] In the nominal condition the experimenter then excused himself from the room to make ready the equipment. For the conditions 3, 4 and 5 he excused himself to provide the desired experimental input.

Observation system
The system used for recording the effect of group member problem-solving statements follows that developed by Hoffman & Maier (1964). A slightly modified version of the valence coding scheme was provided by Hoffman in private communication. In the latest scheme there are five basic acts. These are:

S — Statement: complete or partial descriptions of solutions, additions of details, or elaborations of the character of the solution

J — Justification: describe possible benefits of a solution, draw analogies between the solution and other solutions or situations, indicate aspect of the problem which the solution will overcome

A — Agreement: expression of agreement that the solution is a good one without justification

V — Vote: attempts to gain statements of approval for a solution from another group member or from the group as a whole

Q — Questions: attempts to gain clarifications of statements of a previous speaker without critical implications such as requests for more details.

There are also five correlative negative acts, such as statements of unacceptable ideas (S'), disagreement (A'), negative justifications (J'), attempts to elicit contrary support regarding an idea (V'), and questions which are interrogative and imply doubt or rejection of a given solution (Q').

Of these behaviours only statements (S) and questions (Q) are considered to be neutral affective acts. Justification (J), agreement (A), and vote (V), all refer to behaviours indicating positive affect about a given idea. Negative acts are all considered to be behaviours indicating negative affect about a given idea.

Code-recode reliability T-test comparisons of subject behaviours were made following the method of Hoffman & Maier (1964). T-tests for 28 subjects showed no significant differences between coded and recorded behaviours. For the three behaviour categories where a large number of subjects displayed behaviours (S, A Q), the median Pearson correlation coefficient is .82. For the six most frequent acts (S, J, A, Q, S^1, A^1) the median correlation coefficient is .48. No subject behaviours occurred for 13, 19, 27 and 28 of the 28 subjects in categories Q^1, V, J, V^1, respectively and thus these are not included in the reliability evaluation.

Model development and presentation

Two methods of developing the videotaped model groups were considered. The first was to get a group to 'act' the desired behaviours. Because of the complexity of group processes, this alternative was not considered to be the most desirable. Instead, a number of groups of students were trained in some basic principles of group behaviour and then videotaped in special problem-solving efforts in which they could demonstrate their acquired skills. With this arrangement it was reasoned that subtle interpersonal 'clues' associated with problem-solving activities were most likely to be presented to subjects. Four groups were developed and taped, each performing non-evaluative behavioural approaches to problem solving in one exercise and highly evaluative approaches to problem solving in a second exercise. The two tapes which best demonstrated the desired behaviours were kept for presentation in the two parts of the experiment.

Just prior to viewing the model groups, subjects were told by the experimenter: 'I have a recording of another group which solved this same problem you just attempted. You can watch their attempt. This group was the best group to finish a group problem-solving class in which there were a number of advanced graduate students of business at Berkeley. The class taught these people a great deal about group problem solving. In the final problem-solving attempts, this group did the best of any of the groups from that class.' 'Success' and 'advanced graduate' students were emphasized to encourage imitative behaviour (Baron, 1970).

RESULTS

The intent of this experiment was to test the relative and combined behaviour modification effects of videotape feedback and modelled group behaviour on members of problem-solving groups. An analysis of variance on the change scores for subject behaviours was concluded to be suited to the purposes of the experiment. Change scores for each behavioural variable were computed for each subject by simply subtracting the subject's number of acts in the second problem-solving effort from his number of acts in the first problem-solving effort. Thus a positive change score (ΔV) for variable (V) indicates that during the experiment a given subject demonstrated fewer (V) acts after the experimental manipulation than before.

Subjects in part one of the experiment were set to work on problems which were best approached in a 'non-evaluative' mode. It was hypothesized that behaviour modification inputs would have the effect of (1) decreasing affective behaviours about ideas, (2) increasing affectively neutral statements about ideas, (3) changing the presence of neutral statements relative to affective statements. In order to determine if the experimental manipulations were successful, an analysis of variance was performed on the following scores: each of the behavioural ratings (ΔS, ΔJ, etc), the sum of neutral acts ($\Delta S + \Delta Q$), all affective acts (ΔAAA), comparisons of ($\Delta S + \Delta Q$) and (ΔAAA) with each other and the sum of all acts (ΔAA). The results from this first iteration of the experiment are presented in Table 1. Table 1 shows four significant behavioural changes for the comparison of subjects in conditions 2, 3, 4 and 5.[4] One of these shifts is for all affective acts (ΔAAA). This aggregate term perhaps best reflects the general intent of behaviour change effort.

Table 2 presents results from part two of the experiment in which intended behaviour modification was in the direction of increased affective acts and decreased neutral acts. Table 2 shows six significant behavioural changes for the comparison of subjects in conditions 2, 3, 4 and 5.[5] Two of these shifts are for aggregated terms which reflect the general intent of behavioural change effort.

The data presented in Tables 1 and 2 are not sufficiently detailed to enable complete appreciation of the effects of the behavioural change efforts. Thus examples of more detailed data are presented in Tables 3 and 4. These illustrative data are for conditions 1, 3, 4 and 5 in part two of the experiment. Table 3 shows the two by two factorial array of behavioural findings for subjects' neutral behaviours. Model group presentation is shown to change behaviours in the direction of increased scores and thus neutral behaviour was inhibited. Therefore, the change is in the hypothesized direction for part two of the experiment.

The effects of videotape feedback (VTFB) and social learning modelling (SLMG) on behavioural change scores using the 'Nominal' control condition

Variable	Source	df	MS	f
ΔA: Change in number	VTFB (A)	1	0.07	4.01*
of vote eliciting efforts	SLMG (B)	1	0.04	2.38
(V)	(A x B)	1	0.00	0.05
ΔQ: Change in number	VTFB (A)	1	0.06	0.36
of questions (Q)	SLMG (B)	1	1.08	6.14*
	(A x B)	1	0.40	2.25
ΔS': Change in number	VTFB (A)	1	0.02	0.13
of negative statements	SLMG (B)	1	0.62	4.88*
(S')	(A x B)	1	0.15	1.18
ΔAAA: Change in the	VTFB (A)	1	0.38	0.37
sum of all affective acts	SLMG (B)	1	4.87	4.83*
	(A x B)	1	1.35	1.34

$* p < 0.05$

Table 1. *Analysis of variance — Part one of the experiment*

The effects of videotape feedback and social learning modelling on behavioural change scores using the 'Nominal' control condition

Variable	Source	df	MS	f
ΔA: Change in number	VTFB (A)	1	0.35	1.06
of agreements (A)	SLMG (B)	1	2.78	8.49**
	(A x B)	1	0.90	2.74
ΔQ: Change in number	VTFB (A)	1	0.38	2.88
of questions (Q)	SLMG (B)	1	0.78	5.89*
	(A x B)	1	0.00	0.003
ΔAAA: Change in the	VTFB (A)	1	0.37	0.28
sum of all affective acts	SLMG (B)	1	10.17	7.58**
	(A x B)	1	7.86	5.86*
ΔS + ΔQ − ΔAAA:	VTFB (A)	1	1.19	0.70
Change in neutral minus	SLMG (B)	1	22.67	13.28**
affective acts	(A x B)	1	11.58	6.78**

$* p < 0.05 \qquad ** p < 0.01$

Table 2. *Analysis of variance — Part two of the experiment*

*Significant factor: SLMG, inhibition, change in
hypothesized direction*

	VTFB No. 1	VTFB yes 2	Level means	Probability
SLMG No (1)	−1.047	0.844	−0.101	
SLMG yes (2)	1.938	1.817	1.877	0.043 (SLMG)
Level means	0.445	1.331		
Probability	0.37 (VTFB)			0.308 (interaction)

Table 3. *Variable Δ(S + Q) − Part two, conditions 1 ('control'), 3, 4, 5*

*Significant factors: SLMG and interaction, disinhibition,
change in hypothesized direction*

	VTFB No (1)	VTFB yes (2)	Level means	Probability
SLMG No (1)	1.24	−1.094	0.073	
SLMG yes (2)	−3.67	−1.479	−2.576	0.021 (SLMG)
Level means	1.22	−1.287		
Probability	0.91 (VTFB)			0.047 (interaction)

Table 4. *Variable ΔAAA (all affective acts) − Part two,
conditions 1 ('control'), 3, 4, 5*

Table 4 shows the two by two factorial array of behavioural findings
for subjects' total affective behaviours (ΔAAA). Both the model group
input and the interaction term of model groups and videotape feedback
are seen to account for decreased scores and thus increased frequency
of behaviour. Therefore, these significant behavioural changes are also
seen to be in the direction hypothesized for part two of the experiment.

For the total experiment, twice as many statistically significant
behavioural changes were induced by the social learning inputs (SLMG)
than were the results of either videotape feedback (VTFB) or the interaction term for feedback and modelling. There were 12 statistically
significant behavioural shifts attributable to social learning, seven
statistically significant behavioural shifts attributable to videotape
feedback and five statistically significant behavioural shifts attributable

to the interaction of videotape feedback and social learning. Of five statistically significant changes accounted for by the interaction of videotape feedback and social learning, all were in the hypothesized direction whereas only four out of seven statistically significant shifts attributable to videotape feedback were in the hypothesized direction. Further, the interaction term accounts for no significant changes in behaviour in part one of the experiment, while the impact of videotape feedback and social learning are somewhat more consistent between part one and part two of the experiment. In the first part primarily behavioural inhibition is accomplished while a more balanced presence of inhibition and dis-inhibition behaviour change was attained in the second part.

In summary, model group presentations resulted in the most behavioural change. There was more behavioural change in part two than in part one of the experiment. Videotape feedback tended to inhibit more than to dis-inhibit subjects. And the combination of videotape feedback and model group presentations consistently resulted in the predicted impact when impact was significant.

DISCUSSION OF RESULTS

Support is limited for the notion that videotape feedback can easily be used directly with verbal instructions to change behaviours in desired ways. The four significant behavioural changes in part one of the experiment all involved inhibition and none involved dis-inhibition; two were in the hypothesized direction and two were in the opposite direction. The implication is that while videotape feedback did induce change, it was also inhibiting. This finding is somewhat incompatible with current idealizations of the unfreezing process and role of feedback in that aspect of learning. However, partial explanation of the unintended effects of the video stimuli is provided by Weber (1969) who noted that subjects who were exposed to VTFB became more conscious of process *in general*. Thus, although the intent of the experimental arrangement was to make subjects aware of only a small segment of group process, so as to effect specific behaviour modification, it is likely that subjects became highly aware of and concerned with 'process' to the point of developing feelings of inhibition. Support for the value of videotape feedback for predictable and desirable behaviour change is found in part two of the experiment. Here some dis-inhibition changes were observed as the result of the videotape feedback. Still, enthusiasm regarding this support for the value of videotape feedback in bringing about general behavioural change is limited by the inconsistent findings.

Conversely, there is much support for the notion that the presentation of model groups can change behaviours in desired ways. Of the eight statistically significant changes found which were due to the presentation of the model groups in part two of the experiment, seven are in the hypothesized direction. Further, both inhibition and dis-inhibition are found to be initiated by the model group presentations. Still, impact of the model group presentation on subject behaviour was less pervasive in the first part than in the second. This finding is somewhat surprising since it was the opinion of the experimenter that the development of models for the second part (high affect) was more difficult than for the first part (low affect). The most plausible explanation for this finding is that the high affect behaviours of models yielded more concrete behavioural 'clues' and thus made imitation easier in the second part than in the first.

The explanation is consistent with the finding that while the interaction term for feedback and modelling accounted for *no* significant behavioural changes in part one of the experiment, *five* significant shifts were accounted for in part two. Further, these shifts involved both dis-inhibition and inhibition and were *all* in the desired direction. Thus, while the finding that modelling alone resulted in the most behavioural changes (and thus the addition of videotape feedback to modelling was of limited marginal value in terms of amount of change possible) it is necessary to appreciate that the addition of videotape feedback to model presentations did increase the predictability of change remarkably.

A general point of significance is the presence of behavioural changes of only an inhibition nature in part one of the experiment. T-test findings indicated that subjects in the 'control' condition became more verbal and interactive while solving the second problem. Subjects in experimental conditions became less verbal, less interactive and more inhibited while solving the second problem. This unintended effect is probably due to some reactive aspect of the video stimuli, the experimental arrangement and the laboratory environment or to the difficulty in learning certain non-overt behaviours as noted above.

The contradictory behaviour of control subjects in comparison to the experimental subjects occurred only in the first part of the experiment. Subjects for the first part came mainly from UC Berkeley classes on a voluntary basis. Subjects for the second part came from two classes of commerce students at UBC on a voluntary basis. The Berkeley subjects expressed great curiosity, suspicion and anxiety about possible experimental manipulations between and after the problem-solving efforts in the experimental conditions. Conversely UBC subjects appeared to trust the honesty of the educational arrangement. It is not surprising, therefore, that the relative inhibition between the 'control' condition and the experimental conditions was not found in part two, where UBC subjects were used and that the contradictory evidence concerning the hypotheses was not found. In short, the reactivity of the experimental arrangement seemed to be less critical in the second part of the experiment than in the first part due to the different character of the subjects.

These minor limitations on the results of the experiment take little away from the general strong support for the behaviour modification model described and tested in this study. The limitations emphasize the need for prudence in generalizing findings too far beyond the actual population studied and from the specific context of the study. This study has shown, however, that adult subjects in a group context can acquire specific group problem-solving behaviours which are potentially constructive. The Lewinian learning model discussed above is also supported as are the theoretical arguments for the relative contribution of the presentation of videotape feedback and model groups to the learning process.

The major theoretical conclusion one must draw from these findings and for this context is that providing a goal for change through modelling, and aiding the change process through modelling, is more important than providing an 'unfreezing' experience which stimulates change, and that the linking of the two behaviour modification inputs considered in this study yields behaviour changes beyond those to be expected from the simple summation of the two inputs.[6]

Notes

1. Conditions 1 and 2 each constitute a no-model, no-feedback condition. The 'Nominal' condition was added to provide a second condition for comparison with the experimental manipulation conditions.
2. Separate videotapes were developed for part one and part two model presentations.
3. Subset (1) was told to part one subjects and Subset (2) was told to part two subjects.
4. When condition 1 is used for control instead of condition 2 the results also show four statistically significant behavioural changes.
5. When condition 1 is used for control instead of condition 2 the results show 10 statistically significant shifts.
6. This chapter is a reprint of an article published in *Human Relations*, 28, 2, 121-38, with the kind permission of the author and the journal editors.

REFERENCES

Allen, M K & Liebert, R M (1967) 'Effects of live and symbolic deviant modeling clues on adoption of a previously learned standard', *Journal of Personality and Social Psychology*, 11, 83, 253-60.
Bandura, A (1969b) *Principles of Behavior Modification*, Holt, Rinehart & Winston, Toronto.
Bandura, A & Walters, R H (1963) *Social Learning and Personality Development*, Holt, Rinehart & Winston, New York.
Baron, R A (1970) 'Attraction toward the model and model's competence as determinants of adult imitative behavior', *Journal of Personality and Social Psychology*, 14, 4, 345-51.
Danet, B N (1968) 'Self-confrontation in psychotherapy reviewed', *American Journal of Psychotherapy*, 22, 2, 245-58.
Dunnette, M D, Campbell, J & Justaad, K (1963) 'The effect of group participation on brainstorming effectiveness for two industrial samples', *Journal of Applied Psychology*, 47, 1, 30-34.
Flanders, J P (1968) 'A review of research on imitative behavior', *Psychological Bulletin*, 69, 316-37.
Guetzkow, H & Gyr, J (1954) 'An analysis of conflict in decision-making groups', *Human Relations*, 7, 367-82.

Harrison, R (1965a) 'Cognitive models for interpersonal and group behavior: a theoretical framework for research', *Explorations in Human Relations Training and Research,* (hole No 2), NTL, Washington, DC.

Harrison, R (1965b) 'Group composition models for laboratory design', *Journal for Applied Behavioral Science,* 1, 4, 409-32.

Hoffman, L R & Maier, N R F (1964) 'Valence in the adoption of solutions by problem solving groups: Concept, method and results', *Journal of Abnormal and Social Psychology,* 69, 3, 264-71.

Hoffman, L R, Harburg, E & Maier, N R F (1962) 'Differences and disagreement as factors in creative problem solving', *Journal of Abnormal and Social Psychology,* 64, 206-14.

Hoffman, L R & Maier, N R F (1967) 'Valence in the adoption of solutions by problem solving groups: II Quality and acceptance as goals of leaders and members', *Journal of Personality and Social Psychology,* 6, 175-82.

Kagan, N, Krathwohl, D R & Miller, R (1963) 'Stimulated recall in therapy using videotape: A case study', *Journal of Consulting Psychology,* 10, 237-43,

Maier, N R F (1952) *Principles of Human Relations,* Wiley, New York.

Osborn, A F (1953) *Applied Imagination,* Scribners, New York.

Parnes, S F & Meadow, A (1959) 'University of Buffalo research regarding development of creative talent', in Taylor, C W (ed), *The third University of Utah Research Conference on the Identification of Creative Research Talent,* University of Utah.

Schein, E H & Bennis, W G (1965) *Personal and Organizational Change Through Group Methods: The laboratory approach,* Wiley, New York.

Stoller, F H (1967) 'Therapeutic concepts reconsidered in the light of videotape experience', unpublished manuscript, Child Studies Center, University of Southern California.

Taylor, D W, Berry, P C & Block, C H (1958) 'Does group participation when using brainstorming techniques facilitate or inhibit creative thinking?, *Administration Science Quarterly,* 3, 23-47.

Walter, G A & Miles, R E (1972) 'The impact of task group participation plus videotape feedback on self-acceptance scores', unpublished manuscript, University of California, Berkeley.

Weber, R J (1969) 'The effects of videotape feedback on interaction behavior and role perception in small decision making groups', unpublished manuscript, University of California, Berkeley.

Weber, R J (1971) 'Effects of videotape feedback on task group behavior', *Proceedings, 79th Annual Convention, APA,* 499-500.

11. Stimulated Recall from Video: Its Use in Research on the Thought Processes of Classroom Participants

Perc Marland

SUMMARY

Interest in teachers' mental functioning during preparation and implementation of instructional plans and in how students think as they interact with instructional processes and materials has led to the use of stimulated recall. This method provides access to human thinking. It involves using records of task performance, such as videotapes, to stimulate recall of thoughts occurring during task completion. This chapter reports on the use of videotapes to stimulate teacher — and student — recall of their thinking during classroom instruction or when engaged in classroom-related tasks. An examination is made of the rationale underlying use of stimulated recall in these contexts, the roles assigned to recaller and researcher, and problems and limitations of the method.

INTRODUCTION

Dramatic changes have occurred in the science of psychology since the 1950s (Calfee, 1981). The dominance of behaviourism has been challenged by a new paradigm within cognitive psychology — an information processing paradigm which takes, as its focus of study, the structure and process of the human mind. Consequently, there has been a resurgence of interest in the mental functioning of human beings as they plan, make judgements, diagnose, solve problems, evaluate, make decisions, counsel clients and process textual materials in a range of naturalistic task settings.

Research into the cognitive processes of human problem solvers, judges, clinicians and planners has necessitated the use of techniques that provide access to their mental functioning during performance of their respective tasks. Reviews of some of these techniques appear in Shulman & Elstein (1975) and Shavelson & Stern (1981). One such technique is stimulated recall, a method involving the use of a perceptual record (audio, video) of a subject's overt behaviour during task performance to stimulate recall of simultaneously occurring thought processes. Thus, the stimulated recall approach requires subjects to provide, retrospectively, self-report data on thought processes. It also typically involves, as well as the subject whose cognitions are to be disclosed, an interviewer, whose role is to facilitate such disclosure.

Bloom (1954) and his associates at the University of Chicago were some of the first to report use of the stimulated recall technique. It was used by the Chicago group to study the thought processes of university students during discussion. Their research, which used audio records of discussion classes, was directed towards gaining a better understanding of the learning processes in discussion contexts as a means of improving the quality of tutorials and small group discussions at the tertiary education level. Since then, stimulated recall procedures have been used, but not extensively, to study the diagnostic reasoning of physicians (Elstein, Shulman & Sprafka, 1978), the thinking of teachers and students during instruction (Kagan, Krathwohl, Goldberg & Campbell, 1967; Morine & Vallance, 1975; Clark & Peterson, 1976; Marland, 1977; McNair & Joyce, 1979; Marland & Edwards, 1982); and the interpersonal reactions, both cognitive and affective, between counsellor and client in therapeutic counselling sessions (Kagan, Krathwohl & Miller, 1962; Kagan, Krathwohl, Goldberg & Campbell, 1967; Kagan, 1973). (In the field of counselling and counsellor education, stimulated recall has been referred to as interpersonal process recall — IPR.)

Discussion of stimulated recall in this paper will focus on its use in the study of the information processing of teachers and students in classrooms. In particular, the author will draw mainly on his own experiences in the use of stimulated recall. These include studies of:

☐ teachers' interactive thinking (Project 1 — Marland, 1977; Marland, 1979; Marland, 1982)
☐ teacher planning (Project 2 — Caldwell, 1982; Marland & Caldwell, 1982)
☐ the mediating processes of secondary students during instruction (Project 3 — Edwards & Marland, 1982; Marland & Edwards, 1982)
☐ the mediating processes of external students as they study from textual materials (Project 4 — Store & Marland, 1982).

RATIONALE

Retrospective self-reporting techniques such as stimulated recall are generally used where think-aloud methods would cause an unacceptable degree of interference with task performance. For example, use of a think-aloud approach to study how teachers think interactively (that is, during instruction) would cause a high level of disruption to classroom events and seriously jeopardize the validity of the self-report data. In such situations the stimulated recall approach provides a more appropriate means of access to thinking during task performance because self-reporting by teachers occurs after, not during, the lesson. However, think-aloud and stimulated recall have also both been used in the same project — as a means of checking on the reliability of data (Elstein, Shulman & Sprafka, 1978), and also to pursue further interesting leads presented by a teacher-planner in think-aloud data (Caldwell, 1981).

Users of the stimulated recall technique believe that research into the mental processes of classroom participants will reveal the influences (aims, intentions, plans, perceptions, interpretations, expectations, theories, etc) that direct their behaviour. These researchers adopt the position that what people think influences directly what they do. Hence they argue that behavioural models of human activity are conceptually incomplete and that overt behaviours are best understood in terms of the cognitive processes and states that precede them.

Such data, it is confidently expected, will provide a better understanding of the information processing skills and styles that characterize successful performances in teaching and learning. The expectation is that this research will yield a richer understanding of the processes of teaching and learning and of the ways successful teachers and learners cope mentally with the complex realities of their task environments. It is anticipated that knowledge of the kinds of information processed by competent classroom participants and of the ways in which such information is processed — in short, the 'everyday rationality' of teachers and learners — will provide better bases for educating teachers and learners. (Reviews of the findings of research on teacher thinking have been undertaken by Clark & Yinger, 1978 and Shavelson & Stern, 1981.) Not all persons interested in this type of research hold such high expectations. Calderhead (1981), for example, makes a somewhat less optimistic forecast:

> Stimulated recall techniques may assist the researcher to gain access to the cognitive processing of more global units of teaching ('plans') though perhaps not so easily to the processing involved within such units . . . However, it can by no means provide a complete account of teachers' thoughts, nor is the method likely to be of use entirely on its own. (pp 213, 216)

ASSUMPTIONS

Numerous assumptions, some contentious, underlie use of the stimulated recall technique. Some relate to the nature of human thinking itself; they are given extensive coverage in Simon (1979) and will not be discussed here. Others deal with the issue of whether or not human thinking is susceptible to verbal representation and, furthermore, whether thinking can be recalled and characterized verbally with accuracy. For discussion of these issues the reader is referred to Radford (1974), Nisbett & Wilson (1977), Smith & Miller (1978), Ericsson & Simon (1980) and Calderhead (1981). A third set of assumptions relate to use of records of task performance to stimulate recall of thinking that was co-occurring with overt activity. It is generally assumed that a videotape which provides a continuous and up-close record of the subject's overt behaviours and classroom events, generally will provide sufficient cues to stimulate accurate and near-complete recall of mental processes. The author's research experience provides some subjective justification for this claim though there is no way of verifying it objectively. However, there are times when textual materials which the subject was working on or from (for example, a lesson plan, a text or work pad) also provide substantial assistance in the recall process.

It has also been assumed that a video record would prove superior to an audio record in stimulating recall of mental processes because of the greater number of cues available — visual ones. This assumption has not been empirically tested.

Another assumption which has received extensive consideration in the research literature generally concerns the effect of videotaping on the research subjects and others in the research setting. Because a principal goal of information processing research is to find how humans function mentally in everyday task environments, keeping the research setting as naturalistic as possible is of crucial importance. Most subjects who have co-operated in the author's research have reported feeling, in the initial stages of the research, some anxiety and discomfort because of the presence of recording gear but contend that this soon disappears and that it makes little or no difference to their thinking. In support of this, self-report data also contain very few references to these matters. However, steps have been and must be taken to safeguard ecological validity. Careful preparation of participants in the research project is therefore essential. Thus, it is recommended, for example, that the researcher should:

☐ arrange for a period of familiarization when the research subjects can become accustomed to the presence of the video gear in the task setting and to self-confrontation on video
☐ establish rapport with the subjects well beforehand so that the research is not perceived as a threat and the subjects can 'be themselves'
☐ inform the subjects of the purposes of the research project and provide opportunities for full and frank discussion of them
☐ give assurances of anonymity.

In addition, videotaping should be done unobtrusively and, if possible, with no change to normal routines, class periods, scheduled lesson topics, seating arrangements, and regular teaching styles.

PREPARATION OF THE VIDEO RECORD

In Figure 1 are shown camera locations for preparation of the video records of classrooms during instruction for subsequent use in stimulated recall sessions in Projects 1 and 3 (described above). Some technical guidelines for preparation of video records of classrooms for use in stimulated recall research are provided by Conners (1978). Two black-and-white cameras (National Model WV-314N), one fitted with a 6.5mm wide-angle lens, the other with a 15-150mm zoom lens, were located in the classrooms as shown. The camera at the front of the room (C_1) was positioned to capture as much of the classes' activities as possible and was fixed. (Complete classes were used.) The second camera at the back of the room was manned and was able to be adjusted for tilt and pan to focus on the teacher all the time. A vertical split-screen videorecording, with the teacher in one half and the class in the other, was produced through a video mixing console by a second technician. Two microphones were positioned to capture public discourse by teachers and students but private dyadic

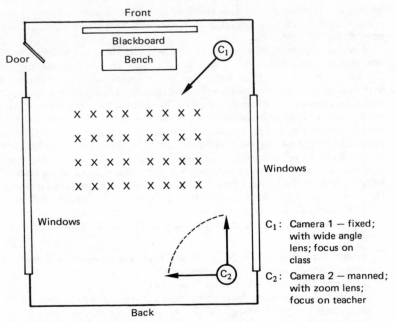

Figure 1. *Arrangements for videotaping in classrooms*

conversations were not picked up. To achieve this latter goal more sophisticated instruments would be needed but these were not available. In Project 3, the position of the camera at the front of the classroom was adjusted slightly so that the four student participants were clearly in focus. The regular seating arrangements were also slightly modified. The four participating students were seated either at, or close to, the front but still with their usual neighbours. Attempts to record the muted discussions within student dyads or small groups with desk microphones were not very successful. However, there usually appeared to be sufficient cues, both aural and visual, to trigger recall of details of events and thoughts. Low light levels in classrooms sometimes caused problems which were overcome by using a studio light pointed at the ceiling to deflect light downwards.

Project 2 involved videotaping the teacher's think-aloud instructional planning sessions. This necessitated a relatively simple set-up of one camera with in-built microphone and proved very satisfactory.

Only the pilot phase of Project 4, the learning-from-text project, has been completed. Again two cameras were needed, one to provide a frontal view of the subjects while studying, the second camera to provide a view from above the student's left shoulder with a focus on the page of text being studied and the notebook being used by the student. As with Projects 1 and 3, a split-screen image was produced but the available cameras were not good enough to produce a readable image of the text on the monitor. Tags carrying the page numbers were used to assist identification of pages. It was also found necessary, in the interests of a fuller disclosure of thought processes, for subjects to have

160

access to a copy of the textual material being studied during recall sessions.

INTERVIEWS

Other threats to validity of the data in stimulated recall research come from interview procedures, the ways in which the roles of both interviewer and interviewee are defined and the relation between these two persons. The conceptualization of roles and procedures formulated by Kagan *et al* (1967) in their research with IPR on counselling has provided a useful basis for stimulated recall research in teaching and learning. Guidelines which have worked well in practice for this researcher are:

1. The stimulated recall session should be held as soon as possible after the record of task performance has been made but, preferably, within 24 hours. Stimulated recall interviews with teachers, for example, have usually been arranged in free periods or after school on the day of the lesson. Bloom (1954) contends that ability to recall would probably decline significantly after 48 hours.
2. Subjects must be fully briefed on the goals of the research project and the purposes to be served by the stimulated recall interview. Without such information, subjects may construct their own theories about the researcher's intentions and could respond accordingly in ways which may distort the data and subvert the research goals.
3. Interviewees are asked to relive as fully as possible the situations in which they were videotaped and to verbalize the thoughts they had during that session. At this time, too, the need for complete and accurate recall is stressed; they are asked to be careful to distinguish between thoughts they had during the actual task performance and any subsequent thoughts (including those they have as they watch the videotape) and to notify the researcher of these differences; and they are reminded that they can stop the tape as often and for as long as they wish in order to achieve full disclosure of their thoughts.

Although in the initial research on teacher thinking (Marland, 1977) teachers were given general instruction about their role in the recall session, including some about the kinds of thoughts they should try to recall, the author has since departed from this practice. A simple general request to the interviewer such as that they report what was going on in their minds is now recommended and in use by the author. Interviewer invitations to recall should also be very general and open-ended; for example, 'Were you having any thoughts at that point?' These procedures are much less likely to lead the interviewee and cause distortions in recall thereby invalidating the data. Calderhead (1981, p 214) pointed out in a recent critique of the directing approach used earlier by Marland (1977) that 'explicit instructions beforehand may have influenced the teaching itself, and the procedure may also have encouraged teachers to place a greater degree of post-hoc rationality upon their behaviour'. It is interesting to note, however, that in a study of physicians' diagnostic reasoning (Elstein *et al*, 1979) instructions to some participants to think in a particular way were apparently ignored. The researchers concluded 'that an experimenter should never assume that a certain set of exhortations is going to have the desired effect on a group of subjects' (pp 249-50).

With the preceding points in mind, guidelines for the conduct of stimulated recall interviews have been formulated. Those adopted for the current investigation into the mental processes of external students as they use distance teaching textual materials are set out in Table 1. These indicate the nature of the interviewer's role which is difficult to enact without at least some practice or training.

LIMITATIONS AND PROBLEMS

Certain limitations, real or imaginary, applying to the use of stimulated recall in research on teaching and learning, have surfaced as a result of experience with the technique. In the studies described earlier, stimulated recall was used with teachers and students in the 12 to 17 age range, all of whom were volunteers and keen to participate. Masses of verbal data were produced but self-report data from the 12-year-olds were much briefer and simpler. This marked decline in volume, complexity and richness of data raised the question of whether use of the technique is appropriate with all school-age children or only with those who can retrospect and verbalize their thinking. Conventional wisdom in the field would restrict use of stimulated recall to children over 10 years — however, this might be an unfair assessment of the introspective and verbalizing abilities of the under-10s.

The technique also worked well with volunteer subjects but some studies (see Fuller & Manning, 1973) suggest that self-confrontation can be disturbing, non-productive and perhaps even harmful. Whether results for all personality types would be satisfactory, or where use of the technique was not optional, remains open to question.

Another limitation concerns duration of the video record. A half-hour video usually resulted in a stimulated recall interview of one to one-and-a-half hours. Overlong interviews tended to become much less productive towards the end so videotapes were usually limited to 30 minutes and recall interviews to about one hour. This meant that task performances had to be either restricted to a half hour or divided into half-hour segments. Both arrangements are infringements of the requirement that performances and settings be naturalistic.

Another unknown is the extent to which quality of the record of performance (visual and aural) affects recall. It is possible, for example, that availability of cues for triggering the subject's recall are significantly related to such features of the record as clarity, visual resolution, depth of vision, size of images and amount of detail.

Use of stimulated recall is also bound up with certain problems. There are the problems of identifying factors (for example, anxiety, prior expectations, ego-protection tactics) which could influence (bias, distort) subjects' recall of thoughts, and the problems of designing measures to minimize them. There are problems of analysis and interpretation of data (see Calderhead, 1981). Other problems arise from the

Gain the confidence of the interviewee by being open and frank about the purposes of the research and by answering questions as fully as possible.

Establish a relaxed, friendly, supportive atmosphere prior to and during interviews.

Assume a respectful set towards the interviewee and the self-report data; communicate to the interviewee that he is being taken very seriously.

Avoid making interpretations of, and judgements about, what appears on videotape or what the interviewee says in stimulated recall sessions.

Encourage and facilitate self-discovery; it is important for the interviewee to believe that he is capable of telling about his mental processes.

Keep the interviewee's attention focused on the TV image; refrain from unnecessary activity as it may actually interfere with recall.

Encourage the interviewee to talk; don't have him become so engrossed in listening to you that he forgets what he is meant to be reliving; remember that the interviewee is the authority on what he was thinking about during task performance — you are there to learn from him.

Immerse yourself in the interviewee's communication rather than trying to figure out what to say next.

Keep the discussion focused on what transpired during the study session and matters relevant to that.

Encourage the interviewee to stop the tape as often as he wishes.

Be prepared to stop the tape (if the interviewee has not done so) at points in the study session where it appears likely to be profitable for purposes of this research. Such points might include when the interviewee:

- (a) underlines; makes notes; prepares a summary
- (b) looks up; stares ahead; squirms; smiles; makes a gesture, pose or movement; 'appears' to be expressing an emotion (perplexity, frustration, surprise, bewilderment, boredom)
- (c) scans; flicks over pages; overdwells; re-reads

Ask questions which invite open-ended recall, clarification, elaboration.

Avoid questions which 'lead' or suggest possible answers, imply criticism, incredulity, disagreement, disapproval; avoid questions answerable by 'yes' or 'no'.

Once the interview has provided some recall data, ask questions that facilitate full disclosure by the interviewee. (NB Questions should be brief and create an intense awareness in the interviewee of himself and his mental processes.)

Check frequently that the interviewee is differentiating between 'a priori' thoughts and feelings, those experienced during the study session, and those subsequently experienced.

Table 1. *Guidelines for the conduct of stimulated recall interviews*

almost total dearth of methodological studies on the use of stimulated recall. Consequently, optimum conditions for stimulating recall are impossible to specify. Answers to such questions as the following are often disparate, unconvincing and atheoretical. How often should the videotape be stopped? How specific should instructions to subjects be? Should the interview be structured or unstructured? Is it necessary for an interviewer to be present at all? If so, should the interviewer be an initiator and to what extent? Should the interviewer stop the tape? The researcher, therefore, receives conflicting advice and few definitive answers. Finally, there is the problem of establishing the validity of data.

CONCLUSION

In spite of these problems and limitations, there is a generally held view among those who have used stimulated recall that the technique does offer a fruitful means of exploring the cognitive concomitants of human behaviour in the classroom and other task settings, and of developing new insights into the nature of important enterprises like teaching.

REFERENCES

Bloom, B S (1954) 'The thought processes of students in discussion', in French, S J (ed), *Accent on Teaching. Experiments in General Education,* 1st edn., Harper, NY.

Calderhead, J (1981) 'Stimulated recall: A method for research on teaching', *British Journal of Educational Psychology,* 51, 211-17.

Caldwell, N B A (1982) 'Instructional planning for year 12 biology: A case study', BEd (Hons) thesis, James Cook University of North Queensland.

Calfee, R (1981) 'Cognitive psychology and educational practice', in Berliner, D C (ed), *Review of Research in Education,* 9, 3-74, American Educational Research Association, Washington.

Clark, C & Yinger, R (1979) 'Teachers' thinking', in Peterson, P L & Walberg, H J (eds), *Research on Teaching: Concepts, Findings and Implications,* 231-63, McCutchan, Berkeley.

Clark, C & Peterson, P L (1976) 'Teacher stimulated recall of interactive decisions', paper presented at the annual meeting of the American Educational Research Association, San Francisco.

Conners, R D (1978) 'Using stimulated recall in naturalistic settings — some technical procedures', Technical Paper 78-2-1, Centre for Research on Teaching, University of Alberta.

Edwards, J & Marland, P W (1982) 'Student thinking in a secondary biology classroom' *Research in Science Education,* 12. Australian Science Education Research Association.

Elstein, A S, Shulman, L S & Sprafka, S A (1978) *Medical Problem Solving: An Analysis of Clinical Reasoning,* Harvard University Press, Cambridge.

Ericsson, K A & Simon, H A (1980) 'Verbal reports as data', *Psychological Review,* 87, 215-51.

Fuller, F F & Manning, B A (1973) 'Self-confrontation reviewed: A conceptualization for video playback in teacher education', *Review of Educational Research,* 43, 469-528.

Kagan, N (1973) 'Influencing human interaction: Eleven years of IPR (interpersonal process recall), paper presented to the American Educational Research Association, New Orleans.

Kagan, N, Krathwohl, D R, Goldberg, A D & Campbell, R (1967) *Studies in Human Interaction: Interpersonal Process Recall Stimulated by Videotape,* Michigan State University, East Lansing.

Kagan, N, Krathwohl, D R & Miller, R (1963) 'Stimulated recall in therapy using videotape — A case study', *Journal of Counselling Psychology,* **10,** 237-43.

McNair, K & Joyce, B (1979) 'Teachers' thoughts while teaching: The south bay study', Part II, Research Series No 58, Institute for Research on Teaching, Michigan State University.

Marland, P W (1977) 'A study of teachers' interactive thoughts', PhD thesis, University of Alberta.

Marland, P W (1979) 'A study of teachers' interactive information processing', in Rowley, G (ed), *Proceedings of the Annual Conference,* Australian Association for Research into Education, Melbourne.

Marland, P W (1982) 'Models of teacher thinking', paper presented at the International Conference on Thinking, University of South Pacific.

Marland, P W & Caldwell, N B A (1981) 'Instructional planning: A case study', paper presented at the Annual Conference of the Australian Association for Research into Education, Adelaide.

Marland, P W & Edwards, J (1982) 'A study of students' in-class thinking', paper presented at the Annual Conference of the Australian Association for Research into Education, Brisbane.

Morine, G & Vallance, E (1975) *Beginning Teacher Evaluation Study. Special Study B: A Study of Teacher and Pupil Perceptions of Classroom Interaction,* Far West Laboratory for Educational Research and Development, San Francisco.

Nisbett, R E & Wilson, T D (1977) 'Telling more than we can know: Verbal reports on mental processes', *Psychological Review,* **84,** 231-59.

Radford, J (1974) 'Reflections on introspection', *American Psychologist,* **29,** 245-50.

Shavelson, R J & Stern, P (1981) 'Research on teachers' pedagogical thoughts, judgements, decisions and behaviour', *Review of Educational Research,* **51,** 455-98.

Shulman, L S & Elstein, A S (1975) 'Studies of problem solving, judgement and decision making: Implications for educational research, in Kerlinger, F W (ed), *Review of Research in Education,* **3,** 3-42, F E Peacock, Itasca.

Simon, H A (1979) *Models of thought,* Yale University Press, New Haven.

Smith, E R & Miller, F S (1978) 'Limits on perception of cognitive processes: A reply to Nisbett and Wilson', *Psychological Review,* **85,** 355-62.

Store, R E & Marland, P W (1982) 'How students use distance teaching materials: Soundings', paper presented at the Annual Conference of the Australian Association for Research into Education, Brisbane.

12. Video as an Educational Research Tool

Stephen Foster

SUMMARY

The purpose of this chapter is to identify the range of uses and possibilities of video as a research tool in presenting stimuli, collecting responses, and presenting data. It discusses research studies in this field as well as the author's own findings from a research project on psychological aspects of anxiety and arousal in teaching with multiple use of videorecordings.

INTRODUCTION: STATEMENT OF PURPOSES

The April 1968 *Review of Educational Research* was devoted to 'Instructional materials: educational media and technology'. In the three and a half pages devoted to educational television, perhaps two dozen studies were reported investigating or evaluating television as a medium of educational delivery. No mention was made of video as a research tool.

Ten years later in the same journal (Barbatsis, 1978), a review of instructional television presented an extensive discussion of uses of television as a medium of instruction, over the period 1950 to 1970. Again, videotape technology was not discussed as a research tool. Most recently, however, under the title of 'Educational seduction' (Abrami, Leventhal & Perry, 1982), a line of educational inquiry is reported which was conducted almost exclusively with video stimuli.

The purpose of this chapter is not exhaustively to review research involving video technology. That would occupy a volume, and a tedious tome it would be indeed. Instead, the purpose is:

☐ to identify the range of uses and possibilities video technology presents as a research tool in presenting stimuli, collecting responses, and presenting data
☐ to give illustrations of innovative uses of video in research such as the studies of Berkowitz and Frodi (1979), including examples of research that could not have been accomplished without the use of video and for which film could not have been an acceptable substitute
☐ to outline the growing research literature on the 'Dr Fox effect' wherein video shows promise for providing 'teacher prototypes' which may greatly enhance research on teaching and learning

☐ to present the author's own findings from a project wherein video-recordings were both a part of the treatment and the assessment.

☐ Videorecordings represent opportunities to present standard visual and audio stimuli to persons, to record data from experimental participants and to present findings of educational research in ways which hitherto were approached but rarely equalled by alternative technologies. This is the thesis of this chapter.

VIDEORECORDINGS IN STIMULUS PRESENTATION

Two kinds of studies will be discussed in connection with 'investigator controlled video'. The first is an example of studies of parent (or teacher)/child interaction wherein videorecording was essential to the design of the study. The other is a series of studies wherein video-recording enhanced the original study in the area and promises to make even further enhancement on this and other lines of research.

The first type is represented by two studies of the effects of a child's appearance on reactions by adults to 'mistakes on a learning task' (Berkowitz & Frodi, 1979). The first study showed a 10-year-old girl who was made up to appear either attractive or less attractive. In a second study the child was a 10-year-old boy who was also made up to appear attractive or unattractive and who spoke normally or with a noticeable stammer. Over 50 female undergraduates in the first study and 40 in the second watched a videotape of an attractive or unattractive child supposedly performing a learning task. Through instructions and a carefully designed procedure, all of the subjects believed that they were watching a live child in the next room on closed circuit television, none reporting that they actually watched a videotape. When given opportunities to punish the child's mistakes by pressing one of 10 buttons graduated to increasing levels of aversive noise, the subjects reliably punished the unattractive child more severely. To assess the fuller educational significance of these studies they might best be replicated by teachers and student teachers with various levels of experience, who are giving both rewards and punishments to children of varying ages, appearances and ethnic identification. That is not the point of interest here, however. Videorecording enabled this research to be carried out in two important ways. First, it was used to simulate closed circuit 'live' television. No other filmic technology could do this. Second, it provided an easily duplicated standard stimulus which could be used in replication or extension studies of these phenomena. Teacher education research stands to be enhanced by employment of the tools of videorecording in studies such as these and in teacher prototype research, discussed below.

There are a large number of research studies in the literature of social psychology wherein videorecordings are used to simulate television, for example, research on the effects of television on aggressive behaviour and also upon pro-social behaviour of viewers (cf Rushton, 1979). When television effects are an object of study, either as a direct educational treatment or for incidental learning or side effects, videorecordings (sometimes off the air, other times specially scripted and recorded) can be used in place of 'live' television to create a standard, replicable set of stimuli.

A second line of inquiry that illustrates videorecording as an invaluable tool in the presentation of stimuli in educational research is the body of literature on the 'Dr Fox effect'. The original study (Naftulin, Ware & Donnelly, 1973) involved a lecture by a live professional actor who was advertised and introduced as Dr Myron L Fox, a noted authority on his subject. After an enthusiastic lecture of less than an hour to an audience of mental health professionals and educators on the topic of 'mathematical game theory applied to physical education', the audience gave the speaker surprisingly high evaluations. The author's conclusions were that through wit, personality and the appearance of authority, an entertaining and charismatic lecturer who speaks deliberate nonsense can 'seduce' students into believing they have learned something and into giving the presentation a high rating. Follow-up studies were performed more in the fashion of experiments than the initial demonstration, by standardizing the presentation into six 20-minute videotaped lectures using the original Dr Fox actor and three levels of lecture content (low, medium and high) crossed with two levels of instructor expressiveness (low and high).

Further studies performed at the University of Manitoba by Ray Perry and his colleagues (Perry, Abrami & Leventhal, 1979), fit a tight two-by-two design wherein levels of expressiveness (low and high) were crossed with levels of content amount (low and high) in a factorial design wherein relevant main effects and interaction results could be identified and studied. As a consequence, we know far more today about the effects of expressiveness and content on both ratings and achievement than hitherto. Videorecording makes this line of research possible, replicable and extendable, and the availability of video as a research tool has been indispensable in developing this line of inquiry in higher education.

The purpose here is not to evaluate these findings or this body of research, but rather to discuss the role of videorecording technology as a research tool. In fact, the literature on educational seduction is based almost entirely on videotape stimuli. Moreover, it could be argued (Ray P Perry, personal communication) that videorecordings give us the possibility of constructing replicable teacher prototypes based on a finite number of specifiable teacher behaviours. If this potential is realized, then videorecording technology will surely take its place as a major educational research tool for years to come. In related lines of inquiry, of course, it is possible to construct counsellor prototypes, school administrators and other role models on video. However, it seems that the teacher in her or his role as information giver/inspirer can best be captured on recordings and studied in this way.

Perhaps the greatest problem in using videorecordings to present stimuli for educational research lies in the possibility that research subjects will 'see' something different from that which the experimenter expects or believes them to. This can be a problem of differing perspective, lack of clear communication, or subjects who attend to different aspects of the stimulus from those intended by the experimenter.

Perhaps the most promising approach to dealing with such problems is Argyris' recommendation (1976) of 'Model II' or participative research designs. Following his advice, participants in research become partners of the investigator in designing and carrying out the investigations. Far from the deceptive procedures illustrated in studies such as those of Berkowitz described above, pre-briefing moves discussion of participants' awareness of the purposes of the design of the study forward in time from the traditional post-experimental de-briefing practices. In higher education research, the intelligence and motivation of participants are resources to be tapped in designing and conducting research studies.

This emphasis upon teacher as information giver and experimenter-produced videorecordings needs to be balanced with alternative considerations. Subject-controlled videorecording in education is a research vehicle worthy of exploration. Like the initial Dr Fox study, activity to date has been largely at the demonstration level of experience. For example, participants in college and university teaching seminars designed and conducted by the author learn to videotape each other's 'microteaching' presentations. Then each participant is regarded as 'owning' the recorded signal in terms of decisions about who will see it and when it will be replayed and how to use it in teaching improvement. Of course, the instructor makes suggestions about possibilities. To my knowledge, this use of subject-controlled video in higher education (for example, Menges, 1978) has not been a part of a systematic program of research published to date, but it shows promise of emerging from the demonstration stage at this point.

Video stimulus presentations controlled by computer program have made great strides since the early development of PLATO (Hicks & Hunka, 1972). Such technical developments make possible a degree of stimulus control and precision in recording response latencies previously unavailable in educational research. If there is to be a technological revolution in research in education, it is through the coupling of the microelectronic technologies of computer programs and videorecording playback devices.

Ethical issues in the use of video in research suggest themselves at this and later points. Whereas it is not the purpose of this chapter to discuss these in detail, brief mention will be made here. Key issues are privacy, informed consent and who 'owns' the images and decides to what purpose they will be put.

VIDEORECORDING OF RESPONSES IN EDUCATIONAL RESEARCH

Just as anthropologists' field notes gave way to audio-tape recordings and recently to portable battery-operated videotape recorders, the availability of videorecording of the responses of experimental participants raises a host of research and ethical questions. This is particularly true when videorecordings form unobtrusive measures as would be the case if videorecordings designed to reduce shoplifting in stores were used in marketing research analyses. That video is but a tool of research

(Birdwhistell, 1970, p 152) does not vitiate ethical questions about how it is used or misused with reference to people's rights.

Here again, Argyris' participative research designs allow for progress. Once participants consent to and become habituated to the fact that videorecordings are being made of their work, they can get down to the tasks at hand. Modern timing devices as well as skilful use of behind-the-shoulder mirrors provide the opportunity for relatively inexpensive, relatively permanent response collection and coding.

Finally, attention needs to be paid to the research potential for the production of videorecordings *per se*. A study of the actions and inter-actions of teams of students who are assigned tasks involving the production of videorecordings is an area of research in its own right likely to yield hypotheses concerning group dynamics, decision making, individual and group creativity, and so on. Educational uses of the products of videorecording production require evaluation — another illustration of video in research. If language students were to exchange videorecordings with their counterparts in other cultural-linguistic groups (say between England and Japan) daily language usage could be supported by cultural illustrations (how one eats or studies, for instance, in another culture) in ways that invite systematic evaluation of the procedure (itself a form of educational research, if properly designed and conducted).

VIDEORECORDING IN RESEARCH PRESENTATION

Conventional films presenting the research of anthropologists such as Margaret Mead and Ray L Birdwhistell have been invaluable in the dissemination of their research to wide audiences of students and others. The potential of videorecordings for such research presentation is still largely untapped but the rapidly growing number of homes and offices with video disc or tape playing equipment enhances the possibility of widespread development of this form of research dissemination.

Such recordings can not only be mailed but can now be transmitted by wire line and satellite (miniaturization and battery-operated equip-ment are available); and it is possible to do or present research anywhere on earth or in space.

Dissemination of research results to professors by means of audio and videorecordings, for review by the recipient in his or her office or perhaps, with a pocket monitor, while commuting to work, is possible now and may become commonplace in the near future.

Write-ups of research procedures that include instructions read to participants only include the text of what was said. Rarely are clear directions given as to how it was said (vocal inflections, facial and bodily gestures, and so on). Videorecordings make attainable this kind of more precise replication of experimental conditions.

MULTI-USE OF VIDEORECORDINGS IN RESEARCH AND EDUCATION — THE HDZ STUDIES

Finally, in collaboration with Michael Heger and the staff of the Higher Education Centre (HDZ) at the Technical University of Aachen, the author conducted a series of studies on psychological aspects of anxiety and arousal in teaching during the 1981-82 academic year. One of these studies featured multiple use of videorecordings and is described briefly here.

Two groups of 20 education students at the Technical University of Aachen participated in a weekend block seminar on microteaching, communication skills, and anxiety reduction. Their videotaped presentations were used as training devices, but their performance was also scored on a variety of indices of observable stress (audio and video recorded) developed by Foster and Heger for the purpose. These results were correlated with scores on published scales (eg Spielberger State and Trait Anxiety Inventory — STAI). In this investigation, videorecordings formed the training task and provided a vehicle from which dependent measures were scored. To the extent that the apparatus formed a part of the 'audience' it also contributed to the stimuli towards which communications anxiety was expressed and eventually ameliorated. Although we haven't done so yet, it would be possible for a videorecording to be made describing the conduct of this research and its findings, thus providing the dissemination phase as well (Heger, 1983).

SUMMARY AND CONCLUSIONS

A number of examples, real and hypothetical, have been given for the use of videorecording as a research tool in higher education. As a means of presenting stimuli, recording responses, as a vehicle for conveying experimental interventions, or to do any combination of these, videorecording technology has been shown as a powerful tool, its use and potential contributions to behavioural research in general, and educational research in particular, being highlighted.

In its flexibility, video represents an improvement on older technologies (audiorecording and film). In other ways, it makes possible new research procedures.

As far as global communications networks are concerned, videorecordings could soon be playing an important role in disseminating research results far more quickly than traditional methods of publication. What is needed now is for textbooks and courses on research methodology to deal with ethical and technical issues concerning the use of video in research to enable today's students to make optimum use of video as a research tool.

REFERENCES

Abrami, P C, Leventhal, L & Perry, R P (1982) 'Educational seduction', *Review of Educational Research*, 52, 446-64.

Argyris, C (1976) 'Theories of action that inhibit individual learning', *American Psychologist*, 31, 638-54.

Barbatsis, G S (1978) 'The nature of inquiry and analyses of theoretical progress in instructional television from 1950-1970', *Review of Educational Research*, 48, 399-414.

Berkowitz, L & Frodi, A (1979) 'Reactions to a child's mistakes as affected by her/his looks and speech', *Social Psychology Quarterly*, 42, 420-25.

Birdwhistell, R L (1970) *Kinesics and Context: Essays on Body Motion Communication*, University of Pennsylvania Press, Philadelphia.

Heger, M (1983) 'Erfassung und Bewältigung von Nervosität und Aufregung in Praxisnahen Trainingssituationen: Auswertung eines Wochenendseminares des HDZ-Aachen für Lehramtsstudenten', Research Report 17, HDZ, Aachen.

Hicks, B L & Hunka, S (1972) *The Teacher and the Computer*, W B Saunders Co, Philadelphia.

Menges, R J (1978) 'Raising consciousness about teaching: New use for videotape'. Symposium paper, 86th annual meeting of the American Psychological Association, Toronto.

Naftulin, D H, Ware, J E Jr & Donnelly, F A (1979) 'The Doctor Fox lecture: A paradigm of educational seduction', *Journal of Medical Education*, 71, 339-45.

Perry, R P, Abrami, P C & Leventhal, L (1979) 'Educational seduction: the effect of instructor expressiveness and lecture control on student ratios and achievement', *Journal of Educational Psychology*, 71, 107-16.

Review of Educational Research 38 (1968) 'Instructional materials: educational media and technology', American Educational Research Association, Washington, DC.

Rushton, J P (1979) 'Effects of pro-social television and film material on the behaviour of viewers', in Berkowitz, L (ed), *Advances in Experimental Social Psychology*, 12, 322-52, Academic Press, New York.

13. Project Orientation Through Video: Concepts and Experiences

Dietrich Brandt and
Karin Schmitt

SUMMARY

Mass media play an important role in our society: they are influential as means of socialization, information, education and entertainment. Today, many mass media users frequently tend to experience reality largely via these means rather than through direct exposure to reality, through action or response within reality. Research has shown that their ability to master reality seems, therefore, to decline. Since 1974-75, the HDZ (Centre for Research and Development in Higher Education) at the Technical University of Aachen, has been running projects for students designed to develop critical attitudes towards the media and to enable them to act differently in terms of both personal communication and public communication.

INTRODUCTION

Over the last 60 years, many authors have been discussing the dangers of merely consuming media products and demanding that radio and TV develop from one-way communication to means of two-way communication. Producers and consumers would, then, appear fundamentally equal: the public would be able to participate in, and control communication in society.

In this chapter, we discuss four of these authors in some detail. These are Brecht (1968), Tretjakov (1972), Negt & Kluge (1972) and Enzensberger (1970). They have been particularly influential in West German discussions on public TV and on alternative approaches to mass communication through video. They have also stimulated aims and perspectives for concrete projects such as the ones we shall be describing here, as well as for quasi-utopian, anticipatory visions of a media future. The first section of this report presents their concepts.

COMMUNICATION, MASS MEDIA AND SOCIETY

Through essays and public speeches on a 'Theory of radio' (1927-32), Brecht (1968) put forward strong claims for a system of communication which takes advantage of progress in technology to improve communication between people.

Brecht's main concern is to democratize radio with respect to

173

content and to organization. He further claims that radio already existed before there was a real need for it: it was suddenly possible to tell everybody everything — but there was nothing really to tell; and only the producer controlling the medium was entitled to speak, not the listener in his passive role. However, radio could be a fantastic means of communicating if it could also be used to make the listener speak, to draw him into communication. Producer and listener may then appear fundamentally equal. Finally, radio should stimulate action. This certainly does not appear acceptable in a society ruled and controlled by a few: but why does it seem quasi-utopian to shift power of control over the media into the listeners' hands as technological progress would enable us to do? Democracy and democratic use of the media may, thus, be inseparable.

In a series of essays on 'The function of art and the role of the artist' (1923-34), Tretjakov (1972) defined the function of art in a democratic society in the wake of the Russian Revolution, at about the same time as Brecht published his theory of radio.

In Tretjakov's view, art is not just for enjoyment during leisure — leisure in contrast to work: it has rather to contribute to building up and developing the democratic society. It is always linked to political beliefs and values; it is either for or against democratization. For Tretjakov, art ought to be on the side of the progress of society towards more democracy. Reality should be its content, and its target for impact and interference. The central issue should be man: his/her experiences and emotions, including those engendered in working life. In this context, the artist is part of society, he is not isolated from it. He commits himself to social change, seeing himself as one among many. Thus, he is taking part in a collective movement in which virtually everybody is entitled to make art.

In their essay 'Life experience and the public' Negt & Kluge (1972) describe characteristics of a society which is moving towards more democracy starting from capitalist conditions.

In their view, one of the main features of this process of democratization is the view that the public is genuinely democratic or 'proletarian' in contrast to the 'middle-class' public as it is currently prevalent in our society. In this context of art and communication, the term 'middle-class' public implies a set of values which refer to areas of experience not necessarily embracing working life. 'Proletarian' public, however, means to organize and develop real needs and experiences of the working class collectively, setting out from the experiences of daily life and integrating them into the larger context of society. This is to be seen as a continuous process: it symbolizes at any time the then state of democratization rather than any stable or final state of democracy. At present, video action groups, free radio groups, students, and so on, are advancing this notion in society. Negt and Kluge describe this movement by the term 'counter' public in order to differentiate this state of development between the pure 'middle-class' public and the quasi-utopian 'proletarian' public. The latter may eventually develop out of these struggles.

In his essay about 'Approaches to a theory of media', Enzensberger (1970) started a new line of argument about mass media in capitalism.

Enzensberger claims that the communications industry is the main pacemaker of socio-economic development in late capitalism, and hence it largely controls technological progress and the direction and extent of production and turnover. For the media have a fascination for the consumers: they appeal to genuine consumers' needs and expectations without fulfilling them — the consumers experience manipulation. According to Enzensberger, any media use is manipulation. The main question is, therefore, how to enable the consumers to participate in controlling manipulation through media. One way suggested by Enzensberger is to enable the consumers to produce their own programs. Thus, the consumers take over the function of those manipulating. Technological progress has made it technically possible for everybody to be a media producer. The means of media production are already virtually democratized. However, only a genuinely free and democratic society could make full use of these means and possibilities. Here, Enzensberger refers back to the authors discussed before: it is not possible to separate the issue of the democratic use of the mass media from the question of power and control in society.

VIDEO PROJECTS AT THE HDZ AACHEN

The theories referred to in the previous section can be summarized as follows:

1. Radio and TV should develop towards becoming a means of two-way communication.
2. The central issue of media products should be man: his/her experiences and emotions including those engendered in working life.
3. Groups within society should organize their collective experiences to communicate them to other groups.
4. Consumers should be enabled to withstand and eventually control manipulation through media by producing their own programs.

These claims have had influence on the development of the use of mass media and video in West Germany. As an example, we shall describe the approach of the HDZ Aachen to put these theories into practice. The HDZ Aachen is a department of the Technical University of Aachen: it is also the centre for AV media in this university. Since 1974-75, it has been running video projects for students at the Technical University of Aachen, and for students in the 10-19 age group and their teachers in institutions of secondary education in and around Aachen.

In this section, we describe three different projects run by interdisciplinary teams of students of social science, humanities, education, architecture and engineering, from our university, followed by examples of projects involving secondary school students and their teachers. The examples show how the four different, albeit overlapping, aspects of media theory mentioned above have been taken up within the projects. Each example stands for a series of similar or related projects.

PROJECTS AIMING AT DEVELOPING TWO-WAY COMMUNICATION IN SOCIETY

A large range of projects at the HDZ deal with urban planning. Through a series of videorecordings, several interdisciplinary teams of students have investigated development in the urban areas of Aachen and elsewhere, as well as in villages on the verge of becoming suburbs of Aachen. Examples of areas of study are the relationships between different housing areas, traffic and industry, shopping areas and playgrounds. The students' videorecordings have been intended to improve opportunities for participation in decision making for those living in areas threatened by uncoordinated development. Video has, thus, contributed to reshaping development according to the needs of the population.

The students have not attempted to 'teach' or 'educate' people, they have merely observed them through video. They have prepared recordings of local daily life and communal activities — bazaars, fairs, parties, excursions, and so on — documents of social life under threat. They have fed these revealing observations back to the people, and shown them to a wider public. The recordings have become stimuli for self-organization and participation in the communal 'power game'. The alliance of 'progressive' students with those members of the public who resist change in their environment on the basis of their conservatism and their understanding of the quality of life, has prepared the ground for the German ecology-based 'Green' movement in Aachen and elsewhere. Traditional values have been modified, but also translated as the claims of a human society, which is more than an arbitrary assembly described by such criteria as income, social status, and traffic patterns. This series of projects is clearly based on Brecht's notion that the people should be enabled to make themselves heard and to make their impact felt by those controlling communal politics. Many video groups follow the same model; rarely, however, are they substantially supported by a university department.

PROJECTS INVESTIGATING PEOPLE IN THEIR WORKING LIFE

Following Tretjakov's understanding of art and the role of the artist, students in these projects are concerned with a variety of human problems and phenomena. Their approach is to document personal and professional lives of engineers, workers, farmers (and their wives), teachers and so on. The documentary videorecording of the life and work of young secondary school teachers is described here as an example of how students go about these projects.

The students in this particular project, moved freely around in classrooms and common rooms as well as in the homes of teachers and their students, in order to record both the attitudes of students and the behaviour of their teachers. In this way, they produced a detailed recording of problems encountered by young teachers after they had left university: isolation from their more experienced colleagues; their inability to translate educational theory into everyday classroom behaviour; the pressure to betray their educational aims in dealing with students; their attempts to build up solidarity among their peers in order to withstand repression exerted by their superiors; and their failure completely to adjust their private lives to new working conditions. The main aim of the recording was to inform teachers themselves about the conditions they are working under, so as to prevent them attributing difficulties to individual failure rather than to objective causes. Subsequently the recordings have been used to inform a larger audience — parents, students, administration and so on — about the difficulties, thus contradicting prejudices frequently brought up in public. In this way, the students attempted to contribute to improving the teaching-learning environment as a whole.

PROJECTS TO ASSIST GROUPS IN SOCIETY TO COMMUNICATE THEIR COLLECTIVE EXPERIENCES TO OTHER GROUPS

Students in these projects work very similarly to those referred to in the previous section. Their aim is to support groups of lesser weight in society (in Aachen) so that they can articulate their experiences in a way which is comprehensible and acceptable to others. With Negt & Kluge, the students try to set up a 'counter' public: as a group within society which has available both the means and the awareness to organize and communicate collective experiences. The videorecorder serves as a means of focusing the process of observation. The observer quickly becomes a part of the life which he intends to record. The interaction between the 'observer' and the 'object of observation' is deliberate. Here, video serves additionally as a research tool to analyse this particular interference.

This series of projects deals with groups such as migrant workers in Germany, unemployed youth, retarded or maladjusted children, drug addicts, members of the peace movement and related groups, students from non-European countries, and also women. We illustrate this range of activities by means of a project dealing with youth in Aachen who consider and call themselves 'punks'. It became publicly apparent through the recording, that they are mostly sons and daughters of middle-class Aachen families with appropriate schooling, collectively awaiting their fate of long-term unemployment. The scornful rejection of them by local citizens had even led to police action against the punk groups: the recording, however, revealed that the police tried not to employ those tough measures expected by the local newspapers. The recording has been frequently shown in small theatres in Aachen — perhaps a contribution to making a wider public aware of collective experiences of a sub-group of society.

PROJECTS TO ENABLE CONSUMERS TO WITHSTAND MANIPULATION THROUGH MEDIA

A large series of projects falls into this category. The main thrust of the projects is on secondary education, in two ways:

☐ to give students in secondary schools, in the age range 10 to 19, the opportunity to experience learning as controlled by themselves, in a limited project

☐ to assist these students in producing their own recordings with the aim of understanding and applying strategies of manipulating messages.

Students of our university assist the teachers to run these projects with their classes, at school or at the HDZ. The projects, which are part of the school curriculum, either spread out over several weeks or are compressed into one week as a full-day activity. They are supported by formal lessons on media use and related issues. Within the projects, the students organize themselves in teams of three to six and set out to produce 'their' recording from the initial ideas to the finished program. In this way, an enormous variety of recordings has been produced. Some of them have found public recognition; one recording was transmitted by the local TV station. The main themes of the projects are:

☐ Let's make our own commercials (for well known or fantasy products)

☐ Let's set up our own 'Top of the pops' show

☐ Let's re-do the TV news as it should be done.

One series of recordings which has been particularly successful was made by 14-year-old girls on how to advertise European-American goods to civilizations different from ours:

☐ motorbikes for the gods of the Ancient Greeks

☐ shaving cream for Red Indians

☐ roller skates for the aristocracy in the eighteenth century.

Thus, the students experience how manipulation takes place and they may gain sufficient insight to withstand messages of this kind in the future. As Enzensberger suggests, they may win back control of a part of their lives, through having produced their own 'TV' programs on video.

These four examples will suffice here. Several more projects have been described in a previous report (Brandt, 1977). The total number of projects is now around 80, each of them involving three to 10 students of our university for one to three semesters. Another 50 projects involving teachers and their students in secondary schools, have been rendered possible by the HDZ. The length of the recordings ranges from 15 to 50 minutes with the average of around 30 minutes. These are facilitated by the HDZ's 20 portable video cameras and recorders; furthermore, the HDZ has set up a video studio which can be used by any participant after a short training period. Hence, students from our university or from school can produce their programs completely on their own: from the first vague idea through script and stage play to the final product, with electronic editing and sound dubbing. Thus, students develop and train all skills generally needed to produce 'proper' programs. Within the projects, these activities are supported by lectures and seminars on the mass media and their role in society, and related topics.

THE EDUCATIONAL CONCEPT OF THE PROJECTS

It has been important for us to design a coherent educational framework to structure the variety of on-going video projects described so far. In this section, we present an outline of the framework based on several investigations by the HDZ's research staff. According to these investigations, each of the video projects goes through certain developmental stages at three different levels:

☐ the level of personal communication
☐ the level of concern with mass media
☐ the level of transfer into reality.

These three levels characterize the principal educational concept of our video projects. They are briefly discussed here (see Table 1).

	Awareness of problem	Concrete experience	Reflection and generalization
Level of personal communication	What are my personal difficulties in communicating with others?	Role play and video self-confrontation	Impact of video on group processes
Level of concern in mass media	What are the characteristics of public TV?	Production of video programs	Impact of video programs on audience
Level of transfer into reality	How can video contribute to advancing society?	Video projects in schools, social work, communal politics etc	Impact of video projects in different settings

Table 1. *The three levels of video projects*

The first level is concerned with personal communication of the project participants among themselves. Reflection of communication in society starts with analysing communication processes which involve ourselves as individuals: observing interactions within the group, video self-confrontation and role play, developing further the participants' communication skills.

The second level is defined by questions relating to the mass media such as: What are the aims, means and impact of public and commercial TV? Starting from a theoretical analysis of the system of mass media in society, the project groups move on to re-production, and re-creation of such products — or to creating their own products — to be made public and discussed according to criteria which the group may consider applicable to analysing professional TV productions. Thus, they learn to assess the impact of mass media on society by observing the impact of their own products on their audience. They may even sense the power which is familiar to media producers being in control of the means to manipulate others (which may include experiences of frustration and defeat).

The third level is determined by aspects of transferring experiences into practice. The participants launch or join projects using video in schools, urban planning and community actions, controversies of local or regional politics, thus anticipating or testing possibilities and impact of media in reality.

The projects usually combine all three levels within the framework of project orientation. The educational model which yields the basis for this approach follows Kolb, Rubin & McIntyre (1974), referring to experience-based learning as a cycle of four stages:

1. Concrete experience; followed by
2. observation and reflection; which leads to
3. the formation of abstractions, generalizations and hypotheses; which require
4. testing in new situations; thus giving rise to new experiences and the start of a new cycle.

Within the projects, these four stages are related to the three levels described before: the students go through the stages at each of the three levels in turn:

1. At the first level, from individual experience of video self-confrontation, to reflection on and insight into, their own self within the group's communication structure
2. At the second level, from analysis and reflection of personal experiences — and the experiences of others — with mass media, to testing their individual hypothesis by producing, showing and discussing their own video programs in public
3. At the third level, from confrontation with reality to developing new projects or models to master reality.

As Boud and Pascoe (1978) have described it, experience-based learning can be characterized by three dimensions:

1. The degree of involvement of the self of each individual student. Within our approach, students experience this involvement through video self-confrontation and through creating a media product for a certain audience.
2. The degree of learner control over the learning experience. This dimension reflects notions of education suggested by authors such as Rogers, Fromm and many others who have a strong influence on students joining our projects. Their thoughts are present in the project reports of these students. This dimension is also related to the second level of our concept: how society is controlled through mass media. By means of these projects, students learn to take over control of their own learning against the opposition of the teaching system of the university — as a model of how individuals or groups can gain control over their lives against power exerted, for instance, by mass media.
3. The degree of correspondence of the learning environment to reality. This dimension reflects the level of transfer of experience into the practice of our concept.

Within the educational framework outlined here, the video projects integrate cognitive aspects of learning about media and affective elements of motivation through video enthusiasm; they combine creativity in producing video programs with developing technical skills; they lead to action outside the projects — or outside the learning environment — in personal life as well as in society at large. These aspects are clearly shown in the four selected projects described in the previous section. They are also discussed in detail and evaluated with regard to their implementation, in a series of research reports published by the HDZ Aachen.

THE PROJECTS WITHIN THE UNIVERSITY

The students working with video consider this activity a part of their curriculum. Their commitment may lead to a master's thesis or it may be rewarded credit — based on course work or an essay — equivalent to a course option in education, sociology, humanities or even engineering. Within a comparatively conventional undergraduate curriculum, the scope for self-determined learning is, thus, considerably enlarged. Our evaluation studies have shown that the students' attitudes are influenced through their encounter with reality outside the academic community as well as through involvement with problems of others who may belong to different social or political groups. Their creativity and imagination is challenged by the production process beyond what normally takes place in undergraduate education. They learn to learn at their own pace; and they apparently reach a higher level of self-responsibility and independence than their peers in conventional courses.

However, in Germany as in any other country, criticisms are levelled at project orientation. Too many negative experiences allow the universities to reject this notion quite openly: there is procrastination and delay with students failing to finish their projects in time; the projects tend to take up more time than conventional courses do; group work within the projects does not stress the achievement of a student for individual assessment; student teams tend to fall apart since the tasks which they usually set themselves are too large to be mastered in time. Project teams need careful guidance and advice to overcome these difficulties, and we feel obliged to put effort into keeping up the overall performance of the teams because our own reputation is at stake. Hence we have resorted to appointing student tutors who — in addition to investing their own intrinsic motivation — receive small grants, to act as facilitators of peer groups mainly in terms of structures and processes within the project teams.

Criticisms of video projects also stem from the fact that these projects cut across the well-established borders of disciplines and therefore do not teach facts of any one discipline sufficiently. Hence, we have set up a communication network between different departments to have project reports, in the form of a thesis, accepted and credited by these departments in compliance with their normal procedures, in order to demonstrate equivalence of achievement. So far, more than 30 master degrees in education, humanities, social sciences or engineering have been awarded in this way, on the basis of the video projects described here: this encourages us to continue with our concept despite all these difficulties and obstacles.

REFERENCES

Boud, D & Pascoe, J (1978) *Experiential Learning,* Australian Consortium on Experiential Education, Sydney.

Brandt, D (1977) 'Approaches to self-instruction in Germany', *Journal of Personalized Instruction,* **2,** 1, 6-13.

Brecht, B (1968) 'Radiotheorie (Theory of radio)', in Brecht, B *Gesammelte Werke,* **18,** Suhrkamp, Frankfurt aM.

Enzensberger, H M (1970) 'Baukasten zu einer Theorie der Medien (Approaches to a theory of media)', *Kursbuch,* **20,** 159-86.

Kolb, D A, Rubin, I M & McIntyre, J M (1974) *Organizational Psychology, An Experiential Approach,* Prentice Hall, London.

Negt, O & Kluge, A (1974) *Oeffentlichkeit und Erfahrung* (Life Experience and the Public), Suhrkamp, Frankfurt aM.

Tretjakov, S (1972) *Die Arbeit des Schriftstellers. Aufsätze, Reportagen, Portraits* (The Work of the Writer, Essays, Reports, Portraits), Rowohlt, Reinbek.

14. The Use of Videotape in the Improvement of Student Study Methods

Alex Main

SUMMARY

This paper outlines the deficiencies in various methods of improving learning skills in tertiary education, and describes how video material can augment the work of teachers and counsellors. It shows how video can be used for self-study, group work and learning feedback. The rationale, content and general approach of the series 'Study Patterns' are described, as are the modifications which have been designed as a result of feedback from students, teachers and counsellors. Effects of study skills video materials on attitudes of teachers are described.

In tertiary education there are three common methods of helping students to improve their study skills. These are: textbooks, courses on learning skills, and personal counselling. Each has disadvantages of some sort.

Textbooks. In 1979 there were nearly 400 books in print in the English language called something like 'How to Study', 'Study to Succeed', 'Pass your Exams'. Many students buy such books — but few read them. Often they sit on a student's bookshelf as a talisman for success or a charm against failure.

There are several reasons why this should be so. Many texts on study methods are aimed at producing the 'perfect' student. The methods described, the routines outlined and the dedication required are often too much for the student whose motivation is average or who is no more disorganized than his or her contemporaries. Sometimes, too, study texts are too dogmatic and didactic, and do not seem to offer the student reader an opportunity to experiment with methods. Then again, the student who is uncertain about his or her study skills (including those of reading and note-taking) may find it too much of a challenge to open a book which requires quite high levels of reading and comprehension skills to master.

Courses. The impersonality of the textbook is often overcome by offering students a course on learning methods, in which instruction can be blended with discussion and the practice of specific skills. The major drawback of this approach is a logistical one: the timing of the course. Most institutions cannot offer courses on demand, and so need to offer them at fixed points in the year. If a study skills course is offered to new first-year students at the beginning of a semester, it is often seen as unnecessary or irrelevant. Students who have just succeeded in entering tertiary education will be suspicious of a course which appears to be for those who are *not* successful. Until new students have experienced some of the challenges of their studies, they will not identify which skills they need to improve; until they have had some feedback on progress, they may have little motivation to seek improvement.

If the course is offered later in the semester, it may equally fail to cater for the differential development of the students. It is difficult to organize and time a learning skills course so that it meets the needs of different students at the optimum time for each student. In addition, study skills courses tend to suffer from their 'remedial' image: students often stay away from them because they believe them to be for 'failures'. The average student who may want some general improvement in methods and techniques may avoid what seems to be something provided for the below average student.

Counselling. Personal advice from a tutor or counsellor can overcome the difficulties of timing mentioned above: an individual teacher or adviser can spot the optimum time to assist a student with a specific skill, and can tailor the advice to suit the student's personal style or approach. Individual help is also often more anonymous, and students can feel more confident in approaching an individual for private assistance than attending a public course.

The problem in tertiary education in most countries at the moment is that lecturers and tutors often have heavy teaching loads and can offer students less individual attention than they wish. Central agencies such as counselling services and advisory centres are often also overloaded or under-staffed, and can cope only with students who are under severe pressure. They may have little time for helping the average student who simply wants to 'check out' different study methods.

In the mid-1970s at the University of Strathclyde we set about looking for a way of augmenting the three methods of assistance described above. Our aims were to:

☐ overcome the impersonality of the study textbook
☐ provide students with assistance at a time when they recognized the need for help, and as immediately as they required it
☐ give students some of the directness and individual attention that is characteristic of personal counselling
☐ avoid increasing the staff of any central service.

The search was motivated by increasing demands from students for advice on study and learning methods and increased referral to the central learning service by tutors, at a time when university resources could not encompass extra staff. The result of the search was a very modest investment in the preparation of videotaped materials for individual student use.

STUDY PATTERNS

It was decided to offer students access to a series of 15-minute video presentations on the topics which were raised most often by those who called for personal counselling on academic matters at the University's Centre for Educational Practice. On analysis there seemed to be three general reasons for students to seek advice:

1. Difficulty in planning or organizing work: timetabling, making effective use of time, concentrating on study, reading effectively.
2. Ineffective cognitive structuring of subject-matter, as evidenced by problems in note-taking, essay-writing, exam preparation and revision.
3. Some personal worry about a cognitive skill, such as speed of reading or efficiency of memory.

(For further details of this analysis, see Main, 1980.)

The topics chosen for the videotape series were therefore:

☐ Personal timetabling
☐ Using your time
☐ Reading
☐ Note-taking
☐ Essay-writing.

The approach adopted in writing and presenting the material was straightforward: it was to present simply and crisply, without undue elaboration or too much detail, some widely accepted 'good practices' in studying. The tapes were designed to act as a basis for students to explore their own study habits and the skills required by their courses; at no time were they meant to be definitive accounts of *best* methods of study. They were unambiguously aimed at first-year students in all faculties of Strathclyde University, and the examples, references and presentation format were selected for that audience.

It was decided to use one presenter, talking for the most part directly to camera, to involve the viewer in an intimate relationship with the presenter. The term *viewer* (in the singular) is used to indicate that the original concept was of the tape being watched in privacy in a viewing-cubicle by one person. The tapes were made available on videocassette on open-access in a specially constructed resource centre: students could view the material without booking it out or informing anyone of their presence. In this way, the three great advantages of videotaped material were harnessed to the improvement of study skills:

1. *Immediacy*. Students searching for immediate advice, or seeking some method of judging their own study methods, had available to them a 15-minute exposition/illustration. They had no need to search through textbooks for material. For those students who were daunted by the 'open-ended' task of reading, the fact that video-cassettes had a fixed time marked on them seemed highly motivating.
2. *Privacy*. No student need attend a public course on study methods, nor acknowledge to any other person, staff or student, that he or she was seeking advice. The private viewing-carrell seemed to attract many who otherwise would have avoided contact with the Centre.
3. *Relevance*. Students could view only those tapes which related to their individual needs — and (very importantly) at the very time

those needs were identified. Instead of reading one textbook or attending a global course on study methods, students could select the tapes in any order, space their viewing out as required, and re-view any tape any number of times.

General monitoring of the use of the tapes over a four-year period indicated that these three characteristics of the system of viewing were widely appreciated. Systematic research has not been carried out on usage, but a conservative estimate is that 20 per cent of all first-year students use the material each year, and about 10 per cent of students in subsequent years. Some of the tapes, notably 'Personal timetabling' and 'Using your time' are in demand by postgraduates. (Further details of the use of these tapes and other audio-visual aids to study are available in Main, 1980.)

GENERAL USES OF THE SERIES

The primary use of 'Study Patterns' has remained as outlined above — for the average or above-average student to check out study methods, to come to terms with his or her individual needs and approaches, and to direct 'fine tuning' where required. We know that the vast majority of users gain some immediate benefit from their viewing: either they find something directly applicable, or leave feeling satisfied that they have little need to alter their learning styles or strategies. However, the series has also been used in a wide variety of other ways at Strathclyde and in institutions in many other parts of the world.

1. *As a screening and preparation for counselling.* A student who has a general, ill-defined worry about learning methods can be directed to one or more of the programs. Viewing can sharpen up the student's self-awareness, and can help him or her to discuss in more effective terms with a tutor, adviser or counsellor.
2. *Augmentation for courses.* Where study skills courses are held, individual viewing of the elements of the series can be used for preparation or revision.
3. *In group work.* Where a number of students are on a common course, the series can be viewed preparatory to tutorial discussion. The general concepts presented on the tapes can be related by the group to the specific assignments, projects, seminars or lectures of their course.
4. *Distance learning.* The material can form part of the general package of advice and guidance for students who do not have immediate and regular contact with tutors or advisers.
5. *To assist learning feedback.* Individuals or groups can review the tapes at the end of a semester as a focus for discussion of the organization of the semester's work and of planning for subsequent semesters.
6. *Transition to tertiary education.* Secondary school students who intend to enter university or college can use the programs as a means of preparing for higher level study.

MODIFICATIONS

John Jones (in this volume) suggests modifications which improve the content of the series and make it much less didactic in approach. These are very much in keeping with the spirit of the original venture, and fit in with the feedback obtained in many British institutions. Other modifications now under way include:

☐ the re-recording of the series in colour and with a wider variety of illustrations, graphics, animation techniques, in order to meet the increasingly more sophisticated demands of the viewing audience
☐ the re-organization of the material into smaller five-minute modules, each module with its own follow-up exercises
☐ the re-vitalization of the material by inclusion of more interactive tasks for the viewer
☐ the extension of the content to include modules on exam preparation, revision, mathematical skills, laboratory study, physical fitness, relaxation and sleep, and library skills
☐ the inclusion of optional modules for secondary school students
☐ the inclusion of some modules for group viewing.

POSTSCRIPT

One advantage of the series has been the effect it has had on teaching staff who have used it in discussion with their own students, or who have seen it as part of a workshop course on learning skills. It has encouraged many lecturers at the University of Strathclyde and else-where to become more explicit about the tasks they set their students, and more direct about the learning aims of their courses. Particularly where the series has been used as an aid to the tutorial program of first-year classes, it has encouraged staff and students to explore more fully together the skills of both teacher and taught. In this sense the series, designed primarily for individual study guidance, has taken on a staff development function in a number of institutions.

REFERENCES

Main, A (1980) *Encouraging Effective Learning*, Scottish Academic Press, Edinburgh.

15. Varsity: The Good Life? Reflections on the Design, Production and Use of a Video Series on Student Study Skills

John Jones

SUMMARY

A series of five videotapes has been produced in response to student demand for learning skills activities. Consideration of the perceived credibility of presentations, and the constraint of local resources, resulted in a program structure and production schedule based on unscripted interviews with students. 'Scripts' were edited out of the student interviews, and appropriate visual materials was then added. It was necessary to include a structured summary in some of the programs. The videotapes have been used successfully as isolated programs and as components of workshops. Some of the factors related to the effective use of the programs are discussed.

INTRODUCTION

In 1977 a student counsellor at the University of Auckland became convinced that there were some students who would benefit from attending sessions dealing with the study skills and strategies which successful students adopt in coping with their university studies. On the basis of his contacts with students he felt that there was a demand, so he went ahead and advertised some voluntary lunchtime sessions. He was hopeful that a few dozen students would be interested enough to turn up: hundreds arrived! It was simply impossible to cope adequately with the demand within the small-group framework which had been envisaged and alternative avenues were explored.

It was at about this time that we became aware of Alex Main's Strathclyde study skills series of five video programs. After obtaining a set of the five programs we considered that an appropriate initial response to the student demand might be to show these videotapes. The thought was that these, together with some printed materials[1] which are regularly made available to all first-year students, might satisfy a large part of the demand from students, at a superficial level at least. So, in 1978, the programs were advertised campus-wide at the beginning of the academic year and were screened during lunchtimes early in the first term. Over a two-week period there were something like 2,000 students attending. Obviously there *was* a demand; and furthermore, informal feedback indicated that at least some students considered their attendance had been worthwhile.

In 1979 we repeated the exercise and also carried out a more systematic survey of students' reactions to the video programs. (Other activities relating to study skills had also developed in the meantime. Some of these are referred to later, but it is not necessary for the purpose of this paper to go into full details.) Generally, students were fairly well-disposed towards the video presentations and considered that useful advice had been offered. However, there were criticisms which can be summarized as follows.

The programs seem 'foreign'

The Strathclyde series was tailor-made and produced *for* the University of Strathclyde. While the University of Auckland is a broadly similar institution, there are nevertheless, points of difference which emerge from the series, and sometimes ring strange in New Zealand. Possibly the most significant difference is related to the 'foreign' accents of those who appeared — particularly the students. Practically all of the advice offered in the programs is applicable in Auckland as in Glasgow; but it seems as though the Auckland students are likely to consider it less appropriate because it is set in an obviously 'foreign' context.

The advice comes from an 'authority', who doesn't really understand students' difficulties

Students often considered the video programs were too didactic and consisted too much of a 'talking-head authority' — albeit a very skilful one! In some cases too the advice was thought to be a counsel of perfection, and not really related to the real world with which students have to cope.

The net result of the students' obvious desire for advice on study methods coupled with the evaluation of the Strathclyde series was a decision to produce an 'Auckland series' of videotapes, aimed more closely at the New Zealand market. The remainder of this article is a description of the development of these video programs and some discussion of the ways in which they have been employed. At the end some general principles for the effective use of such video programs are suggested.

PRODUCING THE VIDEO SERIES

The main resource available for the production of the video series was the Audio-visual Centre at the University of Auckland. This centre has a three colour-camera studio together with good editing facilities. In addition, an experienced TV producer and technical assistance were available. However, this facility is required to service the video needs of a university of 12,000 students, and the time during which facilities and expertise were available was strictly limited. There was no budget available for the production of the video programs, and obtaining specialized help with scripting (or professional actors) was not possible. However, we did manage to obtain the help of an assistant for several months, who was able to act as a liaison person and look after all of the logistics.

Early in the planning stages it was decided to start the series with a program about students' perceptions of the university during their first year and the kinds of problems which confront them. Following this introductory videotape there would be a series of four programs dealing with more specific aspects of coping strategies and study methods. As we wanted a 'non-didactic' presentation, and something with which students would empathize, there was an initial idea of having *students* do the presentation, according to a script. However, early attempts hinted that incredible disasters lay along that path! In fact, there seemed to be the principle that no matter how carefully we structured a program there was no way in which it was going to end up credible, undidactic — and yet get over the messages that we wanted.

Eventually, we went to the opposite extreme and decided that we would do *no* planning whatsoever regarding program structure or script, and to let this emerge from the production process. The sole principle was that the program was to be representative of the perceptions and experiences of five 'typical' students. There were five stages involved in the production of the video programs.

Stage 1

The initial phase consisted of going out and talking with students, around campus, to sort out likely candidates to appear in the series. The main criterion for selecting students was that a student should be 'typically representative'. Over a number of years there has been a fair amount of research carried out into the kinds of problems which different groups of students encounter, and we wanted students whose perceptions were typical. In addition we were looking for subjects who were reasonably articulate and who were representative of the different degree disciplines of arts, science, commerce, and so on. Usually, more than one conversation with students took place, and notes were made to keep track of subjects' perceptions of the various aspects of university. After these initial conversations, possible subjects were interviewed informally in front of a video camera to assess how well they 'came over' on tape. After this, the five subjects who were to feature in the series were chosen.

Stage 2

Armed with the knowledge of what students had said previously, an extended interview (which lasted up to 40 minutes) was carried out with each student on-camera. Questions were simply appropriate prompts to get students to talk about the issues which *they* had previously raised. As far as possible we did not confine students, but simply initiated discussion regarding the ways in which they were coping with the demands of university. The locations in which these interviews took place were varied, and kept as natural as possible: one took place in a student's home, another student was interviewed in her hostel room.

Stage 3

The five interviews formed the basis for the whole video series, and in practical terms represented the pool of possible material from which a script had to be constructed. There were common themes running through what students had said in their interviews, and these broad areas were used to construct an outline for the script. Some of the topics covered by students — and an example of an associated point which we wanted to emerge in the final program — were as follows:

☐ *Reasons for coming to university.* Students come to university for different reasons: one student came because he had a very definite career in mind, another because she had been encouraged by teachers and yet another because he had been 'turned on' during a school visit to a university.

☐ *Workload at university.* Workload seems heavier at university than at school; but some students, far more than others, manage to fit in extra-curricular activities and still cope adequately.

☐ *Differences between school and university climates.* School is much more personal than university; you have to make a definite effort at university to become involved and find the personal element.

By the end of Stage 3, a rough idea of a script and an associated structure for the series had emerged.

Stage 4

This was entirely a matter of deciding which statements from the interviews best illustrated the points arising out of the general script from Stage 3, subject to the constraint that we had to give roughly equal time to each of the five students. When these decisions had been made, the 'script' was constructed by editing together the relevant sections of the interviews. The end result was a series of interview fragments, arranged thematically. For example, the series begins with a brief statement from each of the students on why they came to university — and it ends with the advice which they thought most valuable for intending students.

Stage 5

A collage of interview clips hardly adds up to visual excitement. This missing interest was added by shooting and editing-in appropriate visual material, so that essentially the students' interview remarks became voice-over commentary. The following are some examples:

1. One of our subjects described how there had been very close relationships between staff and students, in small classes, at school, and contrasted this with the impersonality of the mass lecture at university. For these visual shots we took the student back to his school and pictured him in a typical small class, then followed with a shot of him in a large lecture theatre.
2. A second student, who had several younger siblings, was living at home. She found it practically impossible to carry out effective

academic work at home because of the domestic situation. This commentary was put over the top of a visual sequence which showed the whole family at breakfast and the student then rushing off to catch her bus.

3. One student was a karate exponent: we showed her in a practice session as she mentioned this fact in her description of social activities.

This phase had to be 'staged', in that it had to follow on from what students had said, and to an extent it is contrived. However, students were not required to act out situations in which they were not normally involved, and simply had to 'be themselves'. The final effect is credible.

To finish the program, music was added over opening and closing titles and credit sequences. The final product, which runs for 18 minutes, was entitled 'Varsity: The Good Life?'

In principle, this first program was relatively simple to produce; whatever students describe is a true record of the state of affairs for *them*, and is (at the very least) a case study for other students to consider. The 'study methods' programs which followed the introductory video production described above were more problematic. There were some broad principles which we wanted to suggest for students' consideration without being too didactic; students manage to cope effectively with their studies in rather different ways. Having *students* present these principles would not have been credible, as they would not be credible 'authorities'. At the same time, students are not likely to empathize very well with advice which comes from a credible authority figure. It was necessary to make some modifications to the procedures used for the first program, although a similar framework was used.

As before, the first stage involved locating 'typical' students; but this time the students were required to typify the specific study behaviours which we wanted to portray (either 'effective' or 'ineffective'). The process of locating these 'typical' students involved fairly lengthy informal interviews, and these formed the basis of a later semi-structured interview 'on-camera'. Usually three student interviews were selectively edited together to produce the 'script' which was required, and where appropriate, visual material was dubbed over the top of the interview collage, for interest and clarity. In this case though, the edited interview segments were not able to stand on their own and communicate clearly the message that was intended. It was necessary to draw together the main points that the students had been making, via a structured summary/resumé, presented over the top of suitable visual material. The final products are a compromise between didactic, authoritative statements and peer suggestion. Four video programs were produced dealing with the topics of personal timetabling, note-taking, reading and essay-writing, each lasting a little less than 10 minutes.

USING THE VIDEO TAPES

The video programs are currently being used in two quite distinct ways:

first, as self-contained presentations and second as elements of work-shop programs. There are important distinctions between the two contexts from which some general proposals relating to the use of video material of this kind can be drawn. Consider each of these situations, in turn:

Self-contained presentations

Here students simply turn up, as if at a cinema, and watch the programs, in isolation. They come to the presentations 'cold', with little or nothing by way of previous active thought or discussion about what they hope to gain from the experience. Each student who comes along is feeling less than perfectly happy with his/her study methods, and hopes to pick up ideas and get advice which is meaningful and can improve the situation. And here we have the seeds of a paradox.

Students expect fairly hard advice, yet unless they can empathize with the suggestions, and consider them meaningful and credible, they are unlikely to consider the advice seriously. When an authority figure gives the advice, then the chances that students will reject it are increased, simply because the presenter *is* an authority — and hence out of touch with the kinds of difficulties which students experience. But, at the same time, if we have fellow students — at more or less the same level — giving advice, then the audience is likely to reject it because a peer figure will be judged as insufficiently knowledgeable and experienced to make sound suggestions. The compromise solution described earlier, where an authoritative voice summarizes and struc-tures what peer students have been describing, seems to have been reasonably successful. In early 1982, the Auckland series was used for 'mass' showing for the first time, in place of the Strathclyde series. Although student response has not been systematically evaluated, informal feedback has been encouraging. In addition, several university departments have made arrangements for their own particular students to view the videotapes, and a growing number of schools are using the material with older students who are intending to enter tertiary insti-tutions. The evidence suggests that, as 'free-standing' programs the series may be getting through to students fairly successfully. (As this was the total rationale, it would be sad if they were not!) Rather curiously though, they seem to be no more successful — and may even be less so — than the Strathclyde series in a different context, to which we now turn.

Workshops aimed at improving study methods

In one sense it is rather ludicrous to expect that students will be able to improve skills as a result of sitting down and watching video programs. We accept this, and see the video programs simply as a stimulus which might get students thinking about their own behaviours. Any modifi-cation of these behaviours would be as a result of subsequent consider-ation and experimentation on the part of the individual student. Workshops, where students can interact with each other in small groups, represent a much more logical — and effective — approach to the whole business of improving study methods. The procedure which has been adopted at Auckland University is a modification of Gibbs'[2] pyramid approach. This operates through four stages, as follows:

1. Students carry out an appropriate exercise, individually, for a few minutes. For example, in a session devoted to essay-writing students start off by *marking* an essay.
2. Individuals then discuss their efforts, in pairs, for a few minutes. In the case of the essay-writing workshop, students would swap essays, look at the comments of each other, and discuss how the final grade was arrived at.
3. Pairs then combine to form a group, of four or six, and spend about half an hour in generating 'good advice' to other students; one person is appointed as a recorder in each group.
4. Finally, each group volunteers the advice it has generated in a plenary discussion which lasts for up to half an hour.

Gibbs' procedure stops at the end of this plenary session, and the whole structure is totally non-directive. It has the advantage that each participant is 'forced' into being an active discussant, and is projected into a situation where a very serious critical examination of personal study methods takes place in a non-threatening environment. Also, a great deal of informal peer learning occurs. There is often the feeling though that the whole thing is left dangling (some unkind souls have unfairly called the approach a pooling of ignorance) and in need of rounding-off. To get over this problem video programs are used as authoritative statements at a final stage. There are a number of advantages in showing the program at the end of the session rather than at the start. Most importantly much of the advice offered in the video presentation will be identical with that which has been generated during the group and plenary discussion. In this case students have their personal interpretations reinforced by an authoritative confirmation. When advice conflicts with what students have decided for themselves, then the individual is 'strong' enough to reject it — or modify it — with the benefit of the previous peer group support.

There is a fairly strong indication that the format of the Strathclyde series of videotapes (as opposed to the Auckland format described earlier) may be the more suitable as a final stage of the workshop format. This may be because they *are* more authoritative in approach, or possibly because many of the participants in these particular workshops are mature students, and identify more readily with a staff member than they do with students. Whatever the reason, the objections to didactic presentations from authority figures which were outlined earlier do not necessarily seem to hold when the videotapes are only one element of a total program as outlined.

CONCLUSION

In summary then, the credibility of a video presentation is linked very closely to the image of the presenter, the nature of the information which is communicated and the context in which the video is used.

On the one hand we may have information which is objective and impersonal; on the other we may have a message which is value-laden and which each viewer will need to interpret in terms of personal circumstances — such as advice on how to cope with the stresses of university studies. With hard and objective information, successful communication simply(!) consists of presenting the message clearly, in a fashion which is intelligible, in a cognitive sense, for the audience. Presentations are best made by a person who is obviously an authority on the particular topic. There are problems though when the message is of the second kind, and these can be summarized as follows:

1. There is *some* information/advice which can usefully be offered and the aim of the video program is to have viewers consider this seriously and critically.
2. If an authority figure is used to make the presentation, then the advice may be rejected because the authority is obviously not currently in the position of the viewer. ('How can a staff member possibly understand the particular problems which *I*, a student, am experiencing?')
3. If *peers* are used to deliver the advice, then the advice may well be rejected because they *are* peers. ('Why should a fellow student know better than I how to cope? It may work for them, but why for me?')

If video is to be used effectively, as the sole means of communicating such advice, then a synthesis of authority and peer is probably needed. This was the approach which was used in producing the Auckland study skills series, as described above, and it has proved quite successful. But to produce video material which can be used effectively as free-standing presentation is very time consuming — and it is almost certainly not the most effective use for the medium. When videotapes are used as elements in workshops then this is much more satisfactory. This is particularly the case when they are used to confirm (and challenge) the principles and interpretations which participants have constructed for themselves in structured group sessions.

Notes and references

1. Winterbourne, R & Jones, J (1981) *Suggestions on Studying and Sitting Examinations*, HERO, University of Auckland, Auckland.
2. Gibbs, G (1977) *A Guide to Running Group Sessions*, IET, The Open University, Milton Keynes.

ACKNOWLEDGEMENTS

My grateful thanks to all the staff and students who helped in the production of the videotapes; with particular thanks to Richard Smith, Judy Tierney and Chris Watson.

16. The Use of Trigger Films as a Stimulus for Affective Learning

David Boud and
Margot Pearson

SUMMARY

Trigger films consist of short, high-impact vignettes which aim to stimulate learning. This paper examines ways in which learning activities can be designed around trigger films to enhance their use in situations dealing with affective learning. An example of the use of these films in a first-year undergraduate course in introductory clinical studies illustrates this and focuses on classroom activities exploring intrapersonal and interpersonal issues. Some difficulties which tutors experience in using trigger films are discussed and related to general problems of experiential activities. Finally, guidelines for the production of trigger material are presented.[1]

INTRODUCTION

Videotape is a medium that has great potential as an educational resource: the problem is how to exploit it without the resource itself determining methods and style of instruction. It is important that teachers be able to respond flexibly and sensitively to the needs of their students and to deploy educational resources which are flexible in use.

Films and video programs are commonly used to capture and bring reality into the classroom, usually in some form of documentary. They are an excellent substitute for classroom activity; they present a well made product of high quality and coherence; but they are often too long and present the well developed view of the producer. In the area of affective learning such limitations can outweigh the many advantages of the medium. There is a need to introduce the complexity and immediacy of the real world, the visual impact, the movement, the verbal and non-verbal interaction, but in a way that stimulates students to reflect on and to analyse incidents, events and their own reactions, as is seldom possible in the rush of the environment outside the classroom.

This paper looks at one way in which videotape can be subordinated to the functional needs of teaching for affective change by using it as a small but vital component of a variety of classroom activities. It examines, in particular, one of the ways in which the advantages of the medium can be exploited to enhance the impact of learning: the trigger film.

Trigger films or videorecorded triggers[2] have a different purpose from most films and they possess special characteristics. The aim of this paper is to consider the nature of trigger films and to discuss their use in education. It is based upon the experience of staff at the Tertiary Education Research Centre at the University of New South Wales where these types of film have been developed since 1971.[3] It draws on their use in a course for first-year medical students — introductory clinical studies. This context is used to illustrate some more general points about their use in teaching.

WHAT IS A TRIGGER FILM?

The trigger film belongs to a class of educational materials whose aim is to stimulate or provoke learning. These films are not a learning experience in their own right but provide a means of initiating a subsequent activity. They are typically short, high-emotional-impact vignettes designed to trigger a response in the viewer. They are not primarily informative, discursive or instructive. Compared with most film material they appear incomplete and unresolved. This style aims to place the viewer in the position of active learner by presenting incidents which demand a response, emotionally as well as intellectually, to encourage self-reflection and personal engagement in the incident portrayed.

Fisch (1972) attributes the origin of trigger films to the French psychologist Séat-Cohen and its development to the US Air Force, the Film Board of Canada and the University of Michigan Department of Gerontology. At the University of New South Wales, triggers have been produced for a variety of contexts, for the professional development of university teachers (Powell, 1977, 1978), to train nurses and doctors in interpersonal skills, and to help public (civil) service personnel in dealing with the general public.

A CASE STUDY

In the faculty of medicine at UNSW, first-year students take a course concerned with communication skills, awareness of oneself and others, and various social issues in medicine.

Each tutor works with a group of 10 students. They meet once a week for two or three hours. There is no formal syllabus and the content of the course is decided by each tutor in conjunction with each group of students. Many of the normal teaching constraints such as examinations are missing and therefore the course comprises activities which are designed to meet the actual needs of the group. It was within this context that the trigger films were used.[4] Not all tutors used them and the ways in which they were used varied considerably from group to group, even with the same tutor. This was an ideal context in which to examine the range of applicability of trigger films.

In 1978 we conducted an evaluation of the use of these triggers in the course. Attention was paid to the ways in which the trigger films were used and the learning activities surrounding them as well as characteristics of the trigger films themselves. Fifteen out of 23 tutors were either interviewed at length, completed an open-ended questionnaire or engaged in a telephone conversation using the questionnaire items as foci. No attempt was made to gain an exhaustive sample or to obtain consensus about various issues. The aim of the exercise was to explore in depth the varieties of use of the trigger material and to examine the tutors' views about these films.

A series of six episodes was available to the tutors. These portrayed doctors in various situations with:

☐ a relative of a patient about to be bereaved
☐ a patient who expresses uncertainty about the doctor's competency and is unwilling to accept medical advice
☐ a patient expressing gratitude
☐ a patient who is outraged by a diagnosis because of social prejudice
☐ a patient who rejects the implication that he is a hypochondriac
☐ a patient gravely concerned about the prospect of an operation.

These vignettes were presented to students who were then asked for the most suitable response the doctor could make in the situation. Typically the tutors devoted one or two sessions of about two hours to a selection of from two to six episodes.

FORMS OF USE

An analysis of the tutors' report indicated three main forms of use in a course which aims to develop the social sensitivity and interpersonal skills of intending doctors:

1. *To provide an introduction to the course.* The triggers were used to illustrate the kinds of problem with which the course would deal. They were often shown in one of the first meetings of the year by way of orientation to the issues of the course.
2. *To raise general issues.* Certain basic issues are a part of all medical practice: the kinds of relationship between doctor and patient, patients' expectations of doctors, the influence of feelings and emotions in consultations, and so on. The triggers were used to increase awareness of these and similar matters, and to initiate discussion on various ways of dealing with them.
3. *To focus on the personal responses of students.* When used for this purpose the triggers provided a means by which students could explore their own feelings about the doctor's role and behaviour and to initiate experiential activities in which students would role-play various situations and examine their own responses in a direct manner. The emphasis in this case was on experiencing rather than talking about issues.

The latter two purposes are of more general interest. They represent two aspects of a broad range of use relating to both personal and professional issues and focusing on these in the context of interpersonal, community and societal problems. The tutor can arrange to attend to either the personal or professional dimension and to examine the impact of various issues either in terms of the effect on the person as a person, or in terms of the person's professional role. For example, a vignette showing a doctor talking with the son of a dying patient can be used in many ways to focus on the following issues: the way our society deals with death and dying, community provision for grieving people, the kinds of response to expressions of grief appropriately made by helping professionals, or the personal reactions of the viewer to the topic (or indeed any combination of these matters).

We can draw a spectrum to represent a range of classroom activities which might be used in association with the trigger film (Figure 1).

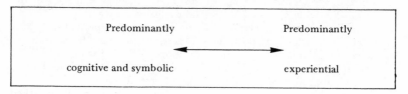

Figure 1. *Spectrum of classroom activities*

So, for example, purely intellectual discussions of matters outside the direct experience of students might be found towards the left of the spectrum, whilst those activities which are intended to impinge directly on the self, involving concern of values, interpersonal relationships and self-esteem, might be found towards the right.

The classroom activities which are deployed in conjunction with the trigger film need to be selected so that they are appropriate for the examination of the kinds of issue on which the tutor wishes to focus. The experienced tutor will select both trigger film and surrounding classroom activity so that they are compatible with the aims he or she wishes to pursue, and the extent to which the experience of individual students is to be developed. Some kinds of learning activity will not be available for the tutor to use unless he or she has had direct personal experience of the whole range of potential methods and is confident in their use.

PROBLEMS IN USE

Even where the tutor is confident and experienced the student group itself will influence what activities and issues will be appropriate. The tutors identified problems which inhibited some uses of the trigger films with their students:

1. There are different levels of readiness amongst students to appreciate the issues which are illustrated in the triggers. Some incidents are so far outside the direct experience of the students that they perceive the episode as artificial and contrived even though it may represent a common event in medical practice. The greater the authenticity of the trigger material the more likely it is that these problems will be minimized, but some aspects of lack of experience of the world

cannot be substituted by the use of any media.

2. There are classroom norms which inhibit acknowledgement of feeling and emotion to be overcome. The tacit rules of classroom behaviour legitimize intellectual discourse at the expense of personal expression. If in other teaching situations feeling and emotion are suppressed it is more difficult to gain access to this dimension of students' response if the context — classroom, tutor, course — is seen to be similar.

3. Some students are not able to cope readily with the expression of emotion shown in these trigger films. Partly through embarrassment and awkwardness, some students take a lot of time and encouragement to appreciate the non-cognitive component of the interactions which are portrayed. This is compounded by the tacit norms mentioned above. It makes it more difficult for the tutor to deploy experiential activities to follow up trigger films without additional preparation and orientation for students.

All of this is clearer if we take one case as an example. In the episode about the bereaved son, the son is interviewed by a surgeon after an unsuccessful operation on his mother. The son, a young man of 20 or so years, reacts to the bad news with despair and is clearly on the brink of crying. The immediate question posed by the trigger film is: what would you, the viewer, do if you were the surgeon faced with the distressed son? The ways in which prior and subsequent classroom activity is structured here will depend greatly on the intended focus of the tutor and the group and the readiness of both parties to handle the issues. It may only be possible or desirable to discuss at a general level the rituals associated with bereavement. It may be important and appropriate for the students to explore immediately their own emotional response to the incident. Only in certain situations can the necessary conditions for experiential exploration of deeply personal reactions be found, but in many circumstances it would be possible to recreate through role-play interactions between doctor and patient to examine more general issues concerning the role of the doctor in that incident.

A scenario which further illustrates these points concerning the effective use of trigger films in the experiential learning context is given as an appendix. Examples of their use when dealing with cognitive or non-personal issues are more commonplace and the reader will be able to think of the many uses without further discussion.[5] On the basis of our experience and our evaluation of the use of trigger films, we would suggest the following list of conditions under which they might be used with maximum effect. There should be:

☐ a climate of trust and openness in the group, both amongst the students and between the students and tutor
☐ a willingness to disclose feelings and personal reactions as well as intellectual ideas
☐ the presence of a facilitative tutor — one who, in particular, can establish the two previous conditions as norms of the group
☐ an informal setting
☐ a relatively small number of students (less than 12). The numbers

should be small enough so that everyone is able to contribute.

Under less favourable conditions they can still be used, but probably only in the issue-raising mode discussed previously (Boud & Pearson, 1981).

GUIDELINES FOR PRODUCTION

Some guidelines have been developed for trigger film production. These arose from our experience in making triggers for both teaching and testing.

1. The trigger should be very short (less than two minutes) and the content simple and not laboured.
2. The trigger must appear to be a real situation for the viewer.
3. The trigger must finish relatively abruptly with as little interaction between the persons portrayed as is necessary for the subject (patient) to indicate his or her affect and concern.
4. The professional (doctor) must not appear to be committed to any particular course of action. The viewers should not be cued in to any response to the affect or concern other than that which they generate themselves. (This point is very important and one of the techniques used for this was to shoot the scene focusing on the patient with only sufficient intervention from the doctor to allow the incident to unfold.)

These guidelines are compatible with Fisch (1972).

To produce trigger films according to these specifications requires a certain amount of imagination and experiment. A balance needs to be drawn between the constraints of time and money on one side and the need to produce an authentic product on the other. In our case the scripts were suggested and improvised by groups of medics, educationists and students. They were rehearsed a few times and then committed to film. The situations were real, but it was sometimes difficult to transpose a feeling of reality to film; sometimes, quite simply, it is difficult to believe that certain events are not contrived without experiencing them yourself.

One factor which compounds the problem of evaluating the trigger films is the anxieties about expression of feeling which students can sometimes experience. These can easily be displaced into complaints about the accuracy, reality and quality of the triggers. Judging trigger films on the basis of immediate student reaction may not be valid because of this and it is important that there are no inherent grounds for complaint: verisimilitude is of vital importance. This does suggest an argument for trigger material which is culture- and context-specific although not necessarily course-specific.

It would be relatively easy for teachers with access to video equipment to make their own triggers, using videotape. Zuber (1978) for example, produced video triggers with faculty at the University of Frankfurt. If triggers were made for specific situations then many of the criticisms of lack of verisimilitude could be met as students would be less likely to compare the products with those that they see on television or in the cinema.

Whether teachers use their own material or not, and whether they use trigger films to start discussions of social or personal issues or not, the material will demand the active involvement of students. Our view is that they are most potent in focusing on the personal and interpersonal aspects of learning because they bypass inappropriate intellectualization. They demand an immediate human response which may subsequently be reflected upon. An added value of trigger films is that they are sufficiently flexible for teachers to be able to guide any exploration to suit the readiness of themselves and the group.

CONCLUSION

This study has identified ways in which appropriately used trigger films can form an important component in a teaching program. They provide a stimulus for students to explore their own interpersonal and intra-personal responses to real-life situations without the distractions of a complex, external environment.

APPENDIX

The use of trigger films in the experiential mode: a scenario
The following suggests some ways in which trigger films may be used experientially to focus on the personal responses of students. It provides an example of one way in which some of the problems of use identified earlier in the case study can be overcome.

Introduction. The room is already set out so that it is easy for students to move around and change seats. The tutor outlines the purpose of the exercise:

> You will see a very brief film which stops abruptly in mid-sequence. It will portray a situation between two or more people and you should look at it first from the point of view of the professional (doctor). The film may appear a little artificial or the situation a little contrived but you should not get concerned about this. It is a reconstruction of an actual occurrence. The aim is for each one of you to become aware of your own feelings, thoughts and reactions in the situation shown. There are no 'right' answers, what is important is your awareness of your own response.

Optional activity. Prior to showing the trigger the tutor may introduce some experiential exercises to heighten awareness: bodily experience, relaxation, communication exercises, and so on. The purpose of this is to orient students to the immediate situation and to enhance a climate of trust and relaxation.

Division into pairs. Either shortly before or after showing the film.

Show trigger. Warning: 'The film is short and there are no captions to signal the end of the scene.'

Tutor. 'Imagine that you were in that situation — how you would feel, how you would react. Pause and consider your own response — not what you should feel, but what you do feel.' The students can either write down their response or respond directly to the person with whom they are paired. In the pairs the students take turns expressing their reactions whilst their partner listens supportively.

Optional activity. Students give sympathetic feedback to each other and discuss reactions before returning to total group.

In the total group (or subgroups if numbers are greater). The tutor elicits individual reactions (to the situation, not the qualities of the trigger film or the acting) and invites students to role-play the situation, stressing the value of role play in involving the person in exploring actual responses rather than imagined or projected ones, and providing by his or her manner the confidence and trust in the students that they can engage in this activity. Students must freely elect to take part without compulsion or authority pressure.

The original scene is role-played and various alternative responses played through. Feedback from other students is invited at various stages to focus on the situation portrayed and their personal response to both the professional and client roles, not to the other students' performances as actors.

As many scenes are played as are suggested within the overall time constraints.

Discussion. The exercise is discussed in the group with the tutor high-lighting certain observations. The tutor may conclude with a brief theoretical input drawing upon the immediate past experiences in the group. The tutor is conscious throughout that some personal distress might have become manifest. The tutor in this situation should have the personal skills which would enable him or her to provide appropriate support.

Notes

1. This is a revised version of an article published in *Programmed Learning and Educational Technology*, Vol 16, No 1, February 1979, pp 52-56, reproduced with the kind permission of the journal's editor and the authors.
2. In the following the term 'trigger film' is used whether the vignettes were produced on film or videotape. The use of the vignettes in the classroom, or with a small group of people, is easier and more practical when replayed on videocassette; the tape can be rewound quickly for repeated viewing of the whole episode or of a particular part, or of several parts, of it. In the latter case the counter on the videorecorder is a useful means to locate the scene which the discussion leader or participant(s) want(s) the discussion to focus on. The room need not be darkened each time as is necessary when projecting a film on a screen. Storage is easier, too. However, the

film version has other advantages. In particular, it can be projected on a large screen to maximize impact. Although many triggers are video productions, the term 'trigger *film*' continues to be used, because of its origin on celluloid film. No attempts are made to change the term to 'video triggers' or other terms related to videotape or cassette rather than film.

3. Information about trigger films produced by TERC is available from: Tertiary Education Research Centre, University of New South Wales, PO Box 1, Kensington, NSW 2033, Australia. They are also available for preview in the UK through: Film Officer, New South Wales House, 66 The Strand, London WC2N 5LZ.

4. The original use in this situation arose out of the need for a test to help evaluate the effectiveness of the course. The test focused on the student's ability to respond appropriately to expressions of emotion in doctor-patient interactions. An account of the test development is available elsewhere (Pearson *et al*, 1978).

5. More examples are discussed in Boud and Pearson (1981).

REFERENCES

Boud, D & Pearson, M (1981) 'Bringing reality into the classroom: the use of trigger films in introducing socio-emotional aspects of learning in the health sciences', in Parsons, R (ed), *Policy Process, Content and Research in Health Science Education*, Proceedings of the Fourth National Health Science Education Conference, Cumberland College of Health Sciences, Sydney, 818-24.

Fisch, A L (1972) 'The trigger film technique', *Improving College and University Teaching*, **20**, 4, 286-89.

Pearson, M, McNeill, P, Magarey, C, Powell, J & Sowerbutts, T (1978) 'The production and evaluation of film materials to assess the interpersonal communication skills of medical students', *Research and Development Paper* 53, Tertiary Education Research Centre, University of New South Wales, Sydney.

Powell, J P (1977) 'The use of trigger films in developing teaching skills', in Elton, L & Simmonds, K (eds) *Staff Development in Higher Education*, Society for Research into Higher Education, Guildford, 138.

Powell, J P (1978) 'The production and evaluation of film material for use in staff development programmes for tertiary teachers', *Research and Development Paper* 52, Tertiary Education Research Centre, University of New South Wales, Sydney.

Zuber, O (1978) 'Trigger Filme als Diskussionsanreger im Hochschulunterricht' (Trigger films as a stimulus to discussion in university education), *Deutsche Universitätszeitung* (1 December), Frankfurt, 728-29.

17. Tutored Videotape Instruction: A New Use of Electronics Media in Education

James F Gibbons,
William R Kincheloe and
Kenneth S Down

SUMMARY

Tutored videotape instruction (TVI) is a teaching method which makes use of unrehearsed, unedited videotapes of regular classroom courses. TVI is most effective when a small group of students watch and discuss the videotape with a (para-professional) tutor. It is less effective for a single student, with or without a tutor. The authors have developed a set of guidelines for the application of video technology to education, and in a number of studies have evaluated the educational effectiveness of the TVI format compared with in-class instruction and live television in engineering and science courses at Stanford University.[1]

INTRODUCTION

In the early 1920s, shortly after radio broadcasting was proved to be economically feasible, Robert Hutchins is said to have predicted that this new technology would undoubtedly have a dramatic impact on education. Subsequent events have shown that his assessment of the educational potential of radio was probably correct but, for a variety of reasons, the potential did not materialize. In the early 1950s instructional television was introduced with a similar fanfare. However, with a few notable exceptions, its potential also failed to materialize. It seems that more recent innovations such as computer-aided instruction and satellite-based educational delivery may come to a similar fate. Why is it that these technological aids to education seldom seem to live up to their potential?

There is of course a different set of reasons in each case, though inconstant financing and the competition with commercial interests are surely among the most pervasive. However, important as these factors are, there seems to be a still more basic problem. The proponents of media-based education describe this problem as a failure of the educational establishment to involve itself seriously with instructional technology. As a result, they say, the changes in the design of the educational system that must be made before instructional technologies can be used effectively have not been forthcoming. This is a valid criticism. However, the educational establishment makes a counter-argument that is also true. The devices of instructional technology are too inflexible. Effective classroom teachers regularly capitalize on unexpected, unplanned opportunities for the achievement of specific goals. As Jackson (1968) says:

Stray thoughts, sudden insights, meandering digressions and other unpredicted events constantly ruffle the smoothness of the instructional dialogue. In most classrooms, as every teacher knows, the path of educational progress could be more easily traced by a butterfly than by a bullet.

Jackson concludes from this that education is best served by tools that can be readily adapted to a wide variety of educational tasks with a minimum of advance planning. Compared to most electronics media, blackboards and books provide at low cost an impressive degree of flexibility. Furthermore, after honest efforts to use electronics media over an extended period of time, many teachers have been unable to see a clear improvement in learning. Hence, electronics media are generally judged by teachers to be inappropriate educational tools for most circumstances.

TUTORED VIDEOTAPE INSTRUCTION

If we accept these criticisms as valid, we are led to seek out ways of using those media that will have the desired flexibility without requiring a major change in teaching styles, and to apply them to situations where the changes in the educational system that are necessary to accommodate them can be easily made. In this article we describe a new technique for using videotaped educational materials that seems to meet these criteria. The method makes use of unrehearsed, unedited videotapes of regular classroom courses, which can be produced at very low cost. The videotapes are used for the instruction of small groups of students (typically three to 10) who are assisted by para-professional tutors as they watch the tape. For this reason, the method is called tutored videotape instruction (TVI).

The TVI method was originally developed to provide course work in science and engineering to off-campus graduate students enrolled at Stanford University. It is based on the commonsense notion that students can learn more from a lecture if they are free to interrupt it at places where they need more discussion or explanation of a point or concept. Experience over the past three years shows that students learn best when the videotaped lectures are stopped frequently (for example, every five to 10 minutes, for periods of three to five minutes). Interactions of such frequency and duration are, of course, impracticable in a conventional classroom situation. Also, TVI is most effective when a small group of students and the tutor watch the tape together. It is less effective for a single student, with or without a tutor.

The TVI technique responds to the educational needs of the students by combining the positive features of lectures with those of small group discussions. The lectures provide for depth and continuity in the subject-matter, while the tutorial discussions afford a means of making the lectures respond to individual needs and differences. Students watching the videotaped lectures feel free to ask questions of both the tutor and each other, and to make spontaneous comments about points of interest. In addition, the TVI students hear the comments that were

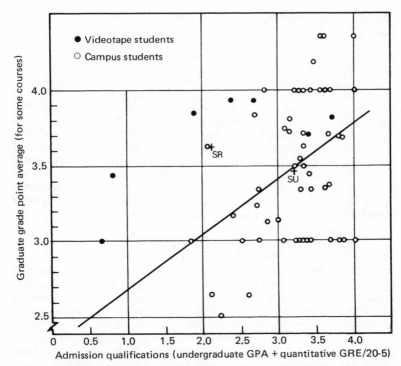

Figure 1. *Results of tutored videotape instruction experiment (October 1973 to March 1974)*

made and the questions that were asked in the classroom at the time the videotape was recorded, and thus profit from those exchanges as well. In effect, the TVI format permits the students and the tutor to manage the lecture themselves and thereby create an intellectually stimulating environment which enhances learning and creates a positive attitude towards the subject.

Although the program to be described relies heavily on the use of video technology, that is probably not its most distinctive feature. Rather, the technology permits us to concentrate attention on some of the most important parameters in the learning process and to begin to understand their effects more precisely. What has been found seems to be applicable in a wide variety of circumstances. It extends well beyond university lecture courses and is in some ways independent of whether or not technological aids are used in the instruction process.

The program was designed to utilize insofar as possible the experience which has been gained over the past two decades concerning the question of how technology can be used most successfully in education. An attempt to summarize this experience led Gibbons (1973) to develop a set of guidelines that could assist educators in planning for the appropriate use of technology in education.

Because those guidelines form the basis of the program to be discussed, it is useful to begin with a brief discussion of them.

GUIDELINES FOR THE APPLICATION OF TECHNOLOGY TO EDUCATION

Current interest in the use of technological aids to education (particularly television) stems from the late 1940s and early 1950s when, following the widespread development of commercial television, the Ford Foundation and later the federal government funded a variety of experiments to study the possible impact of television on the educational process. These experiments included a complete range of educational institutions from elementary school to university, and took as their major emphasis the question of whether students could learn as well from television as from conventional classroom teaching. Surveying the results of 421 experiments carried out from 1950 to 1960, Chu and Schramm (1967) concluded that, across all grade levels from kindergarten through a baccalaureate degree, and for essentially all types of subject-matter, students could learn as well from television as from conventional instruction.

Viewed in its most positive light, this result suggests that access to education can be expanded substantially by communications technology, and indeed this policy has been urged by educational study groups and implemented by both private and public educational institutions for some time, and at substantial expense. However, the educational effectiveness of classroom instruction is itself a matter of increasing concern, and in this light a finding of 'no significant difference in effect between television instruction and the regular classroom' does not provide a forceful stimulus to promote the application of communications technology to educational problems.

This raises the question of whether educational technology has ever established a clear-cut superiority over in-class instruction. From a comparison of some of the most successful ventures in educational technology (such as 'Sesame Street', Chicago City TV College, the Open University in Britain, the Australian School of the Air, and the Bavarian Telecollege) with some of the least successful ventures, we attempted to abstract a set of guidelines that would describe the conditions that seem most likely to ensure a successful application of technology to education. These guidelines, while they may need further refinement and modification, do provide a useful starting point for designing new programs.

The guidelines are as follows:

1. The educational program should be planned for a specific audience.
2. Specific educational objectives that are relevant to the needs and interests of the audience should be clearly defined.
3. Technologies should be chosen in terms of the topic to be presented. Frequently, different technologies are used to present different parts of a course, the choice being determined from a consideration of which technology is most effective for the material being presented. It is desirable (though also expensive) to use both knowledge and media specialists to prepare and produce the programs.
4. Educators who have a clear interest in learning and using the instructional characteristics of various media should be selected and trained.

5. Clear and careful provision should be made for personal interaction, especially among the students.
6. Evaluation and feedback over a period of months or years should be used to monitor the educational effectiveness of the program, and the instructional materials and methods should be changed accordingly.

From the standpoint of educational effectiveness, the guideline that is perhaps most frequently overlooked is the one relating to personal interaction, especially where the use of television is concerned. Television (including lectures that are videotaped for subsequent playback) is most frequently used as a direct substitute for live lectures in large classes or as a means for individuals to view lectures or programs at sites that are remote from the point of origin. These applications are developed primarily to solve problems of cost and access, the assumption being made that courses delivered by television will be as effective as conventional education. However, the experiments that led to this conclusion tested only factual information gained over a relatively brief period. Furthermore, these experiments identified some characteristic weaknesses of television as an educational medium. In particular, as noted by Schramm (1971), television does not stop to answer questions; it does not readily permit classroom discussion; it is an inefficient medium for conducting drill; it does not adjust very well to individual differences; and it tends to encourage a passive form of learning.

These are very serious weaknesses. They can be reduced to some degree by using radio talkback to connect remote sites to the television classroom, or by establishing a regular telephone contact between students and faculty, as has been done by the Chicago TV College and others. However, these techniques for promoting student-faculty interaction do not really remedy the major weaknesses described above. It is critically important for students to be able to stop a lecture or a program when they have questions, and it is highly desirable for it to remain stopped long enough for the question to be clearly answered. It is also highly desirable that the answers to the most important questions be developed as a result of active discussion within a small group of students. Finally, it is important that questions and discussions be used to determine background deficiencies of individual students, so that remedial action can be taken.

The major weaknesses of live television (including videotapes that are simply replayed from start to finish) are related to the fact that it cannot provide the quality of personal interaction that is available in a good classroom. The TVI intellectual community, consisting of a small group of students, an on-site para-professional tutor, and a course faculty member, was invented in an attempt to circumvent these deficiencies. What we seek to do is to provide small groups of students with the high-quality personal interaction that they need in order to learn effectively. What we have found is that TVI can provide a means of achieving this goal.

EXPERIMENTS WITH TVI

We have carried out a number of experiments to evaluate the educational effectiveness of the TVI format. All the experiments to be discussed have been concerned with the delivery of engineering and science courses where the objectivity of the material makes it relatively easy to measure the effectiveness of the method. We believe the method can be extended to a much larger range of subjects and audiences, but there are insufficient data available at present to permit us to define this range of applications with any accuracy. Our description of experiments is therefore intended primarily to provide some general ideas about how the TVI format can be set up and evaluated.

The TVI technique was originally conceived as a means of providing courses to off-campus engineering students employed at a Hewlett-Packard (HP) plant in Santa Rosa, California, about 100 miles north of Stanford. The HP management wished to provide the same educational opportunities to these students as were available to HP employees (and those of other companies) at plants near Stanford where engineering courses given on campus are televised to plants within a 50-mile radius of the university by the Stanford Instructional Television Fixed Service (ITFS) network. The ITFS students also have an audio talkback connection that permits them to ask questions of the instructor while the class is in progress.

Since the courses of interest were already being televised, it was a simple matter to videotape the classes live with no further production requirements. It should be noted that an operating TV system is not a prerequisite for the TVI technique, though it was very helpful in this case because it both facilitated the initial experiments and made possible a thorough comparison between the regular TV students and the videotape students.

It was intended from the outset that satisfactory performance in the courses would result in credit toward a master's degree in electrical engineering from Stanford. Therefore, the Santa Rose students were required to complete the same homework as students on campus, all their papers being graded by the same teaching assistant who graded the papers of the on-campus and regular TV students, and the off-campus students were required to come to the campus to take the same examinations as the on-campus students.

PROGRAM DESIGN FOR THE SANTA ROSA EXPERIMENT

The main features of the program developed for the Santa Rosa experiment can be described in terms of the guidelines listed above.

1. The audience consists of industrially-based students carrying full-time job responsibilities. In some cases the students were studying for a master's degree before they were moved to Santa Rosa and had academic qualifications that were essentially identical to those of on-campus students, but students at Santa Rosa whose academic credentials were known to be inadequate for admission to

the Stanford graduate school were also included.

2. In defining the educational objectives, we knew that the students were interested in graduate training leading to a master's degree. A clearly important factor in their success was that their employer shared this objective, in both its financial and academic aspects.

3. The technology used, half-inch reel-to-reel videotapes, was chosen to permit the clear reconstruction of a given TV frame at the remote sites. The videotapes were of live classes made by a trained student production staff as the class was being conducted. The classroom modifications that are necessary for this purpose are described by Pettit and Grace (1970). Basically, the studio classrooms are organized to interfere as little as possible with the teaching styles and preferences of the instructors.

The videotapes are mailed to Santa Rosa along with class notes, homework assignments, and other materials that are handed out to the on-campus students. The tapes and homework are returned to Stanford in approximately one week. When necessary, the TVI tutors telephone the on-campus faculty after the videotapes have been watched to discuss problems and obtain supplementary material.

4. The educational staff whose courses are to be televised are given a brief training session to acquaint them with the capabilities of the television network and to offer suggestions concerning how these capabilities can be used effectively (how to organize blackboard space, use of a desk pad as an alternative to the blackboard, preparations of demonstrations, and so on).

In addition, Stanford staff members who are responsible for the TVI program visit each site to choose the tutors (from among the company's staff) and to instruct them in the use of the videotape as an educational medium. An alternative that is now being explored is to use as tutors staff members from local educational institutions who have indicated an interest in the program.

In most instances, the tutors are practising engineers without prior experience in teaching. They are chosen primarily on the basis of two criteria: (a) a sensitivity to students and an ability to draw them into a fruitful discussion of issues, and (b) a personal interest in reviewing the subject to be presented. Other criteria, such as recent exposure to the course with evidence of high-quality performance, have been found to be less important.

The tutor's main functions are: (a) to initiate and encourage stopping the videotape playback for the immediate resolution of problems; (b) to answer, if possible, questions that cannot be resolved by the class; and (c) to obtain answers and supplementary material from the on-campus instructor if necessary. Tutors are also encouraged to visit the on-campus faculty once or twice a quarter to become familiar with the course syllabus and to discuss any recurring problems that their students have. The tutor is not responsible for grading homework or assigning course grades.

5. Students and tutors are urged to stop the videotape whenever they have problems or questions or whenever some particularly important concept has been presented. Certain obvious cues are frequently

used by the tutor to initiate these discussions. For example, each time a substantive question arises in the on-campus class, the tape is stopped and the TVI class attempts to generate the answer before the taped lecture proceeds.

In addition to extensive group interaction during the lectures, students are encouraged to discuss problems with each other and with the tutor outside the viewing period. Since the tutors and students are known to each other through their common employment, there is ample opportunity for them to do so.

6. Careful records are maintained of TVI student performance on both homework and examinations. Their performance is regularly compared with that of regular students in the campus classroom and local off-campus students receiving the same courses by way of ITFS.

The homework and test performance of the TVI students is analysed by the Stanford TVI staff and the results are discussed with the tutors by telephone. Corrective measures are suggested when necessary. In addition, course evaluation questionnaires are given to the TVI students in order to assess their attitudes and reactions to the program.

INITIAL EXPERIMENTAL RESULTS

After the first two quarters of operation, the TVI experimental program was evaluated by comparing the course performance of the TVI students to that of both the on-campus students and the HP students taking the same courses by live television. One result of this evaluation is shown in Figure 1, which is drawn from data gathered during the autumn and winter quarters of the 1973-74 school year. This figure shows the grade point averages of the TVI students for all courses taken under the program plotted against their admission qualifications, the latter being a composite of corrected undergraduate grade point averages (GPAs) and the quantitative component of the graduate record examination (GRE) score. (The correction to the undergraduate GPA was based on prior history of performance of students from the same school in doing graduate work at Stanford.) Also shown in Figure 1 are similar data for on-campus graduate students taking the same courses as the TVI students. The regression line shows the best linear least-means-square fit to the on-campus student data, from which the average expected performance may be obtained for a student with given qualifications.

It is apparent from Figure 1 that as a group the TVI students outperformed their on-campus counterparts; that is, the average GPA of the TVI students (represented by the point labelled SR in Figure 1) is higher than that of the on-campus students (labelled SU), even though the average of the admission qualification scores for the TVI students is substantially lower than that of the on-campus students. To make a more refined observation, it is convenient to divide the TVI students into two groups: those with admission qualification scores $\gtrsim 2$, who could have been admitted to the university as regular graduate students, and those with admission qualification scores substantially < 2 who would not have been so admitted. In terms of these sub-groups, the data show that:

1. The sub-group that would have been granted admission did extremely well; in fact, their performance was essentially independent of their actual admission qualification scores.
2. The two students with the lowest qualification scores did quite acceptable work (B or better) even though they could not have been admitted to the Stanford Graduate School based solely on their admissions data. However, on the basis of their continued record of acceptable TVI performance, these students were subsequently admitted to the university and have now completed the master's degree program with creditable performance.

In Figure 2, the grades of the TVI students are compared with those of the on-campus students and those of the students receiving the same courses by ITFS. The 302 on-campus students achieved a GPA of 3.38 out of a possible 4.00 which is typical of graduate electrical engineering students at the master's level. The students participating in the same courses by ITFS with audio talkback capability to the classroom had a GPA of 3.19, still quite acceptable but nonetheless below the on-campus students by almost a third of a grade point. This result is made even more remarkable when we recall that several of the TVI students had marginal academic qualifications that would have made their admission to the Stanford graduate program very unlikely. It is also interesting to note that the performance of students at Santa Rosa

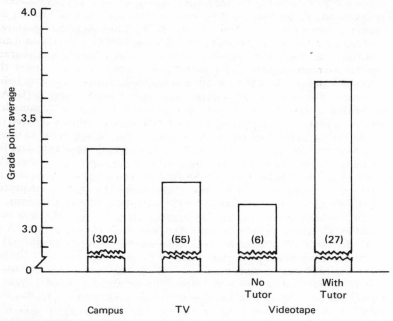

Figure 2. *Results of tutored videotape instruction experiment (October 1973 to March 1974)*

in the videotape courses without local tutors was substantially below that of all the other groups, although the data in this case is very limited.

The total number of courses taken by students studying from videotape without a tutor is so small that the result has no statistical significance. However, a similar result has been obtained recently by Anderson (1977) in a much larger experiment. In particular he finds that both student satisfaction and course performance tend to decrease as the delivery method is changed from on-campus lecture to live TV to non-tutored videotape.

It is sometimes argued that the industrial experience of the TVI students accounts for their outstanding performance in these courses; but the TVI students are drawn from the same population as the students studying by ITFS whom they out-performed, so industrial experience or motivation cannot account for these results. Furthermore, other experiments show that on-campus TVI students also out-perform on-campus students who attend the regular lectures.

It is also natural to question the degree to which the results may be due to a 'Hawthorne' effect. However, the Santa Rosa TVI students have continued their superior performance for three years.

CONTINUATION OF THE TVI INDUSTRIAL PROGRAM

Because of the initially encouraging results with the Santa Rosa industrial TVI students, the university gave permission to continue the program and to incorporate TVI courses into an accredited graduate degree program. New students at the Santa Rosa plant of Hewlett Packard entered the program in both 1974 and 1975; and the program was further extended to include Hewlett Packard plants in San Diego and Boise and the Sandia facility in Albuquerque.

At the end of the 1975 to 1976 school year, after three years of operation, a total of 1,803 quarter-units (approximately 600 courses) of graded course work, plus a considerable number of ungraded seminars, have been completed by 82 TVI students, with 65 different tutors having been involved in the program. The overall GPA of the TVI students for this work is 3.37. If we exclude from this group students whose academic qualifications were below those normally required for Stanford admission, the GPA rises to 3.59 compared to an on-campus average of 3.43 for the same courses. In other words, the TVI students who are qualified for regular admission (48 students) have continued to out-perform the on-campus students; and the poorly qualified TVI students have continued to do very acceptable work.

On the basis of these results it seems reasonable to conclude that, for science and engineering courses, the TVI format is at least as good as the other methods of delivery with which it has been compared. We believe the method can be used successfully for other types of courses, though we have no data to support this hypothesis. We have, however, used the technique in two on-campus experiments to determine whether full-time graduate students could also benefit from TVI.

ON-CAMPUS TVI EXPERIMENTS

The first of these experiments was performed over two successive quarters in a graduate electrical engineering course that was large enough that several TVI groups, varying in size and with different tutors, could be formed for comparison with the large live lecture class. The course was taught by a faculty member who had already established a reputation as a particularly effective instructor for both regular classes and off-campus TVI groups. Three TVI groups were formed, two of these being led by the same tutor. The tutors were chosen from a set of students who had performed equally well in the course during the previous year. Both tutors were very much interested in the subject and were also interested in teaching as a career. However, their possible teaching styles were known from previous experience to be somewhat different. Where one tutor tended to answer questions directly when the tape was stopped, the other tended to encourage his group to find the answer. The first tutor was given a group of six students (labelled groups 3 in the following figures). The second was given two groups, one with 12 members (identified as group 1) and one with six (group 2).

The separate TVI groups were too small for statistically significant differences to be manifested in their educational effectiveness. However, as illustrated by Figure 3, the combined data show that the TVI method was at least as good as live instruction. Furthermore, for students with lower admission qualifications, the TVI method of teaching appeared to be more effective than the regular classes. In fact the regression line for

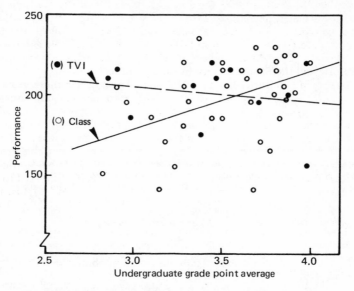

Figure 3. *Classroom and tutored videotape instruction student performance. Foreign students and honours co-operative students were eliminated from both the TVI groups and the in-class group for this comparison because they formed very different proportions of the groups*

TVI students in Figure 3 suggests that the course performance is essentially independent of the standard measures of academic ability. Note that this finding agrees with the results given in Figure 1 for the sub-group of TVI students whose admission qualification scores were sufficient for them to be admitted to the university as regular graduate students.

Student opinions of the TVI format were also collected at the end of each quarter and showed a generally enthusiastic response to the method. Some characteristic features of their responses are shown in Table 1. With respect to the effect of group size, a comparison of groups 1 and 2 (same tutor) shows that the smaller group was generally more enthusiastic about the TVI experience than the larger group. This same general result has been repeated in our industrial TVI groups, and a consideration of all of our present data on group size leads us to the tentative conclusion that the method works best when the group size is between three and 10.

	Groups		
Rating	1 (N=12)	2 (N=6)	3 (N=6)
Question A			
Definitely superior	4	3	
Superior	6	3	1
About equal	2		4
Inferior			
Definitely inferior			
$\dot{X}$	0.58	0.75	0.1
Σ	0.36	0.27	0.22
Question B			
Highly favour	7	6	3
Favour	3		
Neutral	2		2
Prefer not			
Definitely not			
$\dot{X}$	0.71	1.0	0.6
Σ	0.4	0.0	0.55

Table 1. *Student reactions to tutored videotape instruction on-campus. Question A was, 'How would you rate your overall educational experience with TVI as compared to a large live lecture class?' Question B was, 'How do you feel about taking another course in this manner?' To obtain averages and standard deviations a preference scale running from +1 (definitely superior or highly favoured) to −1 (definitely inferior or definitely do not prefer) was employed.*

Table 1 also contains some specific information about the influence of tutoring styles that is consistent with our general observations. The students studying with the tutor who tended to answer questions directly (group 3) were less pleased than students in a group of equal size with a tutor who tended to draw them into the discussion when the tape was stopped.

The second set of experiments, performed during the winter quarter of 1976, was conducted with the second half of an introductory graduate engineering-economics systems course in which the regular course professor was away from campus. In the absence of a suitable lecturing replacement, videotapes of his course from the previous year were shown to the regular class. A professor from the general subject area viewed the tapes with the class and answered questions primarily at the end of the lecture. For technical and scheduling reasons, the tapes shown to the large class could not be stopped during the lecture for thorough discussion.

Two small TVI groups were formed by random sampling from groups of students who had demonstrated high and low performance in the prior quarter, with each group having a separate tutor. A control group was also formed, consisting of 22 students who watched the videotape in the large class.

With respect to course grades, no statistically significant difference was found in the performance of the TVI and control groups, partly because of the small size of the sample groups, although again the data were consistent with the conclusion that the TVI students did at least as well as the regular class, and that the students of lower ability benefited more by the TVI educational method. In fact the comparison was frustrated by the fact that all low-ability students in the control group dropped the course.

However, a pronounced difference was observed in student attitudes towards the use of a videotape with and without the combined tutor and tape-stopping features. These results are shown in Table 2, where the responses to several questions are recorded for the three groups of students (low ability, high ability, and control). Each question was answered on a preference scale which ran from +1 (strongly agree) to −1 (strongly disagree). Note that the high-ability TVI group was on average highly enthusiastic on all counts, though its course performance was almost identical to what it had been during the previous quarter in the live lecture class. In fact, the high-ability TVI group stopped the tape on an average of every five minutes.

OBSERVATIONS

The TVI technique was invented in an effort to provide the benefits of both lectures and small group discussions to off-campus engineering students. Experience gained from three years of operation of the program suggests that the TVI technique is at least as effective as either classroom instruction or live TV with audio talkback capability, for both on-campus and off-campus students. However, our data do not permit a rigorous statistical test of this conclusion to be made. We are also unable to generalize to subject areas other than engineering and science, though we believe the general principles of the TVI format will apply to a wide range of subjects and audiences.

To assist in considering how the method might be applied to simulations other than those described above, we have enumerated the factors which we believe to be critical to the effectiveness of the TVI

Group	SA	A	N	D	SD	$\dot{X}$	Σ
Question 1							
Low	2	3	2	0	0	0.5	0.41
High	1	4	1	0	0	0.5	0.32
Control	0	7	6	6	3	−0.1	0.54
Question 2							
Low	4	2	1	0	0	0.71	0.39
High	5	1	0	0	0	0.92	0.20
Control	1	6	5	5	3	−0.075	0.59
Question 3							
Low	2	2	2	1	0	0.36	0.56
High	4	1	0	1	0	0.67	0.61
Control	1	3	6	10	2	−0.2	0.5
Question 4							
Low	0	5	1	1	0	0.29	0.39
High	3	3	0	0	0	0.75	0.27
Control	0	0	10	7	4	−0.36	0.39
Question 5							
Low	2	4	0	1	0	0.5	0.5
High	2	3	1	0	0	0.58	0.38
Control	0	0	5	9	8	−0.57	0.39
Question 6							
Low	4	1	1	1	0	0.57	0.61
High	4	1	1	0	0	0.75	0.42
Control	0	0	8	7	7	−0.48	0.42
Question 7							
Low	3	3	0	0	1	0.5	0.71
High	1	2	2	1	0	0.13	0.74
Control	1	4	7	6	4	−0.18	0.57

Table 2. *Campus student attitudes toward tutored videotape instruction. The abbreviations are: SA, strongly agree; A, agree; N, neutral; D, disagree; SD, strongly disagree. The attitudes examined were: 1, feel more favourable toward this method of instruction at end of course then when course began; 2, prefer this method of instruction to lectures in large classes (50 or more students); 3, learned more from this course than from other courses due to the instructional method; 4, asked more questions in this class than in other classes; 5, learned more from questions and comments of other students than in other courses; 6, felt more free to ask questions and express myself than in other courses; 7, would recommend this course to a friend exactly as I took it. A numerical performance scale was established for quantification of the data: SA = 1, A = 0.5, N = 0, D = −0.5, SD = −1.0; X and Σ are mean and standard deviation, respectively.*

format:

1. The attitude, personality, and instructional style of the tutor are very important. The tutor should be interested in helping the students in his group. He should attend all or nearly all the videotape sessions. His competence is important, but it is better that he be not so overqualified that he becomes bored or impatient with a lack of understanding in the students. Compensation of the tutors is important for a continuing program.
2. Group size is also very important. If there are fewer than three students opportunity for effective interaction is lacking and the method tends to be expensive. Group size greater than eight to 10 tends to inhibit discussion and reduce the frequency with which the tape is stopped. A group size of three to eight seems optimum, although this can vary with student personalities and acquaintance with each other.
3. Depending on the maturity of the student, commitment to a degree program or similar educational objective seems to be important for sustaining interest and motivation. Certainly for most students completion of graded problems and examinations results in a more productive educational experience.
4. Active classroom participation in the live class is desirable. For the subjects and audiences served to date, unrehearsed, unedited videotapes of classroom lectures may be used and, in fact, may have more 'presence' and be more interesting to watch than tightly scripted, professionally produced lectures.
5. It is important that the instructor be well organized, knowledgeable in his subject, and free of annoying mannerisms. The charisma of a good instructor is emphasized on the videotape.
6. For students employed in industry, attitudes of management play a very important role in the success of a continuing program. Job pressures that create long hours and interfere with family life markedly increase the difficulty of pursuing an educational program.
7. Continued management and evaluation of a TVI program needs to be the concern and principal responsibility of a designated person who should provide liaison between the academic institution and the TVI students. Many details require timely attention that would otherwise not be given by either the instructor or the company.

None of these factors poses unmanageable requirements. With attention to group size, good tutoring, quality of recorded educational material, adequate handling of supplementary materials, and grading of problems and examinations, the TVI methodology can provide an excellent educational experience and opportunities for needed education in otherwise difficult or impossible situations.

Given that it can accomplish important educational objectives, it seems worthwhile to summarize the principal advantages TVI has over both in-class instruction and live television:

1. It is (or can be) educationally more effective than either classroom or televised instruction, especially for marginally qualified students. This is primarily because it permits students to ask more questions

and, through organized discussion, to find more answers for themselves than they could in either of the other formats.
2. TVI is cheaper than either classroom or televised instruction from the point of view of marginal costs. It does not require new teachers, new educational plant, or expensive broadcast facilities. Our operating experience shows that TVI can be provided at a marginal cost of $2.20 per student per lecture for groups of 10 students. The marginal cost of instruction by 'real time' television on the Stanford ITFS system is $2.43 per student per lecture.
3. It makes good use of teaching resources by using faculty for course preparation and para-professional tutors for discussion of the lectures. For this latter function it draws on the substantial (if latent) interest in tutoring that exists in a large segment of the population.
4. It allows instruction to take place at the convenience of the students. It is not bound by either the academic calendar or a broadcast schedule.

These advantages are substantial, and while over-generalizing is dangerous, we nonetheless feel confident that TVI can be successfully extended to large-scale applications, at least for courses in science and engineering. We believe the method can also be successfully extended to other subject areas.

Notes

1. We thank J G Linvill for encouragement and support, J Lindsay and R Latta for assistance with the statistics, and several of our colleagues for helpful reviews of the manuscript. The National Institute for Education provided support for the statistical analysis presented and also commissioned a paper from which this article was abstracted, first published in *Science*, 195, 18 March 1977, 1139-46, and reprinted here with the permission of the American Association for the Advancement of Science.

REFERENCES

Anderson, R M (1977) personal communication.
Chu, G C & Schramm, W (1967) 'Learning from television: What the research says', *Educational Resources Information Centre Report*, Ed-014-900, Stanford University, Stanford.
Gibbons, J F (1973) 'Federal initiatives for bringing communications technology to the service of education', position paper for the Newman Task Force on Higher Education and the President's Science Advisory Commission. A partial summary of the paper is published in Adler, R & Baer, W S (eds) *Aspen Notebook: Cable and Continuing Education*, Praeger, New York, 127-32.
Jackson, P W (1968) *The Teacher and the Machine, Horace Mann Lecture 1967*, University of Pittsburgh Press, Pittsburgh.
Pettit, J M & Grace, D J (1970) *IEEE Spectrum*, May.
Schramm, W (1971) 'What we know about learning from television', *Educational Resources Information Centre Report*, Ed-002-561, Stanford University, Stanford.

18. Individualized Learning with Videocassettes

Björn Hoffman

SUMMARY

This chapter describes an example of students using videocassettes as a source of information for self-paced learning. The main point is that the technical device of video meets its function only when integrated into an educational design. Four didactic aspects of individualized learning with videocassettes are outlined: the concept of 'self-paced learning', the concept of 'learning with instructional material', the concept of 'learning here and now', and the concept of 'individual help for learning'.

DESCRIPTION OF THE INSTRUCTIONAL FORM 'INDIVIDUALIZED LEARNING WITH VIDEOCASSETTES'

This discussion relates to the method used to teach a laboratory course in biology for medical students at the University of Cologne. At other German universities medical students take a similar course for one semester four hours a week. They usually work in groups of 30 to 50 students, sometimes even more in the laboratory. However, in Cologne University students are not required to take the course within a fixed time schedule. Instead they attend a learning centre which is open for their use from 9am to 9pm, Monday till Saturday, from January through to December.

In the learning centre students work in separate study areas. These are equipped with various audio-visual aids, including video players and monitors. Students have the choice of working either alone or within small groups of up to four students. While the learning centre is open, an advanced biology student is in attendance as a tutor to advise students as required. The tutor also maintains a record of students' work.

Course material is divided into 24 units, each unit being represented by an audio-visual program. When a student wants to work on a particular unit, he informs the tutor. The tutor then loads the cassette into a video player which is wired for remote control from an assigned student position in the centre. Before replaying the cassette the student reads the objectives of the unit. Then, using the remote control and headphones, he starts the video program which is designed to contain information and learning material needed by the student to achieve the objectives of the course.

221

In order to avoid passive watching of the video program, the student is requested, after about five minutes, to stop the videocassette and to solve problems. Thus, he can reflect upon, revise and apply the information he has received in the previous five minutes. Some units require the student to perform experiments, to use the microscope, to prepare microscopic slides, to make drawings, or to use models or other relevant illustrative material. The video program provides extensive guidance to all these activities.

By means of the remote control and in addition to the assigned breaks, the student is able to stop the videocassette at any time in order to reflect upon an idea more thoroughly, or to ask the tutor for help, or simply to relax for a while. The student may repeat any part of the cassette or even the whole cassette, for revision or in preparation for an examination. All of these possibilities are used by students extensively.

Students may work alone or within small groups. For about 400 students per semester there are 15 places for individual learning, each with video equipment and two sets of earphones so that two students can work together on a program. There are also separate rooms for groups of two to four students working together.

At the end of the course, a student receives a certificate stating that he has participated 'regularly and with success'. Regular participation in the course means that the student has worked through 16 units (eight additional units are available as electives) during the semester. Award of the certificate is independent of the number of hours spent in the learning centre during the semester. Thus, a student is not disadvantaged if, for example, he becomes ill for two or three weeks or is a slow learner of the subject.

Successful participation is attested on the basis of a student's microscopic drawings, a short essay and two interim tests at a microcomputer.

VIDEOCASSETTES OR 'AUDIO-ALBUM'?

Most of the audio-visual software developed by staff at the learning centre is in the mode of video programs. The centre has also tested other audio-visual aids, one of which was the 'audio-album'. This is a simple and cheap aid, originally developed by Dr Habowsky at the learning centre of the University of Windsor (Canada). The system has proved a success, not only in our learning centre but also in several other departments. It consists of a ring binder containing illustrations, (photographs, pictures, diagrams and other graphic designs) and an audio-cassette with the concomitant explanations and text.

Two disadvantages of the audio-album should be mentioned. First, an audio-album cannot demonstrate motion. Second, to a given text the student has to find the appropriate illustration by himself since the text and the illustrations cannot be synchronized as in a video program.

On the other hand, there are advantages in the audio-album. First, the technical quality of the illustrations is much better than on a video screen. Second, it is easier to review an audio-album than a video program. Third, an audio-album is much cheaper than video equipment.

DIDACTIC ASPECTS OF 'INDIVIDUALIZED LEARNING WITH VIDEOCASSETTES'

Self-paced learning
The most obvious didactic aspect of the Cologne centre's instructional method is the concept of self-paced learning. This concept plays a central role in several forms of instruction. The 'audio-tutorial approach to learning' which has been developed by Postlethwait *et al* (1972) and which served as a model for our own instructional form (Hoffmann & Eickhoff, 1977), and the 'personalized system of instruction' (PSI) developed by Keller *et al* (1968) are the original and most important examples. Self-pacing also plays an important role in different forms of computer assisted instruction (CAI).

All of these examples are based upon the insight that the progress of learning follows an individual time pattern. One student may be able to understand an idea immediately, whereas another student may have to think about it for a while. Differences in previous knowledge, experience, concentration span, distraction or diversion and special motivation all play a role in the learning process.

These are more or less superficial arguments in favour of self-paced learning. The true argument is based upon the fact that real learning hardly ever takes place when the student is just listening passively. Learning instead is an activity that has to be performed by the learner himself. 'Learning is an activity done by an individual and not something done to an individual.' This is the basis of Postlethwait's argument for self-paced learning. Everyday we may observe how 'teacher-paced' instruction bypasses the student without being effectively assimilated. Instead of giving lectures we must allow students to experience that learning only occurs when they themselves are actively involved in the learning process. This is one of our most important functions as teachers, and the concept of self-paced learning is probably our best tool to accomplish this task.

Learning with instructional material
This second didactical aspect has to be clearly distinguished from 'teaching with instructional material'. An example may demonstrate the difference. You probably remember lessons in geography in which the teacher used a wall-map. Imagine what would have happened if the map by itself was supposed to teach you the subject without a teacher being present. It might have been very nice to dream about travelling around the world, but the intended objectives of that lesson probably would not have been reached. So the wall-map alone is not suitable for instruction. It is only a teaching aid. The teacher has to focus the attention of the learner onto details, he has to explain unknown facts, to ask questions, to guide the learner through the subject-matter.

Now imagine that all these stimuli coming from the teacher are replaced by material which is suited to achieve the same aims. Written objectives may show the goal that the learner has to reach. Written text or audio-visual software may explain the facts and focus on important details. Problems and exercises, incorporated into the text, may call

223

upon the learner to repeat some of the content in his own words, to bring several details together, to apply special terms to a different context, and so on. In other words, they may make the learner digest and assimilate the information. Finally, add all the material that a good teacher may use to illustrate the subject-matter — various kinds of illustrations, models, experimental matter, and so on — and you can design instructional material that enables the student to learn without the pacing determined by a teacher in front of the class. It is obvious that this kind of instructional material is an indispensable prerequisite for self-paced learning. And well designed video programs are ideally suited to play a central role in it.

Learning here and now

This concept is closely related to the two didactic concepts that have been discussed so far. It refers to a specific reaction of students to lectures. A lecture like any other teaching in front of a large audience is transitory and cannot be paced by the individual learner. Because of this well known situation students have to catch up with the information later on, or in other words, they are always forced to postpone the real learning activity.

This is one of the serious disadvantages of large group teaching. It is not only often a waste of time for the student, but it also creates an attitude that hinders learning instead of supporting it. Due to the central role of lectures or similar teaching methods in most universities, students tend to generalize this attitude to any form of learning.

Typical student reactions to the lecture type of instruction are:

☐ to listen and simply wait to see whether or not one can remember some of the information
☐ to collect written material and collate it at home
☐ to learn it later when preparing for a test or an examination, and to hope that nobody will recognize one's lack of knowledge.

In order to counteract this attitude of permanently postponing the learning activity, I stress the concept of 'learning here and now'. For this reason, in the Cologne learning centre all instructional material, such as audio-visual programs, experimental material and scripts with objectives and exercises, as well as a tutor, are freely available and may be consulted by the student at any time. In the learning centre there is no reason for the student to postpone his real learning activity. He always has the opportunity of 'learning here and now'.

Individual help for learning

This is the last didactic aspect of our instructional form. At German universities, courses usually end with a test, which the student may pass or fail. Since we at the centre want students to know early when they have to correct their mode of learning, we have introduced two interim tests. The first test is taken after the first five units, and the second one after the five following units. The tests, taken at a microcomputer, comprise multiple-choice items and open-ended questions. If a student reaches 60 per cent or more of all possible marks, he will receive encouraging comments and may continue with the next units. If, however, the student does not reach 60 per cent, he is asked to attend an interview.

Thus this is one of the functions of the computer: to identify, at an early stage and with a minimum of effort, those students who need special help. Whenever a student gets less than 60 per cent in an interim test, the computer prints out the answers that the student has given. At the interview the questions and answers given are discussed, and reasons for the student's poor performance determined. From this analysis the student is advised on how his/her performance might be improved. I first of all try to get the student to agree that his performance was not good enough and that it would be useless to continue this way. We then discuss the possible reasons for the poor result and try to find ways that might lead to the student's better performance.

Together with the second interim test the student writes a short essay about a given topic. This essay is corrected and thoroughly discussed with the student whenever necessary.

The purpose of describing this procedure in detail is to emphasize a very important side-effect of using videocassettes in teaching: that is, they free us (the staff) from time-consuming routine. For if two people had to teach 400 students every semester in groups of 30 to 50, they would never have time to consult with the individual student who needs special help.

CONCLUSIONS

The use of video may be applied to higher education in different ways. In this chapter the method of using videocassettes for individualized learning has been based on and justified by several concepts. On its own, and without support from other elements of our instructional design, a videocassette certainly would not function effectively as an instructional device. It is only in the context of the didactic concepts outlined above and in this educational framework, that video has proved to be an important tool for learning.

REFERENCES

Hoffmann, B & Eickhoff, F (1977) *Individuelles Lernen mit Audiovisuellen Programmen*, Hochschuldidaktische Materialien 63, AHD, Hamburg.
Keller, F S (1968) 'Good-bye teacher . . .', *Journal of Applied Behaviour Analysis I*, 78-89.
Postlethwait, S N, Novak, J & Murray, H T (1972) *The Audio-Tutorial Approach to Learning*, Burgess, Minneapolis.

19. Developing the Use of Videocassettes in the Open University

Nicola Durbridge

SUMMARY

This chapter presents an account of a two-phased development in the use of video at the Open University. It describes the context in which students learn and the way they are currently accessed to video. It describes how in the first instance students are working with videocassette material also available via television broadcasts; the second phase of development involves videos designed to exploit the medium itself. The chapter explains how the university's experience with television and audio-cassettes provides a basis for such video design. Finally, a case study illustrates one format already in use and students' responses to it.

INTRODUCTION

This chapter opens with some brief background information about the Open University teaching system. This sets the context essential to an understanding of how its staff and students perceive the educational roles and functions of audio-vision. The account traces the rapid shift from the use of radio to audio-cassettes and a more gradual but similar trend towards video rather than television. It describes the implementation of a scheme to provide students with access to video equipment on which they may view cassetted versions of television material. The main focus of the chapter, however, is upon the qualitatively different learning potential of cassetted rather than broadcast content, and how this may be exploited from design and user points of view. To illustrate the discussion, one kind of video program is analysed from each of these points of view, drawing upon a case study of an Open University course. The main aim of this case study is to provide insights into the students' perceptions of video work; it does not, in other words, seek to imply general rules about video design, rather to enrich understanding about students' conceptions and experiences of video-related learning.

THE OPEN UNIVERSITY

The Open University was founded in 1969 to provide tertiary level education to any adult British resident. It was primarily conceived as opening doors to people unable to attend traditional universities due to their lack of qualifications or their commitment to full-time employment. Students are allocated places on a first-come first-served basis, regardless of previous educational level and current occupation. It should be explained that much of the organization and administration of the Open University is carried out on a regional basis; each of its 13 geographical divisions has a permanent central office staffed by academics and administrators. Within each of these regions the university rents smaller study centres open to its students, usually in the evenings, for tutorials or for work on university-owned equipment such as computer terminals and television. Adult learning in this context is self-motivated and relatively isolated — students need to be prepared to devote much of their spare time to studying from their home bases — and it is very individual; students bring to their studies a much wider range of experience, abilities and ambitions than in a traditional university setting.

DEVELOPMENTS IN OU BROADCASTING

Early decisions about appropriate media for distance education in this context needed to take on board the wide scatter of its student population as well as students' varying experience of higher, indeed of any level, of formal study. Thus, on pragmatic, as much as on educational grounds, television and radio were chosen to form part of the teaching package. A formal arrangement between the BBC and the Open University was drawn up to provide for the production and transmission of up to 300 new television programs in each year. This televised material, despite its high publicity, was never conceived as carrying the core teaching of Open University courses — this remains the role of a series of correspondence texts sent to students. At the outset then, Open University broadcasts were vulnerable to the criticism that they performed a peripheral teaching role and that their teaching functions were not firmly rooted in educational theory; they were moreover an expensive 'addition' if this is all they were, to the range of components students met as they worked towards their degree. (The cost of such a service in 1980 was $8 million out of the university's total of $50 million expenditure.) Over the years there have been two main developments influencing the role and use of audio-vision.

First, there has been considerable research activity at the university into educational television. Much early work focused on the design end of audio-visual material, on studies of different production styles and how these might influence students' learning. Later studies concentrated on exploring the wider context of learning with television and showed that a multiplicity of factors play a complex and interrelated part in the effectiveness or otherwise of students' learning with audio-vision. The main influence of such studies has been upon decision making; they have provided an empirical basis for allocating funds to courses, and course producers and academics need to make out a good educational case for using television before a program can be made. Experience, in other words, has been illuminating and has provided a rational basis for establishing principles of good and bad educational television; it should be noted that these principles are contextual; they relate to the Open University context, and do not assume the status of general theory.

Second, it is clear that the use of broadcasting has become increasingly problematic over the years, and that the main problem relates to a worsening of the university's allocated transmission hours. The university has found its educational programs squeezed out of favourable transmission slots as competition from general service programs (with their appeal to larger audiences) increases. Meanwhile, the university has produced more courses, most of them seeking to use radio and television. The combined effect has been to present to students broadcast material which is at best inconvenient and often impossible for them to use due to their inopportune viewing hours.

THE DEVELOPMENT OF AUDIO-CASSETTES

These two developments lead in opposite directions: the Open University has developed fairly clear criteria about effective and appropriate programming, but is less able to deliver and thus exploit its expertise. The effect of poor transmission slots upon radio has been dramatic. Students in many cases simply ceased to make the attempt to listen, others tried, but tended to rate the learning experience very poorly as compared with the other media they studied (Grundin, 1980). Part of the explanation for such a rating clearly lay with the timings of transmissions which were often not just generally inconvenient but also poorly synchronized with an *individual* student's coverage of related course material. Some students responded to the situation creatively; they recorded programs off-air for themselves and listened to them when it suited them. They reported that they then found their audio material much more useful. Other students applied for cassette copies of radio material made by the university, a service which was available to them free of charge on a loan basis. Further research showed that if students were sent radio material on cassettes, they found such recorded material twice as valuable to their studies as the *same* material heard on live transmission (Durbridge, 1980). Students clearly appreciated the fact that they could listen at their convenience and replay material according to their needs and preferences. It was not just students who showed certain dissatisfaction with radio; there was a parallel concern amongst academics and producers about the effectiveness of a medium which was so under-used by students, and this was reflected in a general lack of interest in developing new approaches to the medium. Instead of continuing to try and offset the challenge to radio's usefulness by exploring different and attractive ways of using the medium, many decided to switch their attention to the cassette medium itself and to exploit its potential for teaching. Much of the pioneer work in the development of audio-cassettes for use of Open University students was carried out by the mathematics faculty. For example, their Foundation Level Course (M101) for first-year students of mathematics makes extensive use of the medium to teach essential subject-matter. Their approach implemented a combination of sound and vision for concept teaching or problem-solving and audio work was very closely integrated into the course as a whole. Their method-ology is described in more detail in Durbridge (1980). The success of their strategy, in terms of students' responses, fired the growing interest in the medium yet further. It was seen as an exciting option, opening doors to a wide range of strategies which might encourage users to adopt an active and participatory approach to their listening. This was seen as a contrast to a tendency amongst students to listen passively to broadcasts, and to 'receive' but not respond to their content. Implicitly the alternative student approach was seen as a more effective way of learning. From Open University studies of students' use of the cassette medium on this foundation course and others, two characteristics emerged as being particularly valuable for learning (Durbridge, 1981). The first, not surprisingly, related to the pause, stop and replay tech-nology of cassette players, which students found easy to use. Many tapes contained highly structured direct teaching; students were given clear verbal instructions about appropriate activities as they listened; these tended to be directly and informally addressed to students within the commentary itself. Students might be invited to stop and to carry out a calculation, to replay a section and then answer a question or to pause and reflect on a point. These kinds of activities were usually followed with feedback — the teacher's approach to a response; students also used the technology to pace themselves as the commen-tator led them through some activity, perhaps experimental work or an analysis of a variety of data. The effect of such teaching strategies was said by students to create the sense of a piece of co-operative learning; the interactivity they encouraged appeared to be seen not just as between student and hardware, but between student and teacher. This leads on to the second characteristic of cassette work which proved so effective for learning. It was clear that the sound of the human voice could be highly motivational and that this was useful in an individual learning context. Many students remarked especially positively about presentational styles which were informal, encouraging and direct; they tended, for example, to describe learning with cassettes as similar to having a face-to-face tutorial. These are characteristics which will be returned to later; they clearly contributed to the success of *audio*-cassettes at the Open University. The question is, how far can video-cassettes be said to share them?

THE VIDEOCASSETTE LOAN SCHEME

Over 87 per cent of the Open University's undergraduates own, or have access to audio-cassette replay equipment; there is evidence too which suggests that nearly all students will acquire the necessary equipment if audio-cassettes are an important part of course material (Grundin, 1980). Audio, on cassette, can thus be said to be generally available to students and in their own homes. It is also cheaper for courses with a student enrolment of less than 500 to distribute audio on cassette directly to these homes, rather than to broadcast it (Bates & Kern, 1977). Thus while the challenge to radio's effectiveness could be met quite swiftly at the university by a switch to audio-cassettes, the same cannot be said about television and video. Only about eight per cent of Open University students are known to own VHS video equipment although about 18 per cent do have reasonable access to video replay equipment of some kind (Brown & Grundin, 1982) and even with the anticipated growth in this market it is unlikely that all will have purchased videoplayers in the foreseeable future. Clearly, if the university were to encourage an extensive use of video it would need to ensure that students had access to the necessary equipment and probably finance such access itself.

As a first phase of development the university has used video as a supplementary means of delivering televised material; in other words, most videos merely contain copies of broadcasts. Various limited schemes for providing students with access to this supplementary service have been tried out since 1974, but the most recent and most extensive one was put into operation in 1982. All television programs in the scheme are transmitted once and thus available to students in this mode as well as on cassette. However, to supplement the single broadcast a videocassette loan service provides students, on certain pre-specified courses, with access to VHS copies of the televised material. In 1982, the service was restricted to students on low population courses; 21 courses were designated as category A, or first priority courses, and selected because they had populations of under 400 students. A second group of courses, designated category B, were also included; these had populations of between 400 and 600 students, and had a second priority rating. Category B course programs were within the scheme if the demand from category A course students fell short of the estimate.

The loan service operates on a mail-order basis. Students taking A and B courses are provided with blank program request cards at the start of the academic year and with instructions about how to use the service. If they want to see a copy of a program they fill in the card and mail it to the university. They may request up to two programs at a time and may retain copies sent back to them for up to four weeks. A centrally sited audio-visual department deals with the requests. It is equipped with four master videocassette players and 18 slave copiers; on receipt of a request card, its staff make 10 VHS copies, simultaneously, of the BBC master. Nine of these are banked to meet future demand, the other is mailed directly back to the student's home with a new blank request card.

The next feature of the scheme is the network of videorecorders/players established throughout the university's 13 regions. Each region was given a block allocation of money to meet its own assessment of its requirements. This was used to install a total of 243 VHS videoplayers (for the most part on a rental basis), across the country but in locations chosen by each regional office. Regional office staff had considerable freedom to implement and run a service which met their local needs; this meant that equipment could have been placed in a variety of different locations. The scheme is under current evaluation and although final data may lead to adjustments, an interim report (Brown & Grundin, 1982) makes it clear that the vast majority of machines have been placed in conventional Open University study centres. Only some six machines were sited in public libraries, 16 were designated for formal locations such as teacher training centres or local colleges and one was placed in a student's house, on condition that it was made available to other students. In this situation students may have a range of choices about where they see a copy of a requested videocassette. They may use their own equipment if they own it, or indeed borrow the facilities of a non-university neighbour. They may rent a machine specially (this costs about £16 per month) to view videos in their own homes. Some may be able to use facilities at their place of work; teachers, for example, often had this option, and roughly one quarter of Open University students are teachers. Finally, they may go to the local viewing centres designated by the region.

The total cost of this service to the university in 1982 was approximately £238,750, made up largely of the copying and mailing service. The evaluation study mentioned above was set up to guide decisions as to whether, and if so how, the service might be continued. The interim report (1982) recommends that the service does continue and it is anticipated that it will be extended to cover 83 courses with populations of less than 800 students. Interim data show that there were 2,544 student requests for priority course programs, and that each was viewed on average 2.3 times. Information about students' use of different locations and the value they place on the service is still being analysed but what is already clear is that the loan system provides as effective a back-up to courses with single transmissions, as is usually provided by repeat broadcasts. As the evaluators point out, however (Brown & Grundin, 1982), comparisons between cassette viewing rates and repeat transmissions are unfair for a number of reasons, among them, the fact that videotapes provide students with a qualitatively different learning opportunity.

VIDEOCASSETTES

On the face of it then, the use of video at the Open University looks to be restricted and restrictive; students have limited access to a limited kind of audio-vision and a firm commitment to future expansion has not yet been made. Behind the scenes, however, a second phase of development is well underway. Several courses of study intended for presentation in the next few years but under development now, are seeking to use videocassettes to replace broadcasts entirely. The ways in which they will be used will draw upon previous university experience in two areas. First, its experience in designing good *cassette* material, extrapolated from the audio examples; second, its experience in designing good audio-vision, taken from television work.

The word 'good' can be a critical one. It has yet to be shown for example, that a 'good', that is educationally effective, *audio*-cassette design feature will translate with a similar effect to video. The same can be said of 'good' television and video. Indeed, Open University experience (Gallagher, 1978) has already alerted it to the dangers of assuming that features of good television in *general* broadcasting terms will be always appropriate to good *educational* television, and with a change of medium these dangers may be exacerbated. It would be valuable to explore this point a little further as the video case study in this chapter presents recordings of real-life scenes for students to work upon, and this has also been a common use of Open University television. Paradoxically, many of the arguments for this use of television also touch upon the reasons why some students find it a difficult one to handle. For example, it is difficult to conceive of an equally efficient and practical way of providing students with the opportunity to study in common a series of naturally-occurring events — and this is probably true both of more conventional university settings as well as of those using distance teaching methods. On the other hand, since such opportunities are comparatively rare this may partly explain students' unease in knowing how to cope with them. It can also be described as an exciting use of the medium, since the format often effectively conveys a sense of vitality, immediacy and drama. There are parallels to be drawn here with what is generally accepted to constitute 'good' television in general broadcasting terms; the more fluently the events are seen to occur, the more stimulating and 'natural' the film may be gauged to be. The danger of this type of presentation is that it tends to imply that 'good', stimulating television also necessarily implies 'good' teaching material. University studies have shown, however (Bates & Gallagher, 1977), that students are easily sidetracked by film material showing events of personal or of dramatic interest, or that they recognize the format as one met in general broadcasting and may be seduced into considering it as a soft option involving little learning response on their part. In fact, this kind of program usually expects students to exercise the higher learning skills, as Bloom (1956) describes them, of analysis and evaluation, and so may be argued to be more demanding than others rather than less. Students' difficulties are probably compounded if they have not developed a critical stance towards the *televised* presentation of facts. Whereas they may be both aware of the need to be critical, and be relatively experienced at setting about assessing the reliability of written materials (checking references, looking for evidence of bias and so on), regular viewing habits do not encourage a similar stance *vis-à-vis* television. More seriously, many students are unfamiliar with the characteristics of the medium and are probably unaware both of purely presentational factors and of more fundamental factors (such as the editing and structuring processes necessarily involved in film making), which influence their perceptions. The implications of this are argued by Bates & Gallagher (1977) who recommend that the more inexperienced students are uncritical in learning with television; the more didactic, structured, active, neutral and integrated students prefer the production to be factual.

THE VIDEO CASE STUDY

It is useful to have these recommendations in mind when examining how students responded to the video structure in the following case study. The case study is of a series of eight videos made for an Open University course called *Developing Mathematical Thinking*. It was first presented as a course in 1982 and was the university's first use of video material designed specifically for the medium so as to form an integrated study component. The course content was expected to attract enrolment from members of the teaching profession and this influenced the decision to use video rather than television. It was anticipated that such students would be in a more favourable position to undertake video work than typical Open University undergraduates, and would be more willing to study videos in a group context, an approach highly recommended by the course designers. The reasoning behind such beliefs was that teachers were likely to have access to video replay equipment in their schools and to have experienced regular discussion work as part of their teacher training.

The analysis of the videos which follows is in two sections: first it looks at them from a design perspective — their structure and their intended teaching functions; second, it turns to the user perspective and looks at how students responded to the medium, and to the teaching strategies underlying the ways video work was structured. First of all then, the design perspective.

The videos present film of children doing mathematics. There are eight video programs each with a playing time of roughly 23 minutes; six of them focus on a particular mathematical topic, one per program, and show individual, small group or classroom work related to it. The focus in these programs is upon a range of problems children are having in the doing of mathematics. Some structure to students' viewing is given within the video, by occasional voice-over comments; for example, students may be told to focus their attention upon particular aspects of the content, or be asked direct questions about it. The two remaining videos also show classroom work, but with an emphasis this time upon the teaching of mathematics rather than its learning. The live film in these instances is supported by graphics which analyse the planning and scheduling of classroom work, and by rather more voice-over commentary than in the other videos. Two design features principally distinguish these programs from a television treatment of similar content; both seek to exploit the technology of cassette players. First, each program is divided into short sequences. These range from two to six minutes in length and their division is signalled by a flashing star-shaped symbol in the top-right corner of the screen. This instructs viewers to take a counter reading, to stop, take notes on, or discuss, what they have seen. Second, each program is accompanied by notes appropriately bound into correspondence text; 'appropriately' means that the correspondence text deals with the same mathematical topic and draws upon the video to illustrate a discussion of theory and practice. A particular sequence of work is encouraged by the page-ordering of text, and its division into 'study sessions'. It is obvious that students are intended to view the video and to consult their notes about it before studying the remaining 'sessions' in the main text. The video notes are used partly to provide viewers with an overview of the cassettes' contents; so there is a summary page which describes the main focus of each program and suggests a timetable for students' video work. Here, they are told the length of each sequence and how long they might sensibly spend working on each so as to keep to the suggested two-hour limit for an entire video session. The notes continue by providing students with separate pages of activities, and space for comments. An example of their typical layout is shown in Figure 1.

The radical difference between such notes and typical Open University broadcast notes lies in the encouragement they give students to respond thinkingly to what they see and hear. They emphasize, in other words, the potential of having material recorded on video. So, for example, references are made to a *two-hour* session, one which clearly envisages far more from students in terms of work than a passive viewing of a 20-minute sequence of sound and vision. There are, as Figure 1 shows, suggestions about how students might interact with the video (screen 'on' symbol to the left) as they view, and about the kind of inquiry they might pursue afterwards (symbol of screen 'off' to the right). The reminder to take a counter reading implicitly invites replay and so on. A feature of the notes particularly praised by students was the photograph; this was found to be an invaluable memory jogger about content and, with the addition of the names of the children seen and heard, made later textual references back to individual sequences easy to follow.

The videos aim to perform a range of teaching functions, but perhaps most importantly they seek to *lead* the related texts rather than to 'be driven' by them. The videos also provide primary source material which the main text *later* draws upon and uses to illustrate and analyse theory. Students themselves are encouraged to participate in the analysis of each video and to be selectively observant. It is interesting to note that such analysis is not intended to reflect the received interpretation of a particular theory, since students' suggested sequence of work does not allow this. The teaching challenge is thus a much more open one, and invites students' own speculation and probing about the 'meaning' of each video. Nevertheless, students are given some guidance towards avenues of profitable thought — that is to say, towards ideas which will be later taken up by the text. As mentioned earlier, there is some guidance within each video sequence, for example, from voice-over instructions to concentrate on a particular aspect of the subject-matter or from occasional voice-over questions which again aim to focus viewers' thinking. The notes provide similar academic structure to students' video work.

The real-life flavour of the film content suggests that the videos are intended to perform a further function, that is, to give students a sense of an experience. Here, the medium itself carries the teaching burden and, uninterrupted by academic comment, seeks to illuminate by making a direct appeal to students' senses rather than by encouraging rational thought. Thus, the video can be described as having two aspects to its full meaning. One is the *sense* of the problems of doing mathematics, the other involves a *critical appreciation* of these problems. Students need to respond in two ways to understand the whole; they need to be receptive to the stimulus of the 'real-life' sound plus vision and to show a sympathetic but instinctive understanding of it; they also need to pursue a rational inquiry into its fuller meaning along the lines prompted by the notes and voice-over elements mentioned. There are no right or wrong answers to the inquiry encouraged;

1 Subtraction problems

6½ minutes   Counter reading

In a large Outer London comprehensive school Sandy Carter was recorded working one at a time with several children aged twelve to fourteen from the remedial class. This sequence shows three of these children. They are all doing subtractions on a special machine which allows us to record what they write, to hear what they say, and to watch their facial cues. This enables us to observe their difficulties and make some sort of diagnosis.

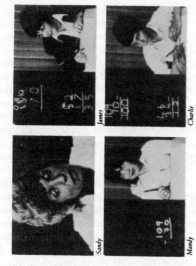

What's interesting about the children's explanations? Make notes on what each child says about handling the subtraction of 0 from 9.

What conclusions could Sandy come to about each child's state of understanding?

20 minutes

Figure 1. *Reproduced from Open University Course, EM23.5, 'Developing Mathematical Thinking'; Topic One: 'Subtraction'.*

what is intended is that students should think about what they see and hear rather than just 'receive' it.

Academic organization is also evident in the way the video is divided into short 'digestible' chunks and supplemented by discrete pages of notes for each sequence; both these design features are clearly orientated towards a teaching strategy which maintains that students learn most effectively if they adopt an inquiring stance as they work on course material. A similar theoretical standpoint probably underlies the fact that students were encouraged to work on the videos in groups; clearly it was believed that group work would stimulate and thus facilitate the open-ended analysis intended and provide a context in which students could exchange perceptions. The context thus would broaden their understanding of the videos, as well as make video work more enjoyable.

Regions were responsible for organizing students' individual or group access to video equipment. Most did so by informing students of places equipped with videos and available for group or individual viewing; they also circulated addresses and telephone numbers of fellow students. The cassette material was available to students in two ways. Students were encouraged where possible to make their own recordings of the video material, and for this reason alone the videos were also broadcast, twice, on midday transmission slots. It was envisaged that many students would have access to recording equipment since the majority were teachers and thus might be able to use school equipment. Sometime after receiving this encouragement, students were informed that the videos were also available to them through the university's cassette loan service as described earlier.

Aside from circulating this general information, regions then left students to make their own decisions about video viewing. They could choose to view alone if this were preferable and more convenient, or take up the initiative to try and form self-help groups. For the majority of students viewing was not home-based since few had the necessary equipment, and thus video work involved considerable forward planning. Students needed to plan their viewing to fit in with the opening times of particular locations; they needed to book a viewing if using a study centre, to order a cassette loan from the university centre, or otherwise arrange to have a copy of the video by appropriate dates as well as to arrange their travel. When compared with switching on the television (even at inconvenient times), or an audio-cassette player, or with reading a unit text, video study involved considerable individual effort. Groups of students moreover needed to find a *mutually* agreeable viewing date and hour and place. How students responded to these requirements will be taken up next, in an analysis of these videos from a user perspective.

In the event, most of the students enrolled in this course *were* teachers, although not necessarily of mathematics. As such they placed great value on the subject-matter of the videos, 'the luxury' as one student described it, 'of being able to concentrate on watching and listening to the children individually and in small groups'. Undoubtedly, the close-up camera work, focusing on children's faces as they tackled various aspects of mathematics, carried a powerful and convincing message which teachers and non-teachers intuitively and quickly accepted. Most students maintained that this kind of material was highly appropriate both to the course and to an audio-visual medium. It was considered valuable to be able to see children of different ages doing mathematics; the videos operated here to 'fill-in' about teaching at different levels and thus to extend (by proxy) viewers' experience. The 'real-life' approach to content was, on the whole, therefore, accepted both in terms of its 'truth' and its relevance.

Resistance to the 'truth' of the video content was most evident when it focused upon classroom work, rather than upon individuals. At these times some students were concerned about the necessary editing and selection processes involved. Teachers, drawing on their experience of 'real' classroom work, tended to become conscious of a certain mis-match between what they heard and saw on screen and 'real life'. This led them occasionally to preface post-viewing discussion or activity with queries about the validity of such exercises. However, these doubts rarely amounted to more than a minor diversion. Both groups of students and individuals tended to be enthusiastic about the course as a whole; they were, therefore, more concerned to get something out of the videos than to allow even genuine doubts about reliability to dominate their responses. In fact, these occasional criticisms were more evident among groups than individuals, and perhaps querying validity was more an attribute of group work than anything else — for example, the need to appear critically aware to colleagues was more evident than *real* discomfort with video content: students were quite willing to *use* the visual material to illustrate and back up their verbal arguments despite their previous criticisms.

A more serious problem with the video content for several students was its lack of background detail. Many claimed it was difficult to say anything much about the nature of the difficulties experienced by the children they saw without knowing more about their educational background. This, at least, is how students diagnosed the problem — they felt they could not answer particular questions with sufficient particularity, and thus demanded more illustrative material to work on. An alternative diagnosis might be that the audio-visual content was adequate for the teaching functions outlined earlier but that the questions and activities put to students did not stimulate the general kind of analysis the course team had in mind. This is a point I shall return to later when discussing students' learning from these videos.

In one sense students tended not to be very video conscious. For example, references were mostly to 'the television programs' rather than to video; indeed, students often compared them to university broadcasts they had watched on other courses. This perception came from students who were praising the relevance and appropriateness of real-life classroom film on education courses. Their attitude to television, in other words, was also positive, and they merely described video material as 'just as good as' or 'very like' the television programs they had previously studied. This view of video as similar in structure and function to television was maintained throughout the course. One difference remarked upon — but this had no bearing on the content *per se* — was that video was much more convenient to use than live programs transmitted at inopportune hours. At the start of the year it was evident that the notion that video and television were the same things but with different names attached to them could be a problem. Students who had *not* found their previous experience with university television programs particularly valuable or relevant to their studies were predisposed not to bother too much with video either. The university may be in a special situation here, and if it is to make extensive use of video in the future, it will need to encourage students to re-think their position on audio-visual media; it will need, for example, to publicize the fact that video and television are two different species and can involve different kinds of teaching, promoting different kinds of learning activity.

In another sense, some students *were* markedly video conscious; this consciousness seemed to be raised by their being encouraged to interact with the hardware of the medium as much as with its content. On the evidence of this study, students had little difficulty in learning how to operate videorecorders in order to play back their cassettes, *provided* that there were some written instructions to follow. If students in future were to be invited to record material off-air, on the other hand, they would need clear advice about procedures, as it was common for students never to have done so before and not to know how to set about finding out how. There were two aspects to interaction with the hardware which caused problems. The first is probably readily solved by providing all official video equipment with remote control apparatus and recommending that private owners purchase this as well. This should alleviate the tedium, inconvenience and disruptive effects of needing to be too physically active when operating video playback, and stop-start devices. The second problem is perhaps more seriously disfunctional; it seems that a number of students felt some considerable discomfort and embarrassment about video work which, as they saw it, turned them into 'part of the machinery'. These students were self-conscious, for example, when explicitly asked to switch on and off, and seemed to feel equally exploited by *implicit* instructions to replay parts of their videos. This is something which could need careful handling on other kinds of video programs; for example, on video material where repeated viewing is requested and where this is intended to form an essential part of the learning activity. It is a teaching strategy which has worked well on some audio-cassettes, a point mentioned earlier, but it seems that many students experience video and audio-cassette work rather differently. Interactive audio-cassette work appears to be seen as only a little less private and less familiar a way of studying than working with a written text, while interacting with video appears to be seen as involving a more *public* response to a more *inhuman* directive. It should be noted though that students' attitudes to the video medium *itself* were not by and large hostile; their negative attitudes tended to be directed towards video subject-matter or, to the ways they were expected to use this content. These are points which will be discussed further in the section on the different ways in which individual students and groups of students used the video material and perceived their learning tasks.

The sequential design of these videos worked very well. It was effective for the way it achieved sensible subdivisions within one program; sensible in that it gave students a breakdown of the audio-visual content and literally began to help them make sense of it. It operated, in other words, rather like paragraphing in a written text. It also proved a useful way of helping students to concentrate on visual material; it was evident that most found it comparatively easy to recall each section in considerable detail if they stopped the cassette and immediately worked on it. If sequences were very short (two minutes on some videos) students were more inclined to replay them *in toto* and to get more out of them on a second viewing. There is some clear evidence here that students found a real-life scene easier to work upon when its content was subdivided in this way; it is one example of how video can exploit both the emotive potential of audio-vision to provide stimulating and 'natural' seeming events and the educational potential of its technology to provide a covert structure to students' learning.

The use of voice-over directives to students to focus on particular content did not appear to work well. Some students said they did not think they had heard them because they were 'more engrossed with the action' on screen; others said they ignored them because they were (for example) 'off-putting as I was concentrating on trying to interpret what they wanted us to see instead of just watching. I preferred the written questions in the manual which you could look at after the program'. The last comment illustrates how easy it is to suggest activities to students which operate as diversions from, or interferences with, individual constructive thinking. This problem was even more marked with the written video notes; these sometimes appeared to students as requiring them to notice and remember points of detail if they were to 'learn' from the video, or, in other words, if they were to use it successfully. There was a wide gap here between part of the teaching purpose of the directives and students' interpretations of their purpose; it meant that the structural devices worked restrictively rather than constructively upon students' perceptions of the general meaning of the videos. On the other hand, they were effective in the way they encouraged some students to observe the content closely.

One voice-over technique however, was very effective at promoting general group discussion. This was the use of a direct question to students at the very end of a sequence; a question which referred them back to the very last item they had seen, and called for some comment on it. This often promoted a snap, yes-no type answer, which was then taken up and explored. On the other hand, questions posed *during* a video sequence were usually lost. Groups of students, who tended to do less replaying than individuals and to be more confident about the 'rightness' of their group approach to video work, rarely picked them up at all. Individuals, if they replayed the cassettes, sometimes did so with the precise intention of hearing the voice-over questions again, but explained that it needed a special and diverting kind of concentration to do so.

On this evidence, it would seem essential for video designers to consider carefully first of all whether it is a genuine function of the video they are making that it should promote detailed discussion of particular questions. If the answer is 'no', then voice-over directives and questions should be omitted on the grounds of their distractive effects. If the answer is 'yes', then the video should supplement the voice-over with other techniques — such as a freezing of action and a print-up of the words and questions on screen; alternatively, a visible presenter rather than voice-over might be used. There is also clear evidence that if questions and directives are highlighted in these ways that they will need to be supported by some indication of the answers or observations students might make. Without such support many students felt both frustrated, and anxious about the quality of their learning. Indeed many students also appeared to have anxieties about the adequacy of their responses to the more open-ended and general questions (those which usually appeared in the video notes). These questions tended to be perceived as requiring precise answers and rarely as starting points for constructive thought or discussion. This perception did not prevent students in groups from using the questions put to them partly as a basis for general discussion but it also meant that they often returned to the questions after making some general observations and tried to answer them directly, as a kind of summary of the group activity. The majority of students working alone, on the other hand, found general questions extremely difficult to answer; some explained that this was so because 'I just go blank and have no ideas', or because they felt they lacked the necessary teaching experience and information to provide a sensible answer. Again, it would seem important for students to be given feedback on their approach to open-ended video material to alleviate the tensions and frustrations they experience and to do so at the time of viewing. If video is to be studied seriously, in most students' views, the points it raises must be made clear and not left to guesswork; if it is relevant to their understanding of the course as a whole, its relevance must be indicated.

There are a variety of ways in which immediate feedback could be provided — it could be *written* and presented, for example, at the end of any accompanying video notes, or it could be contained within the video program itself. The sequential structure of these particular videos suggested a useful approach: the effect of the usual slipback of tape when students re-started a cassette meant that they often heard again the last words of each sequence. This repeated nugget of data often provided a very satisfying summary of students' intervening work. Where a sequential design is used it would be valuable on this evidence, for students to hear some kind of comment or discussion which over-viewed individual sequences in turn. It might be an opportunity too, to provide students with linking comments between sequences and thus provide them with a clearer sense of the video as a whole. It is evident, in other words, that students welcome a structure to their video work and a clear sense of its purpose, but that neither the provision of verbal questions nor voice-over directives in themselves provide a sufficiently supportive framework.

The video notes used in this case study were considered very good in parts. Students particularly praised their retrospective value; that is to say, the photograph, and the summaries were said to be useful memory joggers. More contentious was the value of the questions and note-taking activities. It was clear that almost all students wanted some guidance about what they should 'do' with the material they had seen beyond applying an instinctive appraisal such as 'How interesting'. But the *kind* of guidance about activities and discussion students wanted varied tremendously; it appeared to be related to their general perceptions of what learning entails, and to what they wanted out of this particular course of study. In order to have a clearer idea of students' conceptions of useful and effective video study let us look at individual and group work separately.

INDIVIDUAL STUDENTS

Despite the course team encouragement to students to try and form self-help groups it was clear from the outset (from answers to a questionnaire) that roughly half of them would opt to study video material alone. Problems of arranging mutually convenient meeting places and dates were influential here, but even more marked was the tendency for such students simply to prefer the notion of working on their own. Those who did study the cassettes on their own tended to express more doubts than group members about their adequacy as video learners. It should be pointed out that these doubts were expressed in relation to their one experience of video, and thus to one particular kind of video content. It would not be reasonable to infer from this one experience that students will have similar doubts about their ability to study with other kinds — for example, with video material which teaches more directly. (Whether one can expect students to be so 'reasonable' is another question.) However, a fairly typical comment from a doubting student illustrates their concern:

> When watching alone I try and make notes on *everything*!!, so I probably miss a lot of the visual as I have one eye on what I am writing. I don't recall being aware of being told 'to watch out for' things some of the time. I don't think the way I watched was educationally valuable . . . Although I found the video essential to understand the course material and it made it clearer, I don't honestly think it stimulated my interest!

It may be helpful at this point to remind oneself of the position of individual students enrolled in this course. They are set to watch video *before* reading a text which provides a framework to the illustrative material. Having, in most cases, put in considerable effort to view (ordered a cassette, arranged a viewing and travelled) they are then faced with a suggested study period of two hours. The cassette runs for about 20 minutes. Students quite naturally want to get something out of the precious study hours at their disposal, and as indicated earlier, have clear clues, in the course team's 'two hours' and their questions, that there is some serious learning to be done in relation to the video. Given a written text to work on in a similar situation, students can skim read, go back and forth and underline, make marginal jottings and even if they cannot understand or answer questions they can, in these ways, begin to sort out the text and provide themselves with a visible record of their having done so. They have *evidence* of their study. Given a videotape, students are less sure what to do. Some again begin by skimming — they just view to get the gist of the content: others focus immediately on the questions. Whichever tactic is used, students cannot interact with the audio-visual action in the same concrete ways they handle text. Nor is it a simple matter to paraphrase things *seen*, that is, translate them into another symbol system so as to provide a written and meaningful summary. Most students wanted written evidence of their study period, however, and there were two main approaches. Either students replayed extensively and wrote down much of what they *heard*, in note form; or they replayed extensively and, with a focus upon the referential questions they were given, again made records of words spoken in the video. There are two points to notice about these activities. First, they are orientated towards just one of the teaching functions intended by the designers — that of careful observation. Second, they indicate that students *may* need practice and guidance about how to record visual data. It could be argued that individuals in this instance made no attempt to make such records because they were not specifically asked to do so. Nevertheless, much of the information was visual — for example, scenes of children handling apparatus with hesitancy as they worked on a mathematical problem. How aware were students of these features? Observation of groups of students *discussing* rather than recording in notes what they saw and heard, revealed that they too made little or no reference to visual as opposed to audible information.

Students' own perceptions of the *learning* value of these activities ranged from the fairly satisfied:

> I read the questions and listen very hard to the commentary — I have to go back and replay a lot to do this — then I write down the words I hear and the maths they show. I think it will be useful for answering questions later.

to the more critical:

> Do I really need to make the detailed notes they suggest? . . . I mean, I can answer the other questions in a couple of words, so I'm not sure what is supposed to take me so long . . . do you suppose the course team will want to see what we've written?

It seems in sum, as if the note-taking and referential questions encouraged students to focus on detailed facts, and to attempt an accurate record, particularly of the *audio* content. Some students assumed this was valuable merely because this was a given task, some assumed it was valuable as it provided them with written evidence of children's problems, or written examples of how teachers should teach. Others instinctively felt it was a waste of time since they preferred to think in general terms rather than to note particularities, but nevertheless, felt constrained to follow the instructions they were given.

Lone students, as I have already indicated, when discussing video structure, tended to find general questions difficult to answer in any depth without the support of a theoretical framework, or the help and stimulus of colleagues. The main learning they were thus able to entertain, related purely to the specific video content, and for some students this caused considerable frustration. There was a strong minority voice, for example, claiming that the videos really only could be effectively studied in groups, and that they had clearly been designed with this intention. Students who, for geographical reasons, could not attend group work, or who felt reluctant on other grounds about viewing with colleagues, suggested that it was a divisive and inappropriate use of video in a distance learning context.

On the evidence of the difficulties these students working alone experienced, there would appear to be good grounds for claims that this type of video, essentially involves group activity if it is to achieve its more general learning goals. It seems likely that courses made with these kinds of aims in the future at the Open University will be recommended to warn students, as they apply for enrolment, that group work is important. They are also likely to be recommended to give students advice about ways in which their individual work can usefully be supported by group work 'at a distance'. Three approaches to such support have been tried out and appear to be very successful. First, isolated students can be allocated to a functioning group and sent audio-cassette recordings of the discussions that take place. Second, isolated students can be encouraged to telephone and discuss video questions with a colleague. Third, students can write letters and comment on each others' answers.

It has already been pointed out that the video described here is, in a sense, a unique event, and that many of the problems lone students experienced with it related to the open-ended teaching strategy it adopted. The potential for individual learning with other kinds of video-cassette material has not been argued either way. It seems there may be dangers, however, in assuming that videocassettes will be similarly valuable to Open University students as audio-cassettes simply because both involve work with material delivered on cassette. It is true that audio-cassettes have proven useful for a variety of teaching purposes, and probably for three main reasons already outlined: the control they give students over their learning, their informality and their convenience. While video equipment provides students with the same potential for replaying and pausing as they work through material, I have described how, for some students, this kind of physical interaction can be quite damagingly intrusive upon their learning. Also, as compared with audio-cassettes, video seems to be a less potentially informal or human medium and is certainly less convenient to use unless students have their own equipment in their own homes. Another vital difference of course, is that students using video material presumably need both to watch and to listen; they are less free, therefore, to carry out some of the activities (writing, drawing, setting up equipment) they can so usefully perform while simultaneously listening to an audio-tape. In sum, although the point is often made that videocassettes provide a qualitatively different learning experience from television, less attention appears to be paid to the qualitative differences between audio and video *cassette* work, and the implications for video design inherent in such differences. Students may well prove to feel less comfortable with the medium and less willing or able to engage with the sense of student/teacher co-operational learning which worked so well on audio.

GROUPS OF STUDENTS

It is clear that video functions very effectively as a focus for group discussion. In this situation however, the learning that takes place is likely to be as much a reflection of the inter-student activity as the student-video interaction. Nevertheless, the sequential structure of these eight videos in the case study clearly encouraged some replay of sections of the taped material, and students nearly always stopped the tape as instructed by the flashing symbol. It was clear, however, that groups of students replayed material far less than individuals. They usually only did so if there was a common complaint about the clarity of visual data or a lack of consensus about what had really been seen or heard. For the most part, students relied upon their pooled recollections to reconstruct the scene as a whole, and if there was any dispute about what had 'happened' on screen, the majority view won the day. Indeed, one of the main reasons expressed for working in a group was that it absolved students from needing to worry about details of the visual evidence. One comment illustrates this view:

> I tended to feel more relaxed . . . because I thought the others would pick up things when my concentration wandered and I could discuss things I didn't understand.

Another very important reason for preferring group work implied in these last words was the pool of experience which members could draw upon and contribute to. It was extremely helpful to students on *this* course, for example, to meet colleagues teaching at levels above or below their own. For group discussions to work well it seems that the number attending regularly was less critical than the need for a group to include students with a wide range and mix of experience; thus, the discussion in groups of three could be as lively and productive as in groups of 14. Indeed, the larger the group the less chance individuals had of contributing to the discussion and the greater the need for formalities such as an official chairman.

As had been expected, several students on this course had access to school facilities for watching video and or for recording broadcasts themselves rather than using the cassette loan service. It is unlikely that an 'ordinary' Open University undergraduate would have either of these advantages, and for them the need to do group work might prove very demanding. Even given favourable circumstances, it was evident that as the academic year drew on, the pressures of doing the bare essentials to keep up with the course and other commitments told upon students and argued against the luxury of continuing to do group video work. Group attendance became less regular and often ceased altogether.

The luxury element of group work was the mutual support and encouragement students could give each other, not just in relation to their video work but to other aspects of the course. At the start of the year meetings also helped some students to become more confident about learning with such open-ended material. Unlike individuals, groups of students showed less interest in repeating or rehearsing details of content but used the social context to exchange opinions about the significance and implications of what was seen and heard.

So sessions were mainly used to explore a wide range of ideas in discussion, and then often followed up either immediately or at home by students making a few written notes to record ideas which remained uppermost. Having once gained experience and confidence about this way of studying, some students seemed to feel freer to choose whether to attend regularly or to work on their own. Presumably they felt they had a rational basis for deciding whether video work was essential or not, and showed such objectivity in the way they tended to blame the video rather than themselves if the sessions were not useful; students who always worked alone in contrast tended to blame themselves. Groups were also quicker to sense that the video's true purpose was to lead the text, and to explore the ground before restricting analysis to one theoretical perspective. In this sense, it did not much matter if you missed some of the content of each video, for essential ideas would be taken up and explored later by the text. If individuals found the general questions difficult to tackle, for groups these were the most stimulating and valuable kinds to work upon. Many students claimed that just by being *present* at a group meeting they found ideas flooding in or at least something to say about the general implications of what they saw, and they tended to put this down to the competitive edge such social contact provided, as well as to the stimulus of hearing alternative points of view.

As already mentioned, some very small groups — pairs or threes — worked as well as large groups. Their success seemed to depend partly on a good mix of experience and thus on access to a broad information resource. It depended too on students' attitudes to the course thesis. A student strongly opposed to its line of argument could be very damaging to discussions between two or three other more ambivalent students. In larger groups, on the other hand, a critical voice could stimulate discussion. A third and vital factor seemed to be the individual members' perceptions of learning and their orientation to the course. Students who sought to reconstruct detailed facts or who insisted on searching out the right answers to questions given, tended to narrow the focus of the discussions which took place. Given the presence of a colleague(s) with a more holistic view of the purpose of the videos, small group video work appeared to work as the course team intended. There was too, less anxiety about the time spent on discussing individual sequences, given a good mix of students; they had, in other words, more confidence in their approach to video work *as* a group and felt less constrained by course team 'imperatives', than either individuals or members of small, homogeneous groups.

In sum, it seems that more constructive thinking about the video material took place in a *combination* of video input and group interaction. The group activity was not really an optional extra but vital to a successful match between this teaching intention and students' use of video. In a group, students seemed able to analyse the video content by making links between their own teaching experience or common sense knowledge, and to perceive this as the 'right' response to be making.

CONCLUSIONS

This chapter has traced developments at the Open University in the use of video. It has discussed the two-phased approach to implementing cassettes as a teaching component on its courses, and indicated how the move towards using audio-cassettes rather than radio provided a rehearsal of what is expected to happen in the field of audio-vision. It has drawn attention to the research work at the university which provides its academics and producers with a sound basis for making decisions about appropriate ways in which audio-vision and cassettes can be employed in a distance teaching context. The case study illustrates just one way in which the university anticipates using video in the future. The study shows how valuable the medium can be for promoting learning amongst groups of students when the particular format described is adopted. It is an approach which may be less useful for individual students, however, and it is anticipated that this style of video will be most used in the continuing education area of courses produced by the university rather than on its undergraduate program. Such courses provide material which professional bodies, in, for example, the worlds of medicine, education and industry, may use as a basis for their in-service training programs. In this situation problems of student access to equipment and arrangements for group studying are taken on by the organizations concerned rather than by the university itself. Meanwhile moves are afoot for the university to extend its use of video; the ways it will improve students' individual access to the medium are as yet undecided but this is clearly an aspect which will need adjustment if students can be expected to make effective use of video material. As to the design of video in the future? The case study provides a further resource; from research such as this the university gains insight into students' attitudes to the medium, and into the ways they interpret particular kinds of structure. These kinds of information will, it is to be hoped, help designers to make programs which are sensitive to students' very varying needs and approaches to learning.

REFERENCES

Bates, A W & Gallagher, M (1977) *Improving the Effectiveness of Open University Case Studies and Documentaries*, Open University (mimeo), Milton Keynes.

Bates, A W & Kern, L (1977) *Alternative Media Technologies for the Open University*, Open University (mimeo), Milton Keynes.

Bloom, B S *et al* (1956) *Taxonomy of Educational Objectives Handbook 1 Cognitive Domain*, David McKay Company Inc, New York.

Brown, S & Grundin, H (1982) *The 1982 Video Cassette Loan Service. Interim Evaluation Report*, Open University (mimeo), Milton Keynes.

Durbridge, N (1980) *Audio Cassette Usage on D284, T341 and M211*, Open University (mimeo), Milton Keynes.

Durbridge, N (1981) *Audio Cassettes in Higher Education*, Open University (mimeo), Milton Keynes.

Gallagher, M (1978) *Good Television and Good Educational Practice: Problems of Definition*, Open University (mimeo), Milton Keynes.

Grundin, H (1980) *Audio-Visual and Other Media in 91 Open University Courses: Results of the 1979 Undergraduate Survey*, Open University (mimeo), Milton Keynes.

20. The Use of Video in Distance Education As Applied to Economics

Wolfram Laaser and
Jon Stanford

SUMMARY

This chapter focuses on the production and use of video programs in teaching economics at a distance, based on the rationale of an 'overtly didactic approach' and illustrated by examples from the Division of External Studies at the University of Queensland (Australia), the Fernuniversität (West Germany) and the Open University (UK). An 'overtly didactic approach' puts emphasis on the following principles: academic content and educational objectives (as against presentation and production standards); video interaction with viewers; autonomy of an integral, but text-independent part of the course; and the use of the distinctive features of the medium for teaching.[1]

INTRODUCTION

Despite the widespread use of film, television and video in the community at large these media are not extensively used in tertiary teaching in general and in economics teaching in particular. A review article on economic analysis and film (Moss, 1979) suggests 'that the celluloid future of economic analysis appears to be a bright one'. The use of videotape to show repeat live lectures has been considered by McConnell *et al* (1971) and the use of videotape to enhance teaching skills has been examined by Becker *et al* (1978). Video is widely believed to have a great impact on teaching at a distance.[2]

This paper, while related to the broader background of the use of video in tertiary teaching, concentrates specifically on the use of video as a technique of teaching economics at a distance.

The major arguments of the paper are that one of the most important reasons for the failure to use video more extensively in teaching economics, apart from its cost, is the lack of an underlying rationale which would make most effective use of the medium; and that video is too often seen as a means of imitating traditional techniques rather than making use of its distinctive features as a medium which requires the development of particular skills on the part of the teacher before it can be used effectively.

The aims of the paper are:

☐ to argue for the relative advantages of video rather than television as a technique for teaching at a distance

☐ to present a rationale for the preparation of video programs in economics — this rationale is referred to as an 'overtly didactic approach'

☐ to discuss the production of video programs using an 'overtly didactic approach' based on the experience of the audio-visual project[3] being carried out in the Division of External Studies, University of Queensland

☐ to discuss the production and use of video programs in economics at the Central Institute for the Development of Distance Education (ZFE) at the Fernuniversität in Hagen (West Germany)[4]

☐ to examine the more conventional and better known use of television for teaching economics at a distance by the British Open University

☐ to outline proposals for further research and development in the production of video programs.

TELEVISION OR VIDEO IN DISTANCE EDUCATION?

Central to the issue of the choice between television and video in distance education is the question of how distance education is to be conceived and organized. At the risk of oversimplification, one can draw two stark polar alternative views about distance education: the first is that distance education is a substitute for conventional classroom education. This is the 'surrogate theory' (Stanford, 1981a) of distance education which says that teaching at a distance should be congruent with classroom teaching. The second extreme is that distance education is genuinely innovative and is an alternative to conventional classroom-based education. The implications of these polar views are of considerable importance for the choice of methods and techniques in teaching at a distance. The surrogate theory attempts to provide, as closely as possible, for distance students the experiences gained in the classroom, while the second alternative attempts to use techniques of instruction which make the most of the advantages of distance education. The two most significant advantages to the student in distance education are the relaxation of the constraints of location and time and the reduction in cost of education.

For conventional formal classroom education, students are highly constrained in their activities by fixed location and time. Students may, in general, receive instruction only at a specific location — the site of the educational institution — and only at a specific time — the class times which are scheduled only during particular sessions of the year.

One of the major costs of full-time education, which is often overlooked by teachers, is the cost of student time. According to the economist's concept of *opportunity cost*, the cost of student time in full-time education is the cost of the best alternative way a student could spend his time. Assuming that full-time employment is available, the cost of attending full-time education is the wage or salary income foregone.

However, when viewed as a genuine alternative to classroom instruction, distance education offers significant advantages to students.

In the first place, students may initiate learning at times and locations convenient to them no matter how unconventional or unusual these times and locations may be. Secondly, distance students can avoid the loss of income by combining study with full-time or part-time employment. (It is, of course, true that distance students incur other costs by extending the time taken to complete their course of study.) If we accept the view that distance education is a genuinely alternative education, teaching at a distance requires concomitant alternative teaching techniques. Viewed in this light, video offers significant advantages over television as a technique of instruction at a distance. Television, in distance education, retains the constraint of time; the student may view the program only at the time of transmission which, itself, is often determined by non-educational criteria so that education programs are transmitted at off-peak (and unattractive) viewing times.

The advantages of video over television lie in the fact that students are allowed to initiate and *to repeat* viewing of programs and that they are able to view video at the optimum time for themselves. However it must be recognized that the use of video requires more costly equipment. In general, though, we would conclude that emphasis on the development of video presentations is to be preferred to television when developing techniques for distance education. This general conclusion is supported by the particular advantages of designing video programs according to the principles of an 'overtly didactic approach' which we have developed.

AN 'OVERTLY DIDACTIC APPROACH' TO VIDEO PRESENTATION

The principles of an 'overtly didactic approach' to video production can be stated as follows:

1. The aim of viewing a program is to learn a particular content.
2. The content of the video program should be more important than presentation and production standards.
3. The video program should not aim at passive viewers but at interaction with viewers.
4. The video program should be a self-contained, text-independent, but an integral part of the course.
5. The video program should make best use of the distinctive and unique features of the medium for teaching.

The 'overtly didactic approach' to video presentations is founded on the concept that distance education is, and should be, learner-centred and that, operationally, the ultimate judgement about the effectiveness of the use of video in distance education is based on student performance. This approach requires that the learning objectives to be achieved by the student viewing the video program are specified and communicated to the viewer. Thus, an 'overtly didactic' video program will be closer in intention to an instructional film than a movie or television program designed for entertainment.

An 'overtly didactic' video program should be judged by its content in relation to learning objectives rather than by its style of presentation. This principle is likely to cause differences between media specialists and academics. Film and television specialists have 'production values' of their own which determine their judgements about the artistic and aesthetic merits of productions. Film and television are widely used as entertainment devices so that viewers may gain enjoyment, relief and diversion. Consequently, viewers derive their criteria of assessment from these uses.

However, while these values and criteria are valid in determining the artistic merit or the entertainment potential of film and television productions, for instructional video productions they are invalid, inappropriate and likely to divert attention from the educational objectives to be achieved. This does not mean to imply that production quality in video presentations is not important. Most students are probably substantial consumers of film and television and likely to recognize any production crudities as an amateurish 'home-made' effect which may destroy the credibility of the video presentation.

However, what it does mean is that given the choice between production quality and content, the choice must *always* be made in favour of educational objectives and content. Academic values must always dominate production values and pure presentation.

The third principle of the 'overtly didactic approach' to video production requires the viewer to interact with the instructional material instead of passively viewing it. Again, we must differentiate instructional video from film and television because video allows students to work individually and at their own pace, both in viewing the presentation and in completing the tasks required of them by the presentation. Thus, the video program must require the viewer to respond to signals or direct commands from the video. One technique to do this is to provide a 'work pause' in the program; that is, the viewer is required to stop the videotape and undertake a specific task, such as the solution of a problem set by the program designer. After solving the task, the student restarts the videotape which provides the answer to the problem to enable the viewer to validate his solution. The intention of such a work pause is to activate the student after passive viewing and to raise his concentration and attention level for the next part of the program.

The fourth principle of the 'overtly didactic approach' requires the video program to form an integral part of the formal course work in distance education. The video program should be independent of written texts in the same area rather than simply elaborating a text. Although repetition is a valid and useful teaching device, the time of a distance student is scarce and highly valued and must be economized.

The fifth principle requires a video presentation to capitalize on the distinctive and unique features of the medium for teaching. There are many aspects of video (some shared by film and television) which are uniquely suited for teaching. Some of these features are visual effects of moving graphics, the dynamic nature of diagrammatical presentations and the combination of sound and picture. These features are of special significance in a discipline like economics where graphical, diagrammatic and mathematical analyses are used extensively and to a high degree of sophistication. Taking advantage of these facilities (including playback facilities) means using video as a new and distinct medium for teaching which allows many effects to be created more effectively and indeed to be created for the first time. Many reported uses of video in economics which have not been favoured by students (particularly televised or videotaped lectures) have been inefficient and ineffectual because they attempt only to translate one teaching technique into another medium. The problem is compounded if the original technique is ineffectual or not particularly good; for instance a poor lecture televised or videotaped will be worse and more ineffectual in the new medium.

The implication of this last principle for teaching staff who wish to produce their own video programs is that they either formally or informally need some professional development to acquire new skills and to learn more about the medium and its possibilities.

THE USE OF VIDEO PROGRAMS IN ECONOMICS AT THE FERNUNIVERSITÄT

The Fernuniversität, that is the Distance University of the Federal Republic of Germany, has been teaching since 1974 and has been producing video programs in economics since 1978. The motivation to produce such video presentations arose from the results of course evaluations showing that students had particular difficulties in understanding the more abstract and mathematical reasoning in economics from the correspondence text (ie written material) alone.

The objectives of the project are to produce video programs which can:

☐ explain these concepts and reasonings more effectually than by print
☐ supplant to some extent the exercises held by tutors at traditional campus universities
☐ motivate students in their study of economics.

The general strategy of the video project is:

☐ to select topics difficult for the students to understand
☐ to make considerable use of graphics and animation sequences when explaining these topics
☐ to include exercises
☐ to supplement the presentation with interviews of experts in the field, comments and discussions by authors of the course unit and with illustrations of real-life applications of the problem. These supplements are intended to be the motivating technique in the video presentations.

The general practice of the video programs is to have the topic presented by the faculty staff responsible for the academic content of the videotape, but to use a substantial component (usually more than half the time) of graphics and animation. The inclusion of exercises in the video programs, which is possible only with video and not television, is an attempt to prevent students losing concentration while viewing the tapes and to provide for the interactive element.

The videotapes are available for use in 40 study centres or may be borrowed by students for use on their own video playback machines.

The use of videotapes at the Fernuniversität is illustrated by an example of the correspondence course on econometrics. This topic was chosen because students had experienced considerable difficulty with the mathematical concepts involved in the unit; the video program was to concentrate more specifically on the narrowly defined topic of 'dynamic multipliers in econometric models,' which was, however, quite representative of other economic topics formulated in a mathematical framework.

The procedure to develop the topic for video presentation was:

☐ to define the learning objectives of the unit
☐ to elaborate an alternative written text which paid particular attention to didactic principles and to typographical means of explaining the concepts
☐ to prepare a video script which presented the concept of dynamic multiplier in a manner which used the specifics of video.

After the production of the video program, the alternative approaches to the topic were evaluated in a structured experiment using a small group of students. The results of the experiment of comparing one group of students who used only the printed correspondence course material with another group of students who watched the videotape were that:

1. Economic concepts formulated in a mathematical framework can be learned from a videotape.
2. The test scores of students who used video alone tended to be slightly lower than the scores of those who used printed materials; but this factor has to be counterbalanced by the fact that the students who used video alone took less time to study the topic.
3. Students who used video as a supplement to the written correspondence text were able to increase their test scores.

The experience of the Fernuniversität has been that a relatively low proportion of students make use of the video programs. A restricted study of students living close to the main campus of the Fernuniversität and being contacted by telephone, showed that only slightly over 20 per cent had used the videotapes which were available for their course although some students indicated that they intended to view the video programs.

The great majority of students (approximately 80 per cent) said that they would view the tapes if they could do so at home with their own video equipment but only about 10 per cent had their own equipment. Nearly all students who viewed the video programs did so at the study centres under the guidance of the course tutors. The reasons for not using the videotapes included the following:

1. Students were not fully informed about the existence of the videotapes and of the playback facilities.
2. Many students made no use of study centres and did not attend the sessions given by the course tutors.

3. Some students found the use of video too time consuming.
4. Other students found no major difficulties with the economic concepts.

The general, if tentative, conclusions that can be drawn from the experience at the Fernuniversität are that economics students accept the video programs as an important learning aid and consider that learning from video is easier than learning from a correspondence text. Students also like the change in media and prefer video presentations to the alternative of additional written material.

OPEN UNIVERSITY EXPERIENCE WITH TEACHING ECONOMICS BY TELEVISION

The British Open University uses television programs as a minor component of a multi-media approach to distance education (the major component is print material); the television programs are produced jointly by the academic staff of the Open University and the British Broadcasting Corporation (BBC) and are transmitted by the BBC on channels which can be accessed by anyone with a television receiver. In consequence the television programs are produced to high technical and broadcasting standards. It is interesting to note that the programs attract a significant audience from members of the public who are not enrolled as Open University students. Thus the transmission of television programs may have important side-benefits which help the Open University to receive community support and which may assist in recruiting new students.

While the use of existing television production and broadcast facilities has advantages, it does bring with it some drawbacks, two of which will be discussed in general terms and in relation to economics programs. The use of existing facilities does seriously curtail both the total amount of time available for broadcasting Open University television programs and the times of the day available for broadcast. In general the times available for Open University television broadcasts are those which are regarded as 'off peak' for the public television channels. Open University broadcasts tend to be concentrated in early morning times (eg 6.30 am), early evening times (eg 4.30 pm), late night times (eg 12.40 am) and off-peak weekend times (eg 6.30-11 am). Again, in general, it can be said that there is severe pressure on the available time for television broadcasting by the Open University so that the opportunity to repeat programs is severely restricted. These two aspects of broadcasting timing impose substantial constraints on students (that is, the programs are available for viewing only at restricted times) and impose institutionally determined pacing on students. By conforming to the requirements of this externally imposed pacing, students lose much of the advantage of being distance students.

The difficulty arising from the use of existing television production facilities is connected with the conflict between academic (or more strictly, didactic) and technical considerations. Professional broadcasters are likely to judge the quality and success of their programs by

253

production values and standards. If this is so, then students will find it more difficult to discriminate between programs as entertainment or relaxation and programs which have explicit learning requirements. (Incidentally it may be observed that the popularity of Open University programs with the general public, mentioned earlier, may be attributed to this factor.)

A report on the response of Open University economics students to television programs is available (Gallagher, 1978). The conclusions from that study are important for illustrating the points which have been discussed earlier. The report which examines a second-level economics course states that only 20 per cent of students saw all four television programs which had been broadcast up to the time of the evaluation. This low viewing rate is attributable to 'students working behind schedule' and to the lack of repeat programs.

The student reaction to the style of presentation is substantially divided; 40 per cent of respondents hold that presentation should be polished and sophisticated but 25 per cent of students are more concerned with the issues of program content, structure and teaching approach than with presentation.

The conclusions of the study are:

1. The type of program which emphasizes demonstration/application of economic principles and illustration of theoretical concepts is preferred by students.
2. There is a need to spell out the conceptual basis on which the program topic and material has been selected.
3. There is a need for more guidance and structure overall in the programs.
4. Students regard 'programs which are visually and substantively interesting' as 'no more than interesting'.

PLAN FOR FURTHER WORK

In planning further work in video for teaching economics at a distance, it is important to note that two areas of activity are involved. These are firstly the development of further video programs in economics, and secondly, research into the effectiveness of video for learning economics at a distance.

The results of research into economics education suggest that further work in video may prove to be fruitful. A comprehensive survey of teaching college economics (Siegfried & Fels, 1979) found, among other results, that 'different students learn economics in different ways. The best learning strategy provides alternative learning methods directed towards the different needs of different students . . . Students like self-paced instruction, and it increases learning in some circumstances'.

These results are particularly important in relation to distance education with a more diverse range of students to whom self-pacing is more important than to on-campus students.

The requirements of the 'overtly didactic approach' to production of video programs for economics imply that efforts should be concentrated on video programs which have a strong theoretical content and which emphasize self-pacing and student interaction. The experience of both the Fernuniversität and the Open University supports this strategy.

Some of the problems of student use of video are due to the fact that this is a relatively new learning aid and that the range of video programs available to students is still very limited. At this juncture it is also necessary to teach students how to use self-instructional video.

It would be an interesting experiment to design a complete economics course on video as a single medium and to evaluate the effectiveness in terms of learning outcome.

There are two major problems restricting the production of more video programs. The first, which has been alluded to before, is the shortage of academic economists who have acquired, or are prepared to acquire, the skills to use the new medium effectively and the second is the cost of producing video programs, that is, the costs of preparing a treatment, script and story board and the costs of producing a video program in a studio.

The *preparation* costs for a video program of 25 minutes duration can be estimated as being a minimum of *two months'* time for an academic plus graphic designers' time. (The estimate is very low in relation to actual time incurred in both the Fernuniversität and the Open University.)

The *studio* costs for the same program can be estimated as a minimum of four technicians' full-time for one week.

We believe that an appropriate strategy for further development would be the production of a full range of video programs covering the whole field of economics and designed for a complete range of student experience and level — elementary, intermediate and advanced.

The question of research into the effectiveness of video as a learning-teaching aid in economics has to be raised at this juncture. Although there has been a considerable advance in research in economics education as exemplified by the Siegfried and Fels survey, there is still a great deal of knowledge of teaching and learning economics which remains unknown.

CONCLUSIONS

Although video remains a relatively new technique for teaching economics at a distance, there are a number of tentative conclusions which can be drawn from the above:

1. To be effective, the use of video must be based on a theoretical rationale. We have offered a possible rationale by the 'overtly didactic approach'.
2. Video has a particular role to play in teaching economics. This role is to stress the explanation and development of theoretical concepts incorporating self-pacing and interactive features.
3. Students generally have positive attitudes towards video but may need instruction in the use of video to gain full advantage from the medium.

4. There is a shortage of academic economists who can use the medium effectively for teaching. In addition, the cost of producing video programs is, at present, an inhibiting factor for further development although the increased use of home videocassette recorders will compensate for the high cost of software production.

Notes

1. This paper is based on joint research activities undertaken by the authors. The financial assistance of the DAAD (Deutscher Akademischer Austauschdienst — German Professional Exchange Service), the University of Queensland (Australia), and the Fernuniversität making this collaborative research possible, is gratefully acknowledged. The views expressed in this paper are not necessarily those of the institutions.
2. The internationally accepted term for tertiary teaching by correspondence is 'distance education'; the term 'extended studies' has been used in the past in Australia.
3. Some of the previous results of the project are to be found in Stanford (1981b). The project has produced an integrated slide-tape presentation, 'The Australian Capital Market', and a videotape incorporating the principles of an 'overtly didactic approach', 'Introduction to the New Macroeconomics'. Wolfram Laaser was co-producer of this video program.)
4. Reports of work undertaken by the ZFE are to be found in Laaser (1981).

REFERENCES

Becker, W E, Lewis, D R, Orvis, C, Riezman, R & Salemi, M D (1978) 'Development and evaluation of teaching skills through the use of videotapes', in Saunders, P, Welsh, L & Hansen, W, *Resource Manual for Teaching Training Programs in Economics*, Joint Council on Economic Education, New York.

Gallagher, M (1978) 'Preliminary report on student reaction to economics television programmes', *IET Papers on Broadcasting, 102,* Open University, Milton Keynes.

Laaser, W (1981) 'Video as supplementary material — the impact of an alternative development of study materials in solving formal economic problems', *Working Papers in Distance Education*, University of Queensland, Brisbane.

McConnell, C R & Lamphear, C (1969) 'Teaching principles of economics without lectures', *Journal of Economic Education,* 1, 20-32.

Moss, L S (1979) 'Film and the transmission of economic knowledge: a report', *Journal of Economic Literature,* XVII, 1005-19.

Siegfried, J J & Fels, R (1979) 'Research on teaching college economics: a survey', *Journal of Economic Literature,* XVII, 923-69.

Stanford, J D (1981a) 'The origins of distance education in the University of Queensland', *Australian and New Zealand History of Education XIth National Conference*, Brisbane.

Stanford, J D (1981b) 'Student preference for audio-cassettes — some further evidence', *ASPESA Newsletter,* 7, 1, 10-17.

21. The Use of Video in a Communicative Approach to Learning French

Christine Mestre and
Andrew Lian

SUMMARY

After a short theoretical introduction, this section describes and develops a range of possible uses for video in the context of a French class. Techniques examined include the viewing and analysis of authentic documents, video self-confrontation within the framework of both micro and macro simulations, the analysis of student performances and, finally, computer-generated simulations. It will be argued that video is an excellent tool (a) for developing awareness of critical features of the target language and (b) for defining the individual needs of students.[1]

INTRODUCTION

In this chapter we shall attempt to outline a range of possible uses of video in the context of a French class or, indeed, any language class, whose purpose is to develop communicative competence.

Many of the principles underpinning our suggestions have already been mentioned in other chapters in this book (for instance, Tennyson & Breuer) and in other places (for instance, Mestre & Lian, 1982; Lian & Joy, 1981; Lian, 1982). It might be useful, nevertheless, to review quickly some of the issues as we see them, before proceeding to a description of various techniques.

THE NOTION OF PROGRESSION

Most language courses, commercial or otherwise, present the student with 'increasingly difficult' material. In the context of a normal class of students, the notion of 'difficulty' appears to us to be necessarily problematic and arbitrary as it makes no room for individual differences: the same aspect may be difficult for one student while presenting absolutely no difficulty for another.

We would further argue that each student will necessarily experience difficulties of a different order from those of his/her colleagues. This is due to the fact that students always have different backgrounds and, therefore, that the sum of knowledge and experience that they bring into operation during the learning process will necessarily be different. Given that perception is always mediated by experience, the interlanguages (of Selinker, 1972; Selinker *et al*, 1975) generated in each student will reflect those differences in background. Each student will, therefore, have an optimal progression which will differ from that of others.

Furthermore, most courses have a grammar-based progression which inadequately reflects the communicative difficulties likely to be encountered by any one student. If a progression is to exist, then it ought to take account of the other systems involved in communication.

Given the above, any class of students will necessarily be heterogeneous in character. Moreover, even where great care is taken to establish criteria for membership of any particular group of learners, significant individual differences will still become apparent and will need to be dealt with.

Thus, in our view, the notion of the language class where everyone does the same thing, at the same time, in the same space and at the same rate can only lead to considerable frustration and dissatisfaction. Furthermore, as, in a heterogeneous language class, the teaching process must necessarily be aimed at the 'average' student, the faster learners are condemned to boredom and the slower ones to bewilderment and failure. Only proper individualization can provide a likelihood of success.

UP-TO-DATE INFORMATION

If communicative competence is to be attained, then a knowledge of the way in which communication is successfully negotiated is important. Such knowledge should include not only the more traditional grammatical and lexical systems, but also relevant paralinguistic elements and communicative strategies.

We believe that video can provide an environment appropriate for the development of communicative competence while responding to the needs outlined above.

THE ROLE OF VIDEO IN A LEARNER-CENTRED METHODOLOGY

Video is capable of contributing significantly to a methodology focused on the learner. We believe that whether video is used for viewing authentic documents or for obtaining feedback on one's own communicative performance, it can enable the learner to develop, through a broad range of possible activities, a sensitivity to the critical or pertinent elements of communication.

One of the great advantages of video is that it affords the opportunity of treating the same document at different levels and in different ways. A feature movie, for example, could be experienced visually, and either with or without sound. Indeed, it is even possible to imagine exercises where only the soundtrack was used. As a result of these different ways of accessing the movie the students are more than likely to have retained at least something of the document, something to which they and the teacher can both turn in order to build up an understanding of the language events experienced: a little bit of certainty in the students' insecure linguistic world. In this way, curiosity is awakened and understanding increased. Thus, we are less likely to witness the sort of bewilderment which often occurs when students are exposed solely to an audio-tape recording. Given that the purpose of the exercise is not to test but to promote learning, the use of visual support for the linguistic elements is not to be discouraged *a priori*.

VIEWING OF DOCUMENTS

The kinds of documents appropriate for use in a language class range from very short items, such as advertisements, lasting for only a few seconds, through news broadcasts, documentaries, games, serials and scientific shows to full-length feature movies.

It is because video material is so rich that it is appropriate to a range of pedagogic uses which are no less varied.

Many video documents are created for a specific type of audience. This is an important factor which it is desirable to exploit in order to bring out the constraints influencing language usage. At the same time, however, this sort of document provides a range of speech acts which is relatively limited. Indeed, this kind of material often consists either of didactic speech (such as a documentary) or of interviews where roles are generally predetermined and unchanging. Thus, the status of the speakers with respect to each other and to the spectators varies relatively little.

On the other hand, video recorded feature movies or television series (even soap operas) provide the opportunity of experiencing a broader, richer range of situations.

In the case of a feature movie, the teacher might choose to screen either the whole or parts of it according to the learning approach selected.

In a functional perspective, for instance, appropriate extracts could be used to illustrate different realizations of the same function, for example, all the ways in which greetings can be expressed. Such differences have the great advantage of being in context and, if necessary, the teacher can point out pertinent differences.

In a situational perspective, on the other hand, one might begin with a global viewing of the document, followed by a detailed examination of the situation, focusing upon the critical elements of communication. Special attention might be given to those elements which may have gone unnoticed or which may have been misinterpreted as a result of first language interference or of over-generalization of communication and language rules (such as gesture, accidents of speech, attitudes).

The teacher might also check understanding of certain important segments through the use of paraphrase, or even translation, where appropriate. Other exercises for checking comprehension and accurate perception might take the form of imitation, repetition, simulation and so on. Furthermore, it might be possible to focus on such non-linguistic systems as gesture by removing the sound component and by asking students to mime the scene.

As a last step, the whole movie might be shown once again. The purpose of this is to allow the students, with appropriate guidance where necessary, to see the way in which the elements on which they had been focusing interact within the larger framework of the situation. Their understanding should now be significantly enhanced through a newly acquired sensitivity to elements of communication in the target language.

VIDEO SELF-CONFRONTATION

For the purposes of this discussion, we shall consider 'video self-confrontation' (VSC) as viewing a videorecording of oneself. Although we are convinced that VSC can be of great benefit in language learning, it does sometimes create certain problems which need to be acknowledged and dealt with.

For instance, discovering the image that one presents to the outside world can be deeply disturbing. This is likely to be exacerbated by the fact that such discovery generally occurs in the presence of others who witness both the recording and the discovery itself. In this sense, VSC is very different from many of the activities commonly practised in language classes. It is therefore extremely important (a) that teachers be conscious of the problems involved and (b) that during the recording and, most importantly, during the viewing phase, they take great care to create an atmosphere of security. They should also ensure that the recording of the various scenes occurs in such a way as to reduce rather than increase students' fears and anxieties. In this respect, the ludic side of regression can be used to advantage.

It is almost inevitable that language learning activity will bring out a number of unpredictable and highly individual psychological blockages. These are the symptoms of unconscious resistance to the imposition of a new set of systems which can be construed as threatening students in their very identity. After all, ability to communicate in another language is not simply the intellectual manipulation of certain words according to certain rules but involves the interaction of many systems resulting in apparent changes in behaviour.

Although VSC tends to make blockages explicit we believe that, paradoxically, it can also help to overcome them. In our experience, VSC seems governed by certain constraints which, in most cases, can have a beneficial effect as they seem to have both a stimulating and a creative function.

Here is a typical scenario. The learners are placed in a communication situation in a *limited space*, for a *limited time* and required to perform a well-defined *limited task*. The over-riding 'rule of the game' is that communication should be successful. Responsibility for the interaction therefore belongs to the students. If one of the partners experiences difficulty then it is up to the others to assist, within the constraints imposed by the simulation. For instance, they must not destroy the coherence of the situation, they must not prompt the person in difficulty but should call upon their knowledge of communication strategies to restart the conversation in much the same way as a native speaker of the target language might assist another native speaker suffering from a temporary lapse in memory.

For the students to feel these constraints, indeed moral obligations, is most important and often highly motivating. Our experience in the context of a macro-simulation conducted in one of the courses offered by the French department at the University of Queensland tends to confirm this. Many of the activities in the simulation tended to revolve around meetings of the 'local town council'. It is most revealing to note that videotaped council meetings generally functioned much better than similar meetings which were not videotaped. In fact, some of the sessions lasted between one and one and a half hours, without any break in the flow of the debate and with no interruptions on the part of the teacher. Although this kind of exercise is clearly successful, it takes its toll in nervous energy. If excessive fatigue resulting in flagging interest and spirits is not to set in, then the teacher has to monitor most carefully the negative effects of the situation. Thus, it will be possible to make the most of the very significant advantages gained from the tension of being 'on camera'.

It is also preferable for the teacher to be absent from the room while the recording is in progress; he/she can still keep an eye on things by using a video monitor in another room. This will help to counteract attempts by students to seek assistance, comfort and reassurance from their teacher by glancing up at him/her instead of continuing with the simulation. Such attempts could have the disastrous effect of breaking down the spatio-temporal (and moral) constraints operating.

Of course, acting out a scene in front of a video camera can be conceived of as a game which is 'lots of fun'. However, once the fun wears off tension sets in. It is then a matter of trying to maintain a balance between the sort of tension which motivates and that which inhibits: not an easy task.

According to Green (1975), successful language learning is likely to occur in persons who have the ability to recognize patterns, and to re-create these patterns in a relatively short time. In other words, time is of the essence. One of the major constraints operating on video simulation is precisely that of time. We would argue that a video simulation followed by a VSC session places learners in a situation which requires that they practise mobilizing rapidly, in the target language, skills which, in any case, are already well developed in their own language. Working with video provides learners with the opportunity of becoming aware of the operation of these skills within the framework of the target language, and to develop and modify them according to the demands of the target language. In other words, they have to deal with the demands of something very close to authentic communicative activity (and a video simulation gives them an opportunity to practise these intensively). Such demands are, to a considerable extent, of a temporal and organizational nature, simultaneously and across several systems. In this respect, the notion of systems management appears to be one of the keys to success (Lian & Joy, 1981 : 8). Thus video simulation and VSC provide an ideal

261

opportunity for developing an awareness of that notion at an affective level.

Just as in the case of authentic material, VSC affords the opportunity of performing a large number of different exercises. The same exercises could be carried out as with authentic documents. We would suggest, however, that the principal thrust be directed toward analysis of student performances at both global and micro levels. In other words, both students and teacher will use the recording for diagnostic purposes with a view to correcting errors.

At the micro level, for instance, certain educationists have attempted to use a form of VSC for improving pronunciation, for instance, at the Southern Connecticut State College, New Haven (Ecklund & Wiese, 1981). The exercise, in this case, consists in videotaping students while they read a text aloud. The tape is then used to define and analyse pronunciation problems in terms of tension or articulation. This seems to be reduced, essentially, to an analysis of lip position.

Although some improvement in pronunciation has been achieved, this approach presents us with a certain number of fundamental problems:

1. It makes no allowance for auditory perception.
2. It makes no allowance for individual differences at the articulatory level.

In fact, this appears merely to be a modern version of an outdated technique which has since been replaced by a combination of verbo-tonal and psycho-motor approaches (*cf* Renard, 1971; Lian, 1980; Lian & Joy, 1981; Lian & Joy, 1982).[2]

The reason for mentioning this approach is two-fold. The first is that modernizing for the sake of modernizing is relatively inefficient if the principles subtending the original procedure remain the same. The second point is that despite our fairly severe criticism of the above procedure, we believe that VSC can be effective in corrective phonetics. Indeed, one can imagine a very useful system where viewing oneself could serve to check upon synchrony between speech and general body movements. This system could be further enhanced through the addition of special remedial filtering with equipment such as the SUVAG Lingua[3] and through the development of more sophisticated self-monitoring techniques.

Analytical procedures can also be applied to other systems, such as grammar and vocabulary. These are relatively easy to imagine and will not be dealt with here. However, video usage really comes into its own with more complex, higher-level, integrative exercises which might range from the description of an object to close imitations of different persons, such as a motorcar salesman trying to sell a car to a gullible customer; a priest giving a sermon; or a local politician making an election speech.

Broadly speaking, the more global communication exercises just mentioned can be classed as *short-term* simulations. Before beginning such exercises, it is important to spend some time in establishing with the students (either through observation or discussion) the situational parameters which are pertinent for successful communication. Thus, the students will be aware of at least some of the critical elements likely to influence the development of the simulation.

It is also important for any recording to be made as discreetly as possible so that inhibitions are reduced and students feel less responsible for the final document. Furthermore, when watching the replay of their performance, students are likely to feel less threatened and to be better able to observe themselves in a more detached, more 'objective' manner, almost as though they were impartial observers. This detachment can be observed when a student sometimes refers to the image on the screen in the third person or by his/her 'stage' name.

The practice of referring to oneself by another name appears particularly useful and ought to be encouraged. It seems to establish a buffer zone between learners and their performance and, consequently, their errors. It is a way of reducing error-anxiety. If a mistake is made it is no longer the student's fault but that of the character on the screen.

In the case of *long-term* or *real-time* simulations, it may seem that some of the beneficial creative constraints to which we were just referring disappear. The advantages derived from such simulations, however, stem from the fact that the quality of the communicative activity is enhanced and gains in authenticity. The learner has the opportunity of becoming deeply involved in the simulation through the interaction of his personal experience and the role which he has selected and which he is currently developing. Within the framework of such simulations, it is possible to imagine a number of activities which, quite naturally, incorporate the use of video as television in one's daily routine. For instance, a security guard might be monitoring activity in a bank, a post office or a large supermarket. On the other hand, video can also take the form of an old television set found in a corner of the local café or it can serve its customary function in professional development.

In the last type of activity mentioned above, the learner's attention is shifted away from *linguistic* performance and is now focused squarely on *professional* performance. For example: does the 'salesman' succeed in convincing the client to purchase a particular motor car?

Here is a further example drawn, once again, from our experiments at the University of Queensland. At election time, candidates can make use of video (now operating as 'television') to present themselves and express their ideas. In so doing, the 'candidates' must utilize whatever expressive resources are at their disposal, such resources ranging from facial expressions, gaze and other forms of eye contact, to the use of technical vocabulary and complex sentence structures, all of which contribute to effective communication in the target language.

Another similar example is that of the news broadcast or telecast. This can be produced by the students themselves and can serve as a central and sometimes essential component in the macro-simulation itself.

This kind of situation presents the very considerable advantage of reducing inhibiting factors and of broadening the settings for language activity. Recordings which are made can then be evaluated by the class for communicative success. In addition, several kinds of error analysis can be carried out; such as grammar, pronunciation, speech gambits. As a result of these evaluations or analyses it could be suggested to students that they might benefit from re-enacting the situation in order to improve their performances and, very importantly, to become aware of these improvements.

VIDEO-COMPUTER TECHNOLOGY

Finally, under computer control, video provides us with the opportunity of creating truly individualized learning systems. This is likely to be one of the most significant contributions of modern technology not only to language education but also to education generally.

Computer-assisted learning has much to offer. To begin with, a computer can be the most patient of teachers. Well programmed, and in an interactive setting, a computer can analyse errors and tirelessly guide the student toward correct language production.

With further technological development, specifically the advent of videodisc and the creation of easily accessible worldwide data banks, one can imagine the student taking part in a broad range of activities, including interactive simulations, generated and controlled by computers.

VIDEODISC

Videodisc needs a special mention in the context of modern technology as we believe that it will revolutionize access to information. A video-disc looks somewhat like an ordinary record except that it is used to store both picture and sound. Information is read from its surface either with a needle or with a laser beam. A videodisc player can fulfil all the functions of an ordinary videorecorder. However, its most remarkable feature is that any of the 54,000 frames stored on it (approximately equivalent to a 30-minute film) can be indexed and accessed individually in a matter of one or two seconds, unlike a videorecorder where the tape has to be wound on, sometimes for several minutes, until the right spot is found. Furthermore a picture can be frozen on the screen and held indefinitely with no loss of quality, or a series of frames can be played back at normal rate (just like a movie). They can also be slowed down or accelerated and sound can be turned on or off as desired (cf Kellner, 1982; BYTE, 1982).

As a result of these developments rapid interaction between student and audio-visual information now becomes a possibility and, by the same token, so do real-time simulations. Whenever they feel like it, students will be able to run a simulation in private and in the knowledge that patient and useful guidance will be provided by their teacher's alter ego.

In Australia, the University of Queensland's CASLED team[4] is currently developing a simulation package for trial in English and in German. It consists of a customer in a butcher's shop. In its final form, there are likely to be at least two stages to the simulation, each of which will have a corresponding module.

The first module consists of a dialogue generator which actually 'creates' the dialogue within specified parameters, thus providing the student with the opportunity of experiencing the situation.

In other words, the program has been provided with the information necessary to simulate the situation, including a range of greetings, selections of possible cuts of meat and a series of expressions appropriate for transacting the purchase. These are then selected in the right order to create realistic dialogues of various length and changing content. Thus it is possible for the students to observe many thousands of different dialogues which share the critical features necessary for transacting a purchase.

The dialogue generation can be co-ordinated with a videocassette or videodisc unit which will provide both picture and sound for each of the elements of the transaction. The power of such a program should be obvious. Traditionally, a student is provided with one or two audio-recordings of a situation, which he is then asked to study. The range of possible realizations of language functions to which he is exposed will always remain limited to what has actually been prerecorded. The tapes cannot be altered in any way. This activity is comparable to doing the same set of exercises over and over again. The most significant advantage of the dialogue generator is that, effectively, the student now has access to many thousands of potentially different recordings.

These new dialogues are further enhanced by the video element which provides not only a realistic setting for language activity but also the opportunity for observing non-verbal behaviour, including the important synchrony between speech and gesture.

The second module consists of an interactive program where the student actually plays the role of the customer. Here the students can test the knowledge acquired through observation of the dialogues created by the first module. The computer plays the role of the butcher and cues the students through the various stages of the transaction. Feedback is provided either in the form of positive reinforcement or in the form of appropriate error-messages. Such messages pertain not only to the grammatical correctness of sentences but also to appropriateness with respect to register. For instance, if it is specified that the customer is a northern German and that the transaction occurs in northern Germany, then he is most unlikely to use the greeting *Grüss Gott*. If the student has made such an error then it will be flagged and an appropriate error-message displayed.

Once again, video provides a realistic setting for language activity together with the opportunity of responding to the many non-verbal stimuli occurring in normal face-to-face communication.

At present, the simulation is functioning only in written form on the computer's VDU, but it is hoped that in the foreseeable future it will be possible to implement this simulation on a videocassette recorder, in the first instance, and then subsequently transfer it to the more versatile videodisc when low-cost recording facilities become available.

There is still a very long way to go before all the possibilities of computer-controlled videodisc players have been explored. Suffice it to say that their use will undoubtedly expand and have far-reaching effects on educational practice. Given appropriate hardware, students will have access to an enormous amount of information which will provide them with an opportunity for real autonomy in learning.

CONCLUSION

A crucial point: in our view, there is no question of replacing the teacher with a machine. Technological change provides us with a rare and challenging opportunity for rethinking our language learning methodology and for redefining the framework within which it is to function. Furthermore, a methodology which is centred on the learner and which exploits individualization to its fullest extent seems to demand a radical reorganization of teaching structures, particularly in the case of fairly traditional institutions such as schools, colleges and universities. One of the most important aspects of such restructuring could well be the replacement of set courses (arbitrary progression) with learning networks within which students would be free to move according to their needs as perceived both by themselves and by their teachers.

It is in this new and exciting framework, where video will play a central role, that the language teacher, no longer merely a dispenser of information, will be able to play his equally new and exciting role: that of a *manager of learning*.

Notes

1. Some of the research reported in this chapter was partly funded by a University of Queensland Special Project Grant 1981, a University of Queensland Humanities' Major Project Grant 1982 and by the secondment of A-P Lian to the University of Queensland's Tertiary Education Institute in second semester of 1982.
2. Refer also to the excellent but largely unpublished work of Dr Odile Menot (University of Paris III).
3. This is a set of electronic filters used in corrective phonetics and designed by Professor Petar Guberina of the Institute of Phonetics, University of Zagreb. SUVAG stands for 'Système Universel Verbo-tonal Auditif Guberina'. The equipment is manufactured by SEDI in Marseilles.
4. CASLED stands for 'Computer-Assisted Second Language Education'. The team consists of Barrie Joy (Education), Rosalie Russell (German) and Andrew Lian (French) who is also the team's co-ordinator.

REFERENCES

BYTE (1982) (Special issue on videodisc), 6 June.

Ecklund, C L & Wiese, P (1981) 'French accent through video analysis', *Foreign Language Annals,* 14, 1, 17-23.

Green, P S (ed) (1975) *The Language Laboratory in School: Performance and Prediction: The York Study*, Oliver & Boyd, Edinburgh, quoted in Hawkins, E *Modern Languages in the Curriculum*, Cambridge University Press, 1981, 219-20.

Joy, B K, Lian, A-P & Russell, I R (1982) 'Introduction to computer-assisted second language education', paper read to the 21st AULLA Congress, Massey University, Palmerston North, New Zealand, January, to be published in the *Proceedings and Papers* of the Congress. Also to be published in *The New Zealand Language Teacher*, (forthcoming).

Kellner, C A (1982) 'V is for video disk', *Creative Computing,* **8**, 1, January, 105.

Lian, A-P (1980) *Intonation Patterns of French* (Teacher's book), River Seine Publications, Melbourne.

Lian, A-P (1982) 'On interlanguage and naivety', *SGAV Review,* 2, (forthcoming).

Lian, A-P & Joy, B K (1981) 'Verbo-tonalism, research and language learning', *SGAV Newsletter,* 4, July, 7-12.

Lian, A-P & Joy, B K (1982) 'Prosody: the crossroads of language systems', *SGAV Review,* 1, (forthcoming).

Mestre, M-C & Lian, A-P (1982) 'The use of video in a communicative approach to language learning', *SGAV Review,* 2, (forthcoming).

Renard, R (1971) *Introduction à la Methode Verbo-tonale de Correction Phonétique,* Didier, Paris.

Selinker, L (1972) 'Interlanguage', *International Review of Applied Linguists in Language Teaching,* 10, 209-31.

Selinker, L, Swain, M & Dumas, G (1975) 'The interlanguage hypothesis extended to children', *Language Learning,* 25, 139-52.

22. Video in Foreign Language Education

Ortrun Zuber-Skerritt

SUMMARY

This chapter illustrates how the various uses of video, as discussed in the other chapters of this book, can be applied to a particular discipline in higher education. Mainly two forms of application in foreign language learning and teaching are discussed: video self-confrontation (VSC) and the production of video programs; the latter in the form of simple recordings, video programs produced by staff and students, video triggers, commercial productions and interactive video/computer programs. In addition to VSC other uses specific to foreign language education are discussed, such as live video laboratory (LVL) and the video split screen auto tutorial model (Video SAM).

INTRODUCTION

Foreign language education is not defined here, in the narrow sense, as the acquisition of language skills in the target language or as applied linguistics, but rather is meant to include the interdisciplinary study and understanding of the culture of the particular target language. The study of culture, in turn, comprises, for example, geographical, historical, political, anthropological, sociological, literary, and economic studies or experiences.

If students learn linguistic skills without the cultural background knowledge, they will misconstrue and misuse that foreign language. If, on the other hand, students study some aspect(s) of a foreign culture, such as its literature, translated into, and expressed in, their mother tongue without having the knowledge and skills of the target language, they will miss a great deal of authenticity of the original.

Therefore, in foreign language education (FLE) today, the study of the target civilization and the acquisition of the target language skills should be integral parts of any course. Thus, every foreign language course should be part of an integrated, coherent, interdisciplinary program. The single, salient characteristic of FLE which distinguishes foreign language programs from other interdisciplinary programs is the fact that students of foreign languages have to perceive and communicate (that is, speak, hear, write and read) the multifaceted knowledge in a foreign tongue. Video can be a most valuable aid in this whole learning process.

Elsewhere (Zuber, 1979; Skerritt, 1981) I have developed a taxonomy

268

of the major uses of video in higher education in three main cateogies: video as an aid in classroom teaching, video as a replacement for classroom teaching, and video as an instrument to improve learning and teaching. This chapter deals mainly with two forms of video application in FLE: video self-confrontation and video production. I am not attempting to present a complete list of all the possible ways in which videotape has been, or can be, used in foreign language education, but to outline some of the various methods which I have used or seen used in Queensland and elsewhere in Australia, America and Europe. I refer to other chapters in this book to illustrate how various uses of video can be applied to a particular discipline, in this case to foreign language learning and teaching.

VIDEO SELF-CONFRONTATION (VSC)

Foreign language teachers can make use of VSC in the same ways as were suggested by Kagan, Perlberg and McAleese earlier. For example, the recording and subsequent video analysis of lectures, tutorials, language laboratory and consulting sessions are a useful instrument in staff development. It is advisable, though, that teaching or faculty staff discuss their VSC with an experienced colleague whom they trust as having a positive, supportive, non-competitive and non-threatening attitude. As long as this colleague is relied on as a friend and helper, it does not matter whether he/she be in the same department, from a different faculty, or from the institution's educational research and development unit/centre, although a colleague from the latter is more likely to devote all the necessary time and interest to this exercise and to be better trained in VSC consultancy. This colleague will know that his/her role is not to criticize the performance, but rather to balance the teacher's self-criticism, which is frequently too harsh, and to discuss possibilities for improvement.

In teacher training, one special technique of using a two-track U-matic videotape may be worth mentioning: while the trainee's teaching is being recorded on a videorecorder in a separate room, the teacher trainer in that room is observing the student teacher on monitor(s) (or through a one-way mirror wall if this is installed between the classroom and the recording room) and is simultaneously recording his/her comments on the second audio track of the videotape. This has the advantage that the student teacher — although aware of being observed and criticized — does not actually see, and might in fact soon forget, the trainer, and thus be less inhibited than he/she would be in the physical presence of the trainer.

Another advantage is that the trainer need not sit through the replay with the student, frequently stopping the tape in order to make comments; the student can pick up the tape immediately after the lesson and replay the recording first on soundtrack 1 only, or at once on soundtrack 2, that is, first without or straightaway with the trainer's comments. The actual contact time between teacher trainer and trainee can thus be more usefully spent on discussion of the evaluated lesson and of possible improvements in the student's presentation, content, pronunciation, intonation, syntax, grammar or whatever might be recommended to the student. The possibility of simultaneously recording the trainer's comments and corrections of the trainee's mistakes is particularly useful in foreign language teacher training because of the additional language errors which can be corrected in the orginal context and immediately after they occurred.

Without a two-track sound system on a videotape the trainer would have to note down the errors and to correct them hours or days later. Thus the trainer might miss a few mistakes when writing instead of observing and commenting; and the impact on the student is not as great as immediately after the event, when the student replays the lesson with the instant correction of mistakes recorded on the videotape.

Foreign language students can make use of VSC when improving their language skills in the live video laboratory (LVL) or the video split screen auto tutorial model (Video SAM) both developed by Peter Collins.[1] LVL and Video SAM are described in detail here because they are innovations which might stimulate other foreign language teachers to experiment with, or further develop, this model of individual learning.

LIVE VIDEO LAB

The audio-visual equipment of a live video lab consists of a video camera, a videorecorder, a monitor and about five microphones running through a sound mixer.

There are usually four students (at the same level of proficiency) with an instructor (faculty member or graduate assistant) for 30 minutes.

The instructor must be an expert in speaking and teaching the foreign language as well as trained and proficient in operating the video equipment. The content of the video laboratory is not a conversation in the target language, but exercises which are linguistically sequenced very carefully; for example, idiomatic expressions in French (verbs conjugated with 'to have' — *avoir*) which are different in English (conjugated with 'to be'), for example, *j'ai faim* — 'I'm hungry'.

The instructor's task is to design various exercises and questions to which the students have to respond individually, thus practising the use of these idioms. The session is structured as follows: after a warm-up period of about eight minutes, there is the recording phase of about four minutes, followed by the third phase, the discussion and replay of recording to each of the four students. They all learn from each other.

The instructor can use the pause switch in the second phase to stop the recording when a student is nervous or confused; and in the third phase he can stop the replay when the student wants to explain something, or when the instructor wants the student to comment or to correct a word or phrase. The video laboratory instructor's task is very demanding. He or she has to be sensitive, positive, reinforcing, encouraging, and to prove that the video equipment is not a machine to trap students, but to help them learn. Surveys conducted at San José State University have shown that the initial feeling of intimidation on the students' part is overcome quickly and replaced by an intense interest.

The video laboratory facilitates the most intense language learning, for example, when the student is watching the replay, anticipating the errors and talking to himself on the TV monitor. This experience enables the learner to be outside himself which no other teaching method can do.

There are two further advantages of the video laboratory in foreign language learning: it helps to overcome the 'unauthenticity problem' and it is a confidence builder.

Students who learn a foreign language in a classroom situation, never really believe deep down that it is for real. They know that they are not German, French or whatever. They feel conspicuous and unauthentic. I think this feeling is one of the greatest impediments to foreign language learning. But once the initial shyness phase is over, the students become used to seeing themselves on TV, and it even helps the least confident students to overcome their inhibitions and to build up their self-confidence. Students seem to pay more intense attention to themselves (on TV) than they do to any teaching. Apart from improving the physiological aspects of pronunciation (position and movement of the mouth and so on), the video laboratory helps students both to express themselves in a foreign language, and to accept themselves as speakers of that language.

The advantages of the video laboratory to the learner are enormous. But, as mentioned above, the instructors' task is very demanding. They have to teach directly, videorecord parts of the session, and even edit the recording as they are working, because they have to cut out (by pressing the pause button) moments when students show ignorance, confusion or anything that makes them embarrassed. Some confusion and probing can be useful for the student's self-correction, but an experienced instructor will know what to record and what to leave out.

An obvious drawback for universities to introduce the video laboratory might be the fact that it is expensive in terms of teaching time. At San José State University it was decided to reduce the regular conversation classes from five to four hours per week and to train graduate assistants to teach in the video laboratory. Another drawback seems to be that the instructors' task is very tedious, if they have many small groups doing the same exercises. This problem can be overcome by reserving the video laboratory for individual work and by programming standard and more mechanical exercises (drills) in the Video SAM.

VIDEO SAM

The video split screen auto tutorial model does not require the teacher to be present, while the students work on a program. A typical SAM program takes about 10 minutes to view and 10 minutes to replay, so that three students per hour can view it and be recorded.

How can students learn with SAM? A student can view a situation (dramatized episodes) on one half of the split screen and simultaneously, on the other half, see and hear the instructor explaining the situation in the foreign language and asking a question which prompts the student to think and respond (Figure 1). The same scene is repeated, but this

| Episode | Instructor's explanation or student's response |

Figure 1. *Video split screen of a SAM program*

time the instructor's comments are replaced by a video recording of the student's response.

The master tape is produced as follows: once the dramatized scenes on the one hand, and the instructor's comments and questions on the other, have been recorded separately, they are edited together on a split screen, and each episode is recorded twice. When the master tape is first played to the student, the camera is aimed at the student whose performance is recorded while the master tape is recorded onto the student's tape. Thus, the student's tape is a second generation of the master tape in juxtaposition with the original of the student on one half of the screen, next to the second showing of the episode.

The advantages of SAM are:

1. In terms of salaries a technician replaces a faculty staff, and eventually the recording will be automated to the extent that even the technician need not be there.
2. The students do not passively watch TV, they *are* on TV in action.
3. The students do not merely repeat what the instructor said before them, but they have to provide and create for themselves the phrases which are suggested by the actions seen.
4. When the module is completed, students are given:
   - ☐ the written script of the questions and correct answers
   - ☐ an audio-tape cassette with all possible correct responses
   - ☐ an audio-tape cassette with their own interchange for comparison and correction at home.

5. The students can see themselves on replay and if they are not satisfied, they can do it again (and again). They can experiment and correct themselves until they become proficient and confident in speaking the particular phrases in the foreign language. It can be an advantage for a student to learn independently, without a teacher there as a superior and potentially judgemental person. Unless the student requests otherwise, the videotape is erased and never viewed by the instructor.

The disadvantages of SAM might be:

1. The production of video SAM programs is initially very time consuming. On a one-year basis at least 30 video units of instruction are needed.
2. When making a mistake students are not directly corrected by an instructor. They have to recognize mistakes themselves by reading the correct answers on the handout sheet and by listening to the audio-tapes.

I think, however, the advantages of SAM greatly outweigh the disadvantages. It is a very effective learning method, if the objective is to improve confidence in conversation, grammar, idioms and so on, rather than pronunciation. Students can compare their responses on video (copied on audio-tape to take home) with an answer sheet giving them the various possibilities of correct responses. The objective to improve the students' pronunciation must be achieved by different methods, such as the video laboratory.

Video SAM is only a prototype which can be used by students and teachers as a starting point, but which could be experimented with, and further developed into a learning-teaching model of individualized instruction in FLE.

VIDEO PROGRAMS

Video programs in foreign language learning and teaching can range in technical quality from simple recordings of teaching, educational programs produced by staff and students and research projects (all on half- or three-quarter-inch tape using portable equipment) to the most sophisticated, professionally produced, commercial programs (using broadcast-standard studio equipment).

RECORDINGS

Students who have not had the opportunity to go abroad and to get to know the foreign language of their choice as it is used by native speakers, can replay video recordings of guest speakers from abroad who visit their institution. Recordings of broadcast news or of other cultural events in the foreign language will also be appreciated and of use.

In a country like Australia, which is a great distance from any country whose language is being taught in Australia (mainly French, German, Italian, Japanese, Chinese and Indonesian), it is important to motivate students to attempt to understand that language in its normal-pace, everyday usage with the various vernacular colourings. Video can bring this language world into the classroom. Being a multicultural society, Australia could also draw on its large resource of ethnic languages. Videorecordings of migrants being interviewed or of discussions or cultural events in migrant centres could be useful in FLE and contribute to a better understanding of ethnic groups in Australia.

In foreign language teaching at a distance (or 'external studies') videorecorded lectures, discussions, explanations, demonstrations and so on, will be of increasing importance and value since more and more students will be able to afford home video-replay equipment.

The argument against the introduction of video technology in distance education and against the integration of videotapes into the learning materials of FLE at a distance has been, and will continue to be, the high production costs. However, even though this might be true for sophisticated programs which need a lot of editing (as in the Laaser-Stanford productions) or need broadcast facilities (as in the BBC-Open University productions), this argument becomes insignificant when normal, on-campus live lectures are videorecorded for external students as, for instance, at Stanford University (USA). At most universities teaching departments are provided with an advisory service from the university's audio-visual centre on the preparation and presentation of videorecorded lectures. Teaching staff can either have their normal lectures (which they have prepared for on-campus students) video-recorded or they can improve their lectures with the use of audio-visual aids and other presentation techniques. *Let's Put It on Videotape*[2] is a video program in which a faculty member of Brunel University explains how lecture programs are produced in the audio-visual centre at Brunel University using pre-prepared graphics and objects, and camera techniques such as overhead camera, when writing or demonstrating something, or the autocue, which enables lecturers to read their notes when looking straight into the camera lens — a technique normally used by broadcast TV newsreaders. These lecture programs are usually viewed by students individually at their own time and pace and then discussed in small groups with the teaching staff. They are also used (hired or bought) by other universities.

One could easily envisage such videorecorded lecture programs prepared by foreign language teaching staff, especially for external students who are unable to attend lectures and other language classes in which the visual impact is an essential element in the learning process.

Many foreign language teachers might be reluctant and too self-conscious to be videorecorded and therefore prefer the continuous use of written material. However, once they have overcome the barrier of seeing themselves as others see them and subjected themselves to VSC and simple videorecordings of their teaching, they will realize that there is no real difference between being seen by an audience of on-campus students in a live lecture and of being viewed on a monitor by off-campus students.

They might be concerned that, once videorecorded, they cannot revise or up-date their lecture material. But written lecture notes too have to be constantly up-dated and replaced by new versions. Students can be asked to return the videotapes in exchange for new ones. The tapes can easily be erased and used again for new recordings.

Videorecorded lectures also have valuable side-effects for foreign language teachers themselves: staff development and self-development. Seeing themselves from the outside they will more critically evaluate the effect and effectiveness of their teaching and make a greater effort to improve and develop their teaching in content and presentation.

While faculty staff normally know their subject content well, they have never been formally trained in methods, techniques and skills of presentation and evaluation. When preparing a lecture for video-recording, foreign language teaching staff have the opportunity to discuss their presentation with an educational media specialist and to be advised. They can make use of the institution's facilities, for instance have their audio-visual materials prepared by graphic artists, photographers and technicians. They can learn from this experience and improve their teaching. Ultimately, they will get more enjoyment out of teaching and see the video program as a positive end result of their teaching efforts, just as they see an article or book publication as the result of their research.

There are also considerable advantages for the foreign language students, especially in external studies: they get the lecture material presented more clearly and with more visual aids. They can pause in a tape and think or take notes. They are able to view a section again (and again) which they find difficult to understand or which they would like to repeat aloud in order to practise the pronunciation, intonation or idiomatic expressions. Finally, they can make better use of the contact time with their lecturer(s) by asking questions and participating in a discussion on a sound basis of factual knowledge.

Videorecording can be used as a research tool for analysing linguistic phenomena or non-verbal behaviour related to language content and compared across cultures. For example, videorecordings of native German speakers who have lived in Australia for a number of years would enable an analysis of the influence of the Australian English or vernacular on their oral language. There could be at least two groups of subjects: one living in a German settlement, such as Marburg in Queensland, and another group living in a totally Australian language environment.

Another example of video as a research tool would be the following para-linguistic study. Actors from different cultures, such as Italy, Greece, France, Germany, England and Scandinavia could be asked to act out a basic dialogue in which one person informs another in their mother tongue of the sudden death of a relative or close friend. They could be asked to show surprise, disbelief, shock, gradual realization and dismay. Then the videorecordings of all the simulations of this same dialogue in the various languages would be analysed and compared with regard to gesture and non-verbal expression. I would expect the Mediterraneans' gestures and expressions to be quite different from the Northern Europeans' non-verbal behaviour. A large number of subjects in each experimental group would, of course, be necessary in order to exclude the variable of individual manners and differences within a culture.

Another application of videorecording as a research aid is in translation studies, particularly drama translation. The translation of drama from one language and culture into another consists of the linguistic translation of the literary text and the transposition from the dramatic script to the stage performance. Everybody involved in this translation process — translator, director, producer and actors as well as students and scholars of drama — can be greatly aided in their interpretation of the play if they see a recording of various productions of the original, even though they might not understand the language in which the original play was written. Video can become a substitute for a written text (report, research data) and, moreover, can record non-verbal stimuli and responses. Thus video can be a valuable tool for the study of a foreign language and culture and for comparative research.

VIDEO PROGRAMS PRODUCED BY STAFF AND STUDENTS

While unedited videorecordings are less time consuming, simpler and cheaper than the production of video programs, basic editing equipment can facilitate the production of simple, yet educationally more effective programs.

The simplest way of producing a program is to edit a number of different recordings to extract segments which are relevant to a particular topic and to the achievement of certain objectives. For example, a one-hour videorecording of a group of people from a target country can be edited to become (a) a 10-minute program on the use of dialect or on other linguistic topics and/or (b) a 15-minute program on a cultural topic such as customs, festivals, folk music or folk dance, and/or (c) a one-to-five-minute video trigger. In all three cases the original sound can be erased or superimposed by a commentary, questions or music to suit the particular intentions of the program designer and the particular purposes for which the program will be used; that is, in the examples above: (a) for the study of linguistics; (b) for the study of the target culture and civilization, or (c) to stimulate discussion in conversation classes.

More complicated techniques of producing video programs include video inserts (graphs, maps, still pictures and other visual materials) and the use of studio cameras. For example, a linguistic discussion on phonetics with video demonstrations of native speakers can be made much clearer by the additional use of simple or even animated diagrams or charts of the mouth showing the origin and production of sounds. Or when portraying and explaining cultural differences in various parts of the same country, a geographic map would be a useful insert.

It will always depend on the staff and students themselves; how much time they are prepared to devote to the production of a program, what their aims are, and whether they want to produce programs for their own purposes only, or to make them available to other people as well. My own experience suggests that students involved in the foreign language video production itself are the ones who derive the most benefit, not those for whom the program is designed. For example, a student had only one line of German to speak in a play I wrote and produced in 1973. In a staff-student meeting at the end of the semester, this student maintained that from all courses he had enrolled in, he had learnt most in the oral course consisting of conversations which led to the video productions. Although he had only *one* line to say in German, he said he knew every part of the dialogue by heart because he had attended all rehearsals.

There is no doubt that video can be attractive and motivating for students in learning, memorizing, rehearsing and initiating actual-life situations in a foreign language and in viewing themselves immediately on a television monitor. It can be a thrilling feeling of achievement, success and satisfaction for students to watch themselves in the role of someone from a foreign culture speaking a foreign language which appears to be more and more familiar to them and not impossible for them to acquire.

The play mentioned above is part of a video project entitled *Deutschland in Ton, Bild und Diskussion*. This series of eight amateur video programs (three plays and five documentaries) was produced for the German department under the auspices of the Tertiary Education Institute at the University of Queensland. The videotapes are accompanied by exercises on audio-tapes and a textbook with the dialogues (in German and English) and with the exercises. The titles give an indication of the contents of the programs:

1. *Eine Reise nach Deutschland* — A trip to Germany (14 mins)
2. *Hotel Seehof* — Booking into a hotel (9 mins)
3. *Alpenländische Hausmusik* — Alpine music (14 mins)
4. *Weihnachten in Deutschland* — Christmas in Germany (15 mins)
5. *Auf Wohnungssuche* — Looking for a place to live (15 mins)
6. *Sport an Deutschen Schulen* — Sport at German schools (23 mins)
7. *Verkehrserziehung* — Road safety instruction (16 mins)
8. *Skilehrfilm* — Skiing instruction (18 mins)

Tapes 1, 2 and 5 are plays based on everyday situations, performed by students and staff of the department of German, University of Queensland. The remainder are documentaries mainly recorded in Germany with native speakers. These recordings were mostly made in on-the-job situations with portapack equipment, and for this reason lack some of the quality of staged productions. Tapes 7 and 8 contain specialized vocabulary for higher advanced students.

The objectives of the plays are:

☐ to expand students' command of vocabulary and idiomatic expressions used in everyday conversation
☐ to stimulate students of German to try to act out these situations themselves.

The documentaries were recorded and scripted:

☐ to show normal German cultural situations which differ from those in Australia
☐ to foster a higher level of performance in pronunciation, intonation,

fluency and speed in responding to everyday situations in Germany.

It would be somewhat pointless merely to entertain students with the videotapes. The full value will be obtained by following up the video-tapes by discussions in German based on the material presented and by working through the exercises on the audio-tapes.

Having tried out various methods of using this video course, I would recommend the following strategy:

1. Study the *text* to get familiar with the dialogue or commentary and try the written exercises before following the normal speed of speech on the video and audio-tapes.
2. View the *videotape*.
3. Practise the exercises on the *audio-tape* in the language laboratory.
4. Devote approximately 10-30 minutes to questions, *discussions* or acting out the situations.

The programs can be used as modular units, that is separately as additional teaching material, or as a classroom course, or as a pro-grammed self-instructional course. In the latter case, students would use the textbook in conjunction with the audio-tapes in private study and see and discuss the videotapes in private group sessions.

Although these amateur video programs are used by other insti-tutions in Brisbane at tertiary and secondary levels, they arose out of and reflect my work with my students. They were certainly most useful for those students, but also for students in subsequent years who knew, and could relate to, the students on the video screen. However, the usefulness of these amateur productions for other students is doubtful, because technical and acting deficiencies might detract from learning rather than arouse student interest.

In general, I am convinced that students who are directly and actively involved in the video production benefit more in real terms (that is learning outcome and motivation) than those who learn from merely watching, listening and reproducing the language content. Therefore, I wish to encourage foreign language teachers and students to become familiar with video technology and to make their own recordings and programs. Since video is such a strong motivating force for most students to act and speak with their fellow students in front of a camera, their foreign language learning turns into an in-depth study with more precision, better understanding and subsequent long-term retention.

VIDEO TRIGGERS

Video triggers, can easily be produced by staff and students in foreign language education, especially for use in conversation classes. The main aim of a video trigger in a foreign language class is to 'trigger-off' or stimulate a discussion. This is often a difficult task. The program must be brief (one to five minutes) so that the students are not tempted to lapse into passivity. It must be controversial, thought-provoking, causing affective reactions (for example, emotionally difficult situations where foreign customs are different) and/or cognitive judgement. The trigger can present a model of desirable behaviour or an example of inappropriate behaviour or may juxtapose the two so that the students are provoked to express critical comments. In contrast to a documentary video program, a video trigger does not contain documentation and factual information devoid of any emotional impact. All extraneous, irrelevant and misleading information must be avoided. Sometimes a video trigger has an unexpected or shock ending for impact. All these features of video triggers have emerged from efforts to achieve the following aims:

- ☐ to motivate shy students to actively participate in a discussion in a foreign language
- ☐ to arouse students' interest in a topic
- ☐ to raise students' awareness of a problem
- ☐ to contribute to their understanding and appreciation of foreign behaviours and different viewpoints
- ☐ to develop discussion skills and critical thinking in a foreign language
- ☐ to emphasize that communication is more important than precision of grammar
- ☐ (possibly) to lead to a conscious behavioural change.

The success of a video trigger in terms of the aims stated above does not only depend on its brevity, degree of provocativeness and other features of content, but also on the teacher's ability and method of leading the discussion on the particular trigger. For example, it would be counter-productive if the language teacher, immediately after the showing, gave his/her own comments in the form of a mini-lecture, thus reducing the students' opportunity and motivation to talk right from the start. It would be just as wrong to ask closed questions which do not lead to a free discussion. The teacher should play the role of a moderator and remain in the background. Unlike lectures, a session with video triggers is not teacher-centred, but student-centred. The foreign language teacher has several methodological possibilities to make use of a video trigger:

It may occur that a video trigger is so provocative and the students are so keen to speak that the teacher need not say anything except to summarize the results of the discussion or even ask someone else to give a summary.

However, since the teacher cannot count on such an ideal situation, he/she has to prepare a number of questions which should be designed in such a way as to make a longer discussion possible. Very often a few of these open questions are sufficient. Thus the dialogue between the teacher and the students widens to a discussion in which everyone participates.

Another method would be to structure the discussion by means of questions or problem-solving tasks on handouts or overhead transparencies.

Even in classes of 100 students or more discussion topics and working tasks can be incorporated in such a way that, stimulated by a video trigger, students can discuss these problems in the foreign language in small groups; after a certain time, the results can be summarized and presented to the plenum by one representative from each group.

Although students might prefer passive participation in lectures and seminars, their natural shyness to participate actively in a discussion can often be overcome successfully by a provocative video trigger.

With any of these methods it is possible for the teacher to write up interim conclusions of the discussion on the blackboard, on an overhead transparency or on a flip chart, thereby clarifying difficult points and making it easier for students to follow the course of the discussion.

COMMERCIAL PRODUCTIONS

Professionally produced language programs have the advantage that they are of better technical quality. They may, or may not, be designed in collaboration with educational technologists and subject specialists. More money and effort can be invested in video programs which are for sale to a larger audience. One could assume that therefore these language programs are superior to self-produced ones. But at least as important as technical quality is the appropriateness of the presentation, teaching methods and language content for tertiary students. However, assuming that language programs are produced for tertiary students by university staff in collaboration with video specialists and instructional designers, they can still have the disadvantage of a lecture, film or television program, if they are used as if they were ephemeral. The advantage of a videorecorded film or TV program or of a professionally produced video program is that it has all the positive characteristics of an educational TV program or film (usually more interesting, informative, captivating and visually stimulating than a lecture) without being transient and proceeding in a linear fashion. The tape can be stopped, rewound or forwarded as required. It can be viewed at any time, at the student's own pace, in the classroom or at home, in the office, in a library or in a study centre.

Staff and students should be aware of the particular aims of language study when actively selecting sections to be viewed. Students can be guided in their viewing by certain tasks so that they concentrate on and understand the language content. In these interactive video programs it is advisable to keep the learner's creative language production (such as a talk or essay), at least at the elementary and intermediate levels, to a minimum in order to avoid too many mistakes. Lonergan (1982, p 51) recommends viewing guides for beginners which require a predictive linguistic response, for instance, in the form of ticks or crosses on grids or charts as reproduced in Figure 2.

To ensure effective use of a video program the following provisions should be made:

☐ the availability of suitable support material, usually in written form
☐ a transcript of the programs
☐ interactive videotape instruction with tasks to activate students by rehearsing the language content in breaks provided on the tape or by responding to questions built into the program
☐ tutored videotape instruction in small groups to discuss the program, to clarify any difficulties and to solve any problems.

1. **Studio: In a living room**
   Put + for what people would like to do.
   Put — for what people do not want to do.

	go to the museum	go to a concert	play chess	go out
Mary				
Jane				
Francis				

2. **Loc Spot: At a travel agent's**

Where does the man want to go?   ☐ to Italy   ☐ home   ☐ to Rome
When does he want to go?   ☐ next weekend   ☐ in the morning   ☐ next Wednesday   ☐ in the evening

Figure 2. *Two simple viewing guides from the West German elementary program 'Follow Me'*

In the next decade, as more university staff will become interested in and versatile with the use of video and computer technology, there will be more productions of interactive videotape and videodisc programs combined with computer programs in foreign language education. The previous chapter is an example of this progressive development.

With the evolution of TV, video and computer technology and better information and communication systems we should soon be able to use the best, professionally produced video programs in foreign language education and supplement them with our own in-house materials tailored for the particular needs of our students.

CONCLUSIONS

In the 1980s the student population at tertiary level will become more and more heterogeneous: from young school-leavers, mature-age students with anything up to 40 or more years' work experience to pensioners and retired people with a backlog demand for higher education. I think McMahon (1982, p 78) is right in assessing the new trends at the tertiary level as follows:

We lack a cheap, reliable, easy to use and easy to understand technology which allows the individual to tune into the exploding world of knowledge and information, to select not just the time and place for learning, but the content and style as well, so that the substance and conditions of learning suit personal needs and purposes and those of family and local community.

McMahon believes that this new privately controlled technology is the microchip technology. The control mechanisms should not remain in the hands of a technologically literate elite with professional educators determining the direction, terms and conditions of learning; the learner himself should actively control the immediate learning process. This change in student characteristics and needs, and the potentials of the new technologies (video, microcomputer, videotex, teletext and viewdata, etc) will lead to a more individualized mode of learning. And FLE will be no exception.

The traditional lecture, tutorial/seminar and language laboratory classes will be replaced by packages of learning materials for individual study at home or at a place and time convenient to the learner. Faculty staff will have to change their roles from lecturers/instructors/teachers to designers of individualized learning materials and to managers and assessors of learning. This change is already in the process of taking place, but hopefully it will not develop too fast for academics and teachers to adapt to. Media resource units have a vital function in assisting staff with their adaptation and self-development and with the design and production of packages of individualized learning materials for use within the institution and for sale to a wider audience. These learning packages will not replace the foreign language teacher but will make time for his caring about individual students. For example, he will be able to pay attention to students' particular strengths and weaknesses, to their study methods and communication skills.

I hope to have shown that video in foreign language education is a useful aid in:

☐ the development of language/communication skills (through video self-confrontation)
☐ the design and implementation of the content of the target language *and* culture (through video recordings, commercial and in-house video productions)
☐ linguistic and paralinguistic research
☐ student motivation (video programs produced by staff and students)
☐ staff development (through VSC and videorecorded lectures)
☐ stimulating discussion (through video triggers)
☐ providing individualized language learning packages (including interactive video-computer programs).

Notes

1. I wish to acknowledge Peter Collins' work which he described to me in a personal interview, 5 September 1978, in the Instructional Resources Centre at San José University, San José, California. He is a senior lecturer in the Department of Foreign Languages, San José State University, San José, California 95 192.
2. Available from The Audio Visual Centre, Brunel University, Uxbridge, Middlesex UB8 3PH, UK.

REFERENCES

Lonergan, J (1982) 'Video recordings in language teaching', *Media and Development,* 15, 1, 49-52.

McMahon, H (1982) 'Making time for individuals', *Media and Development,* 15, 2, 78-81.

Skerritt, O D (1981) 'The use of video tape in teaching and learning foreign languages', *MLTAQ Journal,* 12, 10-18.

Zuber, O D (1979) 'Major uses of video tape in higher education', *ASET Newsletter,* 3, 5-10.

23. Students' Use of Videotape Programs as Resources in the Library

Duncan Harris

SUMMARY

The paper outlines the use of videorecordings for student access in a university library. The sources of the recordings are given (for instance, Open University off-air recordings, internal productions, and so on). The way that some students used such recordings and how they reacted to them is outlined. A comparative costing of the recordings is given according to their source. Suggestions are made for implementing the ideas into current and potential systems.

INTRODUCTION

Many universities and polytechnics have videotape programs available on access to students in a library or resource centre. Such systems have been available in the United Kingdom for 10 years or so. The systems themselves were reported in a range of journals (for example, Noordhof, 1974; Walton, 1974; Clarke, 1975). The systems enabled good co-operation between production services and libraries (Harris, 1976). The earlier systems used reel-to-reel recorders, later systems videocartridges and videocassettes. There were advantages and disadvantages to each with ease of operation and reliability as conflicting attributes.

INVESTIGATION CARRIED OUT IN A LIBRARY WHERE VIDEOCARTRIDGES WERE USED

An investigation was carried out at the University of Bath in 1977 to attempt to find answers to the following questions:

1. Who uses the materials and when?
2. How are the materials used?
3. How do the materials relate to the students' course and assessment?
4. What is the main purpose of the materials?
5. What is the cost of assembling and administering the materials?

The questions were necessary because the library and the educational services unit (the TV facilities were in the latter) were unaware of a rapid escalation in the number of recordings available on videocartridges in the library (see Table 1).

Year	1974/5	1975/6	1976/7
Number of video cartridges	13	147	204

Table 1. *Increase in videocartridges on free access to students*

	Architecture & Building engineering	Electrical engineering	Management
Open University	47	17	27
Other universities	—	9	—
Internal	—	12	—
BBC/IBA	—	—	10
Total	47	38	37

Table 2. *Number of videocartridges initiated by departments*

The types of recordings used fell into four categories. Open University materials were recorded off-air under licence with a fee paid for each recording. Materials from other universities varied from purchased copies from master recordings to free copies. Internal recordings were materials specifically produced for a lecturer. BBC/IBA materials were either schools or further education programs recorded off-air.

The videocartridges were available in a side room in the library with double glazed windows to reduce the sound transmission. It was possible for about eight students to be present (Harris, 1977). The whole basis developed from a collaborative venture between the educational services unit and the library (Walton, 1974 & Harris, 1976).

The principal methods of collecting information were by:

☐ observation
☐ questionnaires
☐ interviews with students, individually and in groups.

Full details and all the data are in the report of the evaluation (Harris & Kirkhope, 1978b).

The findings are based on:

☐ questionnaires (109 were returned)
☐ interviews (27, including three group interviews)
☐ observations (which were carried out by one of the investigators working at a dry carrel near the room and observing what students did when they were using a videocartridge).

The sampling was not systematic because students did not have to book the videocartridges, they were available on free access. Questionnaires were in the room and students were requested to fill one in. Interviews and observations depended on the investigators being present — a natural rather than an experimental basis for the evaluation was considered essential. At the time of the investigation, 35 lecturers had videocartridges on access; 16 lecturers' resources were sampled covering a range of disciplines.

SOME FINDINGS

A large proportion of students found the videocartridges by browsing on the shelves. Even though many recordings from the Open University had been requested by lecturers, they had not informed the students (according to the students) that the recordings were available. Most of the borrowers found the facilities, not having known that there were television facilities in the library! The criticisms on publicity included:

☐ 'only found the system of video replay by chance by talking to a member of staff'
☐ 'cataloguing terrible — took 10 minutes to find cassette required'
☐ 'more emphasis on the availability of this material is required in the school' ('school' = university department at Bath).

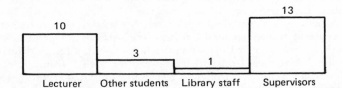

Figure 1. *Source of information about videocartridges*

Other reasons for students using the materials, with typical responses, included:

Related to lecture (29 responses)
☐ 'aid to understanding theory'
☐ 'visual aid'
Related to course (17 responses)
☐ 'supplementary'
☐ 'it *is* our course'
Interest (seven responses)
☐ 'personal interest'
☐ 'viewed for general interest'

The way that students used the material was only possible to glean from interviews and observation.

One of the first surprises from the questionnaires was to find that a large proportion of viewings were carried out in groups. Out of the 87 questionnaires where a response was made to this question:

63 viewed individually   24 were from groups viewing.

The group viewing questionnaires were filled in by one of the group. In terms of students, as some groups had six or even eight when observed, it would appear that group viewing was an important aspect for students.

Other responses included:

Use handout/notes/book (12 responses)
☐ 'consolidated material already in associated book' (This particular comment refers to a well designed series of TV programs which related to a short book designed and created simultaneously with the programs.)
Run straight through (five responses)
Replay/rewind used (three responses)
☐ 'stopped, rewound and replayed when unsure'

The questionnaire incorporated some questions asking students to rate the programs in relation to interest and clearness (see Figures 2 and 3).

The results from these questions were very similar to those from an investigation into the use of study packs carried out at the same time (Harris & Kirkhope, 1978b).

Similarly, a scale relating to ease (Figure 4) was similar although the distribution was skewed towards the easy end for TV and the difficult end for study packs. The most surprising scale related to use of printed handouts (Figure 5). It was clear that most students did not receive handouts. Certainly some of the programs had handouts which the lecturer held. The Open University materials had associated books — many students did not seem aware that these books even existed:

☐ 'access to appropriate OU test would be helpful' (In this case the text was actually on the library shelf.)
☐ 'printed material would be helpful for formulae' (Nine of the 27 students or groups interviewed identified their need for a handout.)

Particular technical problems raised by the students included:

☐ updating content of recordings (four responses)
☐ improving the quality of the recordings (four responses)
☐ noise of machine was tiring (four responses)
☐ improve sound (four responses).

The 'four responses' were not all the same four students!

There were also problems of finding the videocartridges required and of finding the machines free:

☐ 'hard to find tape — would like catalogue' (There was a rudimentary catalogue.)
☐ 'found by looking along shelves'
☐ 'cataloguing terrible — took 10 minutes to find cassette required'
☐ 'machine already in use when arrived — shown how to operate it by other students . . . thought instructions could have been put in a more prominent place'
☐ 'machinery simple to use . . . had tried last week, both rooms occupied, but no difficulty today'
☐ 'several times have come and found machine out of action — nc queuing problem!' (He had not realized there was a second machine.)

Video in higher education

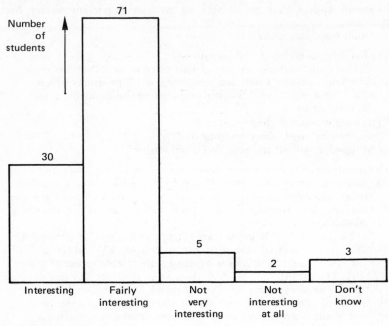

Figure 2. *Did you find this material interesting?*

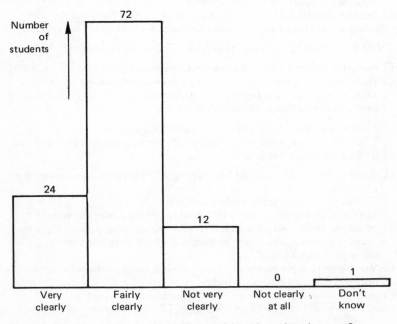

Figure 3. *How clearly do you think this material put its main points over?*

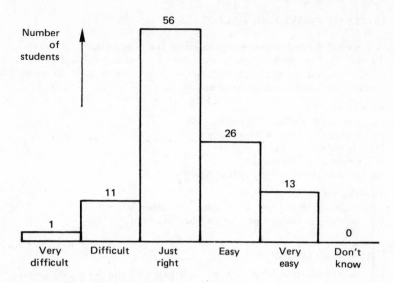

Figure 4. *How difficult did you find this material?*

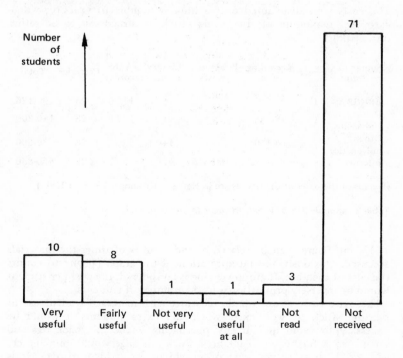

Figure 5. *How useful did you find any printed handout for this program?*

COSTS OF PROVIDING FACILITIES

A detailed costing was incorporated in the study (Harris & Kirkhope, 1978a, 1978b). Because currency values have changed, the figures have been included here as relative values. The costing took account of certain fixed and variable elements.

Fixed elements:
(a)   television studio equipment
(b)   replay facilities in the library
(c)   furnishing of replay rooms
(d)   servicing of equipment
(e)   automatic off-air recording equipment.

Variable elements:
(a)   licences (IBA, Open University, television licence)
(b)   recording charge made by another university
(c)   videocartridge.

Certain costs not included:

(a)   overheads (buildings, heating, lighting, cleaning, local taxes, etc)
(b)   central university administration related to television (eg finance office).

The costs were distributed over a limited number of years (eg video-cartridges maximum life five years — which turned out to be rather optimistic).

Source of recording	Licence	Recording fee	Production costs	Library facility	Auto recording	Cartridge	Total
BBC/IBA	1	—	—	44	17-50	28	90-120
Open University	1	48-75	—	44	17-50	28	140-200
Other universities	—	0-450	—	44	—	28	72-600
Internal	—	—	480-675	44	—	28	550-830

(Details of the bases of the figures are in Harris & Kirkhope, 1978a, 1978b.)

Table 3. *Annual costs of videocartridges (arbitrary units)*

The same figures can be related to the number of times the materials are used. Obviously the interpretation of the graph (Figure 6) counts the cost of each use. If group viewing is considered, the cost per student would be inversely proportional to the number of students.

There are reservations on the costing. With increased student use of existing stock or with extra stock and extra students it would be necessary to avoid queuing by purchasing further playback rigs and setting up a further playback area. Such a change would immediately add 22-23 units to the cost of providing each videocartridge. It is clear that step functions occur which will then reduce in the same

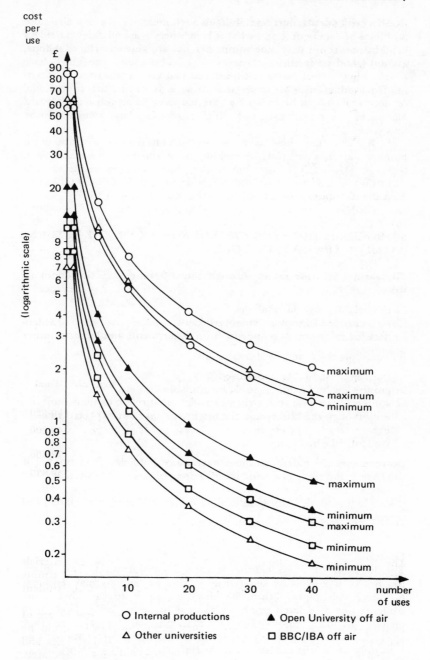

cost
per
use

£

(logarithmic scale)

90
80
70
60
50
40
30
20
10
9
8
7
6
5
4
3
2

1
0.9
0.8
0.7
0.6
0.5
0.4
0.3
0.2

maximum
maximum
minimum

maximum

minimum
maximum
minimum
minimum

10   20   30   40   number
of uses

○ Internal productions   ▲ Open University off air

△ Other universities   □ BBC/IBA off air

Figure 6. *Videocartridges: cost per use*

manner with further increases in load. Such increases of stock also raise problems of cataloguing and what is kept where — are all videocartridges kept in one room with side rooms nearby, are videocartridges shelved as books, and are facilities nearby?

The high cost of internally produced material (a relatively small set-up for production with minimal staffing is found in the educational services unit) could be offset by external sales incorporating a 'profit' margin to cover real costs, but a high charge and large sales would be necessary.

It is clear that these services involve considerable investment in money, materials and staff. A build-up of self-instructional materials in this format, which is not monitored, uses precious resources at a surprising rate. The cost of 200 videocartridges is 35,000-63,000 units with the distribution of tapes that were in use at Bath in 1977.

SOME SUGGESTIONS FOR SYSTEMS NOW AND IN THE FUTURE BASED ON THE INVESTIGATION

The main criticisms raised through the different collecting methods were:

☐ the need for a good catalogue
☐ notes needed to support videocartridges
☐ detailed information requested from departments and lecturers.

By analysing the data it is also clear that:

☐ the system should be monitored
☐ group viewing facilities should be available
☐ students may wish to see videocartridges that relate to their subject, even though the library and the originator have not expected that use
☐ students like browsing.

However, should videorecordings have more publicity than books? Is the library the right place for the videorecordings to be available? The lecturers who initiate the production and the department concerned have a key responsibility in informing students of what is available, and where.

Location
The location of a system needs careful consideration. The library has books and in many universities it also has audio-visual resources including videotapes. From our investigation it appears that many students like associated printed resources to be available. These may include graphics, photographs or mathematical formulae as they appeared in the program. Are these printed materials to be available on loan only or for the student to keep? How do students know where the playback machines, the recordings and the associated printed materials are stored?

The department often has equipment and study areas. Are the

resources better placed here? Would multiple sets of equipment be more expensive? Is the dream of button access to centrally stored discs which are automatically fed feasible? The costs may be too high compared with centrally located, simple playback facilities. The departmental base almost excludes browsers who constituted a large proportion of our viewers. Cynics might add that by placing the resources in the department it is a further disincentive to use books!

Printed resources
Students seem to need printed resources associated with the production because they feel more security in being able to have access to some of the ideas in a format which is the basis of their study, success and expectations in an academic community. The integrated design of resources seems crucial if such resources are to be made available for independent learning by an individual or group. Equally important is that any resources — whether explanatory, extension or core material — should bear a clear relationship to the course concerned. This helps to motivate students to use the resources.

Production
Groups of students appear to have discussions during viewing (usually stopping the recorder); and because it is possible to rewind and stop as often as required, it is not necessary for the production to be a typical video mass communication. The production style for individual and group viewing needs very careful consideration. Most producers are trained to produce materials for mass viewing, but how much do we know about individual or small group viewing in an academic community? We were surprised to find that in 1977 very little work had been carried out in this area.

The purchased or off-air recording is far cheaper than an internal production, even with relatively simple studio facilities. Modern information systems may enhance the transfer possibilities between institutions.

Cost-effectiveness
For cost-effectiveness multiple uses are necessary, as for all audio-visual and library resources. Audio-visual resources are about one order of magnitude more expensive than printed; video is a further order of magnitude more expensive. Checking the amount of use is difficult — free access means that no staff are available to issue the materials and monitor their use. It is feasible to incorporate counters, timers and electronic checks to provide such information.

Unfortunately, the sale of products at the present time is to lecturers. Ultimately, when the learner has more control, the product may look very different. Videorecorders may become so cheap that students will have their own, the recording will be in digital form, for students to use on their personal micro-information system. Future designers certainly need to take account of the diminishing boundaries between micro-computers, video equipment and other information systems.

REFERENCES

Clarke, J (1975) 'A carrell system for an institution for higher education', in Baggaley, J P *et al* (ed) *Aspects of Educational Technology,* **VII,** Pitman, London.

Harris, N D C & Austwick, K (1973) 'TV or not TV', *Programmed Learning and Educational Technology,* **10,** 3, 124-29.

Harris, N D C (1976) 'Co-operation between educational technologists and librarians', in Harris, N D C (ed) *Educational Technology in European Higher Education,* Council for Educational Technology, London.

Harris, N D C (1977) 'The use of non-book materials in the library', *IATUL Proceedings,* **9,** 11-12.

Harris, N D C & Kirkhope, S (1978a) 'Cost analysis of videocartridges as self-instructional materials in the library', *British Journal of Educational Technology,* **9,** 2, 94-102.

Harris, N D C & Kirkhope, S (1978b) 'Evaluation of self-instructional materials in the library', *Collected Original Sources in Education 2,* 1, Microfiche 1 B4-D7.

Harris, N D C & Kirkhope, S (1979) 'Uses of and students' reactions to videocartridges as self-instructional materials in the library', *British Journal of Educational Technology,* **10,** 1, 18-31.

Noordhof, G H (1974) 'The development of self-replay videotape facilities at Brunel University', *Programmed Learning and Educational Technology,* **11,** 1, 10-16.

Walton, E (1974) 'Outlook No 7: John Lamble and Duncan Harris of the University of Bath', *Educational Broadcasting International,* **7,** 142-47.

List of Conributors

Boud, David
Senior Lecturer in the Tertiary Education Research Centre (TERC),
University of New South Wales, Sydney, Australia

Brandt, Dietrich
Director of the Centre for Research into Higher Education, Technical
University, Aachen, West Germany

Breuer, Klaus
Research Fellow, Department of Education, University of Paderborn,
West Germany

Down, Kenneth S
Associate Dean of the School of Engineering and Director of the
Stanford Instructional TV Network, Stanford University, Stanford,
California, USA

Durbridge, Nicola
Research Fellow in the Institute of Educational Technology,
The Open University, UK

Foster, Stephen F
Associate Professor, Department of Educational Psychology and
Special Education, The University of British Columbia, Vancouver,
Canada

Gayeski, Diane M
Assistant Professor, Department of Corporate/Organizational Media,
Ithaca College, and partner in OmniCom Associates, Ithaca, NY, USA

Gibbons, James F
Professor of Electrical Engineering, Stanford University, Stanford,
California, USA

Harris, Duncan
Director of Studies for Research and Senior Lecturer in Education,
School of Education, University of Bath, UK

Hart, Ian
Director of the Instructional Media Centre, Canberra College of
Advanced Education, Australia

Haynes, Bob
Technical Manager of the Advisory Centre for University Education
(ACUE), University of Adelaide, Australia

Hoffman, Björn
Professor of Medical Biology, Biologische Institute der Universität
Köln, University of Cologne, West Germany

Hutton, Dean
Senior Lecturer in Educational Technology, South Australian College
of Advanced Education, Salisbury, Australia

Jones, John
Higher Education Research Officer, University of Auckland, Auckland,
New Zealand

Kagan, Norman
Professor, Department of Counselling Psychology, and Professor,
Department of Psychiatry, Michigan State University, East Lansing,
Michigan, USA

Kemmis, Stephen
Professor of Education, School of Education, Deakin University,
Belmont, Victoria, Australia

Kincheloe, William R
Adjunct Professor of Electrical Engineering, Stanford University,
California, USA

Laaser, Wolfram
Senior Academic in the Zentralinstitut für Fernstudienentwicklung,
(Development Centre for External Studies), Fernuniversität, Hagen,
West Germany

Lian, Andrew
Lecturer in the French Department, University of Queensland,
Brisbane, Australia

Main, Alex
Adviser on Educational Methods, University of Strathclyde, Glasgow,
Scotland, UK

Marland, Perc
Senior Lecturer in Education, James Cook University of North
Queensland, Townsville, Australia

McAleese, Ray
Director of the University Teaching Centre, University of Aberdeen,
Scotland, UK

Mestre, Christine
Lecturer in the French Department, University of Queensland,
Brisbane, Australia

Pearson, Margot
Education Officer, Curriculum Services Division, New South Wales
Department of Technical and Further Education, Sydney, Australia.

Perlberg, Arye
Professor in the Department of Education in Technology and Science,
Israel Institute of Technology, Technion, Haifa, Israel

Schmitt, Karin
Research Assistant in the Centre for Research into Higher Education,
Technical University, Aachen, West Germany

Stanford, Jon
Senior Lecturer in Economics and Co-ordinator of External Teaching in
Economics, Division of External Studies, University of Queensland,
Brisbane, Australia

Tennyson, Robert D
Professor of Educational Psychology, Curriculum and Instruction
Systems, College of Education, University of Minnesota, Minneapolis,
USA

Walter, Gordon A
Assistant Professor in the Faculty of Commerce and Business
Administration, University of British Columbia, Vancouver, USA

Williams, David V
Associate Professor of Psychology, Ithaca College, and partner in
OmniCom Associates, Ithaca, NY, USA

Zuber-Skerritt, Ortrun D
Lecturer in the Centre for the Advancement of Learning and Teaching,
Griffith University, Brisbane, Australia